WORLD CLASS
DIVERSITY
MANAGEMENT

Other books by R. Roosevelt Thomas, Jr.

Beyond Race and Gender
Differences Do Make a Difference
Redefining Diversity
Building a House for Diversity
Building on the Promise of Diversity

WORLD CLASS DIVERSITY MANAGEMENT

A STRATEGIC APPROACH

R. ROOSEVELT THOMAS, Jr.

BK

Berrett–Koehler Publishers, Inc.
San Francisco
a BK Business book

Berrett-Koehler Publishers, Inc.
235 Montgomery Street, Suite 650
San Francisco, CA 94104-2916
Tel: (415) 288-0260 Fax: (415) 362-2512 www.bkconnection.com

Ordering Information
Quantity sales. Special discounts are available on quantity purchases by corporations, associations, and others. For details, contact the "Special Sales Department" at the Berrett-Koehler address above.
Individual sales. Berrett-Koehler publications are available through most bookstores. They can also be ordered directly from Berrett-Koehler: Tel: (800) 929-2929; Fax: (802) 864-7626; www.bkconnection.com
Orders for college textbook/course adoption use. Please contact Berrett-Koehler: Tel: (800) 929-2929; Fax: (802) 864-7626.
Orders by U.S. trade bookstores and wholesalers. Please contact Ingram Publisher Services: Tel: (800) 509-4887; Fax: (800) 838-1149; E-mail: customer.service@ingrampublisherservices.com; or visit www.ingrampublisherservices.com/Ordering for details about electronic ordering.

Berrett-Koehler and the BK logo are registered trademarks of Berrett-Koehler Publishers, Inc.

Printed in the United States of America

Berrett-Koehler books are printed on long-lasting acid-free paper. When it is available, we choose paper that has been manufactured by environmentally responsible processes. These may include using trees grown in sustainable forests, incorporating recycled paper, minimizing chlorine in bleaching, or recycling the energy produced at the paper mill.

Strategic Diversity Management (SDM) and the Strategic Diversity Management Process are trademarks of R. Thomas and Associates, Inc.

Library of Congress Cataloging-in-Publication Data
Thomas, R. Roosevelt.
  World class diversity management : a strategic approach / R. Roosevelt Thomas, Jr. — 1st ed.
      p. cm.
  Includes bibliographical references and index.
  ISBN 978-1-60509-450-2 (hardcover : alk. paper)   1. Diversity in the workplace.   2. Personnel management.   I. Title.
  HF5549.5.M5T465 2010
  658.3008—dc22   2010008303

First Edition
15   14   13   12   11   10   10 9 8 7 6 5 4 3 2 1

To my wife, Ruby,
and our sons and daughter—
Walter, April, and Jarred.
To our grandson, Montré.

To the CEOs and other senior executives
who have influenced my thinking
over the past twenty-five years.

CONTENTS

Preface   ix

Introduction   1

PART I   23

The Four Quadrants Model: Introduction

1. Managing Workforce Representation   25
2. Managing Workforce Relationships   45
3. Managing Diverse Talent   87
4. Managing All Strategic Diversity Mixtures   125

PART II   155

Operationalization

5. Strategic Diversity Management Process   159
6. Managing Complexity   185
7. The Dynamics of Strategies and Paradigms   205

Contents

Part III 221

Application

8.	Jeff Kilt	225
9.	Reflections of Jeff Kilt	239
	Closing Thoughts	265
	Acknowledgments	269
	Notes	273
	Index	281
	About the Author	287

PREFACE

This book has evolved from four streams of my diversity work over the past twenty-five years and comes together at their intersection.

The first stream is my focus on understanding the field. Over the years, I have been thinking and speaking about the Four Quadrants in one form or another as a way to organize the various approaches in the arena of diversity. I have not sought so much to determine what is right, wrong, or useful, but rather simply to understand what exists and their interrelationships. My thinking at this point is that all diversity approaches can be lumped into at least one of four strategic categories: (1) Managing Workforce Representation, (2) Managing Workforce Relationships, (3) Managing Diverse Talent, and (4) Managing All Strategic Diversity Mixtures.

The second contributing stream has been an expanding personal exploration into what constitutes (or would constitute) world class in diversity and diversity management. By "world class," I mean "best in class," according to worldwide standards.

When a consulting colleague suggested that we strive to help clients become "world class" in diversity management, I initially responded, "How can we talk about being 'world class' when we can't agree on what diversity means?" Flashing through my mind were the many discussions I had experienced with practitioners about professionalizing and making sense of the field. All had ended in frustration.

Later, as I was preparing for a speaking commitment, the same colleague suggested that I present on world-class diversity management. He subsequently recommended that we author an article on the topic, as well. In less than a year, I moved from saying the notion was unrealistic to thinking seriously about how to make it a reality. I knew that the world-class manufacturing movement had succeeded. Why couldn't world-class diversity management do so, too? I began the project in earnest.

The third stream of contributing activities has been my work with chief executive officers (CEOs) and other senior-level executives. From the beginning of my involvement in the diversity field, I have encountered senior leaders who have been thoughtful and engaging around the topic of diversity.

Some will find this statement surprising, since many hold a stereotypical view of action-oriented executives preoccupied with obtaining the five "to-do's" and having little patience for exploring concepts and frameworks. The skeptics believe that those leaders subscribe to the philosophy of "Fire, ready, and aim" rather than "Aim, ready, and fire."

I have experienced my fair share of such people; however, I also have interacted with a substantial number of executives who desire to engage in thoughtful dialogue on diversity. Consider two examples below:

- Upon first entering the field as a consultant, I presented a proposal to the staff of the human resources (HR) department of a company that pioneered in the diversity arena. They concluded that my proposal calling for a multiyear process of cultural change was so different that I needed to speak to the CEO and the chief diversity officer (CDO). I agreed to do so and was given "exactly" fifteen minutes to make my point. I prepared accordingly. As matters turned out, the two senior executives engaged me in a lively discussion that lasted an hour and fifteen minutes.

- In another setting, I again presented to an HR department responsible for screening potential consultants. I made it past the initial hurdle and received a meeting with the CEO. He responded favorably. I subsequently had approximately twelve three-hour sessions with senior executives, and the CEO attended each one—not just to show his support but as an engaged learner. Because he was willing to be a "learner" and to probe, he provided a contagious model that made the sessions very productive.

I have benefited enormously from exchanges with leaders like these. They have helped me over the years to refine and extend my thinking as they engaged me with questions and affirmations. Collectively, these open-minded and inquisitive executives provided the model for this book's composite case study of Jeff Kilt, a composite leader of a corporate team seeking to be "world class."

Fourth, my twenty-five years of observations of the field (internal and external practitioners) have contributed to the conceptualization of this book. Among the most significant observations have been the following:

- While enthusiasm and energy about achieving social justice and human rights gains persist, practitioners appear less certain that diversity and diversity management are the most promising routes for making progress. When speaking to people active in the field, I often sense weariness, hopelessness, or a sense of surrender. Some are even unclear or confused about what would constitute success. Many admit to "diversity fatigue."

- Many—if not most—internal practitioners and their general managers see diversity as a problem to be solved and pushed aside. I have heard internal diversity professionals say, "My goal is to work myself out of a job." CEOs often share that view. They may, for example, see the "problem" as not having an environment that welcomes minorities and women. With that diagnosis, they set out to create such an environment with the expectation that once that is accomplished, it will be behind them. Their priority is to demonstrate that their organization embraces diversity.

- Despite the perceived declining morale of practitioners, an enormous number of activities remain in place after being institutionalized as part of an organization's fabric. Once institutionalized, diversity activities in many settings are seen as an ongoing given—part and parcel of the business routine. Conviction, energy, and fire are often missing, however. Change, in particular, frequently does not appear to be a goal or expectation.

- No silver bullet is in sight. When I talk with practitioners who have attended a professional gathering designed to advance the field, they report such things as, "I heard little that was new. We keep reworking previous approaches."

- CEOs and other senior general managers rarely play a leadership role in the diversity arena. When the field was new, little of significance could happen without senior-level endorsement *and* operational involvement. Now, as a result of institutionalization, many enterprises have appointed chief diversity officers and delegated major operational responsibilities to them. While CDOs typically are talented, accomplished men and women, an unintended consequence may have been a perceived—if not actual—drop in CEO push. The establishment of institutionalized diversity departments may have made it less clear who is really driving diversity. Indeed, inherent in the concept of institutionalization is the notion that advocacy is no longer needed. This sentiment may have been premature for the diversity field.

In sum, I sense that that the field is at a turning point. It can move into decline, stagnate, or grow into a bigger, disciplined purpose.

In the absence of certainties, I am comfortable arguing that what we are seeing today are the field's growing pains, and that the discipline will overcome them and become an established, respected, and valued vehicle for addressing *all* kinds of diversity. The proverbial glass for diversity is half full, not half empty.

What will be required to overcome these growth challenges? For starters, a framework for organizing the field's various thrusts and their interrelationships would be immensely helpful. Such a structure would assist senior executives and other practitioners in designing effective diversity management strategies and action plans, and also aid academicians in further advancing the field's development as a discipline.

This book offers the Four Quadrants as a candidate for that organizing task. Also, what we are describing as world-class diversity management capability would provide an enormous boost toward overcoming the growth pains.

It will also provide a foundation that can be used to advance the field beyond its growing pains and toward realization of its potential as a managerial tool for managers in general and for CEOs and other senior executives in particular. If, as I hope, the book successfully targets the field's critical needs, it should greatly benefit the field and its development as a discipline and a managerial tool. Without world-class diversity management, or something akin to it, the practice of diversity management will languish.

Seven premises or themes have driven my conceptualization of the book and, indeed, the book itself. All flow from the four streams of activities that I have pursued over the past twenty-five years. These premises follow:

1. The field of diversity can be conceptualized as a "world-class" ideal that can be a source of inspiration and energy.
2. The development of world-class diversity management can parallel the developmental dynamics of world-class manufacturing.
3. The field's primary emphasis should be on building capability for generating solutions to problems, rather than on solving the "diversity problem." Manufacturing professionals, for example, don't envision solving the manufacturing problem and moving on, but rather aspire to develop a capability that will allow effective ongoing problem solving in the manufacturing arena.
4. All diversity approaches can be categorized into at least one of the Four Quadrants. Individuals might differ in their judgments as to which quadrant or quadrants, but the categorization is possible. Further, each of the quadrants is supported by an undergirding diversity paradigm. Accordingly, managing quadrant-paradigm dynamics becomes a prerequisite for effective management of diversity.
5. Diversity generates tensions and complexities, and these by-products must be accepted and worked through in the process of managing diversity.
6. CEOs and other general managers must be operationally re-engaged in the pursuit of excellence in diversity management. Any significant push for excellence with diversity most often will require the visible, operational engagement of senior leaders.
7. While a desire for simplicity has dictated that most of the examples in the book focus on diversity management as it applies to race and gender, the author's Four Quadrants Model applies equally to a multitude of additional diversity dimensions. It applies, for example, to people dimensions beyond the traditional ones of race, gender, and ethnicity to those such as time within

an organization, experience level, member of an acquiring or acquired organization, etc. It applies equally as well to all of the non-people diversity dimensions—function, product, process, etc. As such, the book benefits readers seeking a framework for maximizing the benefits of all of the various types of diversity that can exist while also minimizing the tensions they inevitably create.

As the book has evolved from these mega themes, the idea of building a world-class diversity management capability has emerged as its core. Interestingly, while I focus primarily on organizations, I believe that my insights and prescriptions also hold for individuals, the whole diversity field, and, indeed, society. This for me has been one of the most exciting aspects of the book.

I anticipate that what I say in the following chapters about world-class diversity management capability will not be the definitive word. Rather, I hope it will be the definitive beginning of an engaging evolution toward making the concept a concrete and meaningful aspiration for advancing the work of individual practitioners and the collective reality known as the field. I further believe that a significant part of this evolution will be moving the ongoing dialogue beyond diversity demographics and toward diversity management. Only then will the world-class diversity management concept reach its full potential to provide maximum benefit.

INTRODUCTION

A s I begin this introduction, I have been reflecting on previous situations where I have seen accelerated learning and growth through quality dialogue. The situations have been varied, but they have shared one characteristic: Before the discussion began, time was taken to establish a context for the discussion. Often that time was used to establish agreed-upon definitions.

Given the wide variety of perspectives on "diversity" and my experience in working with senior organizational leaders, I propose that we seek some common ground around definitions—if only for the purpose of discussion. Toward this end, I offer a set of definitions for the diversity-related terms that I have used throughout the book.

BASIC DEFINITIONS

Below are definitions that will make the reading of the book more enjoyable and profitable:

Diversity—the differences and similarities, and related tensions and complexities, that can characterize mixtures of *any* kind. When you speak of diversity, you are describing a *characteristic* of a collection or mixture of some kind, such as employees, customers, vendors, functions, organizational participants in an acquisition or merger, citizens, family members, or congregants in a religious setting.

This means that when you talk of a group's diversity, you have to specify the dimension. In the United States, when someone says a group is "diverse," he typically means with respect to race, gender, or ethnicity. In reality, the dimension possibilities are enormous, thus the need to specify.

In addition, with diversity (differences and similarities) come tensions and complexities. The greater the diversity, the greater the likelihood of tension and complexity.

Diversity tension—the stress and strain that come from the interaction and clashing of differences and similarities.

Complexity—that which makes something difficult to explain.

Diversity management—the ability to make quality decisions in the midst of any set of differences and similarities and related tensions and complexities.

Complexity management—the ability to make quality decisions in the midst of factors that make something difficult to explain.

Capability—the wherewithal to think through diversity issues of any kind in pursuit of quality decisions that support an entity's overarching objectives. A critical assumption is that the individual or organization (represented by its leaders and managers) can be the actor.

Achieving this wherewithal requires understanding and operationalizing concepts, principles, theories, and paradigms; developing and mastering skills and competencies; and sustaining a high level of craftsmanship through continuous learning and introspection.

WORLD-CLASS DIVERSITY MANAGEMENT

Defined

Practicing World-Class Diversity Management means operating at a level that is the best in the world with respect to diversity management. At a minimum, it suggests the use of state-of-the-art strategies and approaches for addressing *any* diversity issue in *any* setting in *any* geographical location.

Achieving this status doesn't require an enterprise to operate beyond its country's borders. It might practice diversity management at a world-class level within its community, state, regional, or national boundaries. The determining factor would be that the quality of its practices cannot be beaten anywhere in the world.

Consider the realm of baseball. The "World Champion" New York Yankees may never play a team from outside the United States; yet, because of their understanding—rightly or not—that United States baseball is the best in the world, they can claim that winning the World Series entitles them to say, "We are world champions." As the quality of professional baseball outside the United States grows in perceived excellence, World Series winners will not be able to claim "We are the best in the world" without engaging in some competition to prove that point.

With respect to diversity management, we still have to define the game and then determine what it means to play at a world-class level. To date, practitioners and managers have expressed relatively little interest in establishing and pursuing the standards that would allow us to do that.

Writing on the meaning of World-Class Diversity Management has brought to mind my first encounter with World-Class Manufacturing and Total Quality Management (TQM) in the mid-eighties, when the emphasis was on achieving world-class status in manufacturing. One of our first diversity clients placed great stock in being world class. The company viewed world class as the gold standard against which any self-respecting manufacturing organization must measure itself. As this company expanded its global manufacturing operations, its managers found that being competitive required familiarity with the best philosophies and practices of TQM and other manufacturing philosophies and tools. This was true for other corporations with global operations and for some with domestic sites only.

This reality led our client to send groups of its managers to attend seminars on different manufacturing approaches, to visit the sites of enterprises that advocated innovative strategies, to invite leading practitioners to tour and assess their facilities, and to devour books on various methodologies—TQM and others. Our clients and other corporations did make significant progress toward world-class status and touted that progress widely internally and externally.

As we began our diversity management work with the organization, its representatives told us that they wanted to be world class in diversity as well as in manufacturing. Given the embryonic nature of diversity at that time, we could not guarantee that our offer was world class. We were comfortable, however, in saying that our approach had the *potential* to become world class. We also gained credibility by relating our diversity approach to the company's World-Class Manufacturing practices and philosophies.

My point here is that being world class had become a way of life for our clients wherever they operated a manufacturing facility in the world. As these manufacturing managers interacted with global functions, they often cited manufacturing philosophies and principles. The notion of world class had become ingrained in them.

The diversity field has not progressed to this point. We in the field have neither established what world class is nor specified how it might be achieved. Further, we lack agreement on our most fundamental philosophies, principles, and concepts, as well as consensus as to what best practices are. Indeed, it is not clear that we want to be world class. Some feeling exists that because the field is diversity, practitioners should be diverse (fragmented) in their thinking.

Requirements

Several elements must be in place if we are to establish and achieve world-class status in the diversity arena. These include the following:

Universal philosophies. We must have sets of universal theories, principles, concepts, and frameworks that can be applied to any type of diversity mixture at any geographic location. Aspirants to world-class stature need universal tools as a basis for world capability and applicability. Such tools are not currently readily available in the diversity arena. This book is intended to be a step toward filling that gap.

An approach that fosters ease of comparison, discussion, and analysis across the globe. This data gathering capability will be key to establishing the meaning of World-Class Diversity Management. Diversity means different things to people in different countries. This can be a major barrier to efforts to identify and understand different diversity management philosophies, unless there are a framework and process that fosters global dialogue and affirms and enhances world perspectives.

An approach that fosters awareness and understanding of the field of diversity and not just its individual dimensions. If practitioners are to understand and address the diverse dimension (race, ethnicity, gender, etc.) priorities around the world, they must possess familiarity and competency with diversity per se. That is, they must have access to both individual *and* collective perspectives. Without that access, they must develop an expertise for each possible dimension. While doable, this can become onerous. A framework with universal and transferable concepts and principles that apply to all dimensions provides a head start with any given issue, by eliminating the need to begin from ground zero in each instance. Most efforts designated as diversity focus on the workforce. That limits the capability to deal with *any* type of diversity issue.

An approach grounded in a universal process for addressing any diversity issue. Given the multiplicity of approaches to diversity around the globe, world-class status requires a process that can be adapted to any approach and used with any mixture.

Infrastructures to foster the establishment and pursuit of world-class standards. For example, the Malcolm Baldrige National Quality Awards program fosters excellence in TQM, while within organizations, entire departments and task forces often are dedicated to the achievement of World-Class Manufacturing.

Obstacles

My initial personal reaction to the notion of world class reflects some of the obstacles. Four in particular merit mention:

1. **Lack of professionalization and rationalization.** This lack impedes the development of universal frameworks and significant consensus among practitioners. Organizations, practitioners, managers, and individual contributors are struggling to make sense of diversity. Some are so confused that they want to discard the notion. Others have

institutionalized diversity into increasingly meaningless rituals. Many organizations are seeking ways to relaunch, reboot, or otherwise rejuvenate their diversity efforts.

While some want to dismiss the idea of diversity, most organizations and communities still struggle explicitly or implicitly with the notion. So there are practical reasons to sort through the ambiguity.

As part of the effort to make sense of diversity, internal and external practitioners are searching for new frameworks. For some, this is a desperate search that leads them to embrace any semantic change that *might* reflect a substantive modification in approach. Their search would be aided by a rationalized perspective of the diversity field, which would provide a context for assessing the fit between organizational needs and a particular framework—and therefore for assessing its likelihood of success. This would also set the stage for establishing world-class standards.

2. Inability to focus on the big picture—to see the forest as well as the trees. The individual dimensions—race, gender, ethnicity, sexual orientation, thought, globalism, political, functional, or generational—consume the attention and time of many organizations, which emphasize them one at a time and seek practitioners and consultants with expertise in the priority of the moment. *Rarely do organizations or community leaders focus on learning about diversity as a field. Instead, they continue to reinvent the wheel as they move from dimension to dimension.* This mindset and corresponding behaviors hamper the establishment of a world-class standard.

3. Lack of discipline. Inattention to sets of widely accepted, well-defined philosophies, theories, and practices that apply to the whole field of diversity has hampered discussion among those in the field. Developing the field as a discipline will require focusing on the forest *and* the trees.

4. Lack of face validity. With World-Class Manufacturing, face validity as a legitimate discipline and organizational function has not been an issue. Lack of face validity for diversity, however, has been most apparent in today's recessionary economic times. People frequently ask me, "Are companies still engaged with diversity?" Among those people are some who never believed corporations were serious about diversity and therefore never had expectations that diversity training would endure. Some observers note how well they are getting along now and express surprise that diversity is still needed. Others suggest that since the United States has elected an African American as president, the country no longer needs diversity work. And still others declare, "Given that we have been 'doing diversity' for so many years, surely we can relax now and move on to something else." The common theme is that diversity lacks face validity and, therefore, has a tentative status and will soon disappear—if it has not already done so.

5. Seeing diversity as a problem to be solved and then removing it from the "to do" list. This perspective contributes to a lack of face validity for diversity and also to the view that an intervention with a beginning and an end is needed—as opposed to the need to build and maintain a *capability* to cope with issues around differences and similarities on an ongoing basis.

6. Leaders confusing their personal beliefs and behaviors with those of their organizations. This confusion can make it difficult to realize and address collective realities regarding their enterprises.

Potential Benefits

In light of so many obstacles, why is now a good time to pursue World-Class Diversity Management?

One major benefit would be the enhancement of global competitiveness. As globalization increases, few enterprises anywhere in the world—regional, national, or international—will be immune to global competition. To return to the earlier baseball analogy, the more teams around the world play the game, the more U.S. teams must become competitive within national *and* international boundaries. Enterprises must expand their focus if they aspire to become world class.

A second benefit would be greater organizational consistency across the nation and the globe. Globalization demands that we make sense of diversity and think in terms of *world* philosophies and practices. Yet there is little consistency with respect to diversity across national boundaries. For example, U.S.-based global corporations are finding that other countries resist American-style diversity activities—rightly or wrongly—on the grounds that they do not have the same issues as those related to America's history of slavery and race relations. These companies do understand the need for consistency between global and domestic diversity thrusts, however, if they are to demonstrate commitment to diversity and also achieve efficiency and effectiveness with their efforts. A rationalized world perspective of the field would facilitate such consistency.

Without understanding the forest (the whole) of diversity, organizational diversity leaders treat their domestic and international arenas as two unrelated trees (dimensions). Chief diversity officers sometimes say with pride, "We are doing global diversity now." An implication is that "global" is better and represents a move to the next level, that the domestic issues have been mastered. A rationalized perspective would encourage integration of the two arenas within the context of the diversity forest.

A further benefit of developing a World-Class Diversity Management concept is that it would free organizations and individuals from their current imprisonment by domestic diversity paradigms (mindsets). The resulting independence of thought would help organizations to move toward the next level with their diversity management efforts.

For some time, I have known about the impact of paradigms on the behavior of individuals and organizations and their ability to greatly inhibit change. However, a recent personal experience heightened my understanding of this phenomenon.

I found myself in the new Jacksonville, Florida, airport. As I prepared to wash my hands and exit the men's room, I noticed there were no wash basins; instead, a marble slab under faucets with a drain at the back of the flat surface served the function of the bowls. As you wash your hands, water runs down on the marble slab and flows backward to the drain.

At first, it took me a minute to be clear that I had not walked by the wash basins—to realize that what I saw was a new approach to hand washing. Several questions flashed through my mind: "What is this?" "Why did they do this?" "Is it more sanitary?" "Is this more cost effective?" "More green?" "Why?!" "What was wrong with the way it was?"

For that moment, I was in paradigm shock. My paradigm for airport washrooms collided with the reality of the new arrangement in the Jacksonville airport, and for a moment the collision immobilized me. If I had had the option of a traditional arrangement, I have no doubt that I would have chosen it.

Individuals and organizations can be imprisoned by their domestic diversity paradigms in much the same way. For example, U.S.-based corporations tend to focus on workforce diversity from the perspective of the civil rights movement. Going global has forced many to rethink their diversity paradigm and to broaden their perspective. Outside the United States, enterprises tend to be adamant that they do not share the United States' issues.

Not long ago, I made a presentation in England. The client requested that I arrive early so that I might be oriented. Our orientation meeting began with me talking about my approach to diversity with respect to acquisitions, nationalities, products, and functions. When I had finished, I asked what I needed to know for my presentation. "You're fine," the client's representatives replied. They simply had wanted to be sure I had not come with a way of thinking about diversity that was at odds with their thinking; in particular, they did not want me to bring a race and gender perspective that they considered to be peculiar to the United States. My model and its assumption of a global application to any diversity issue appeared attractive to them.

As United States managers bump into other diversity paradigms in pursuit of world-class standards, the result hopefully will be an increase in innovation and movement toward the next level.

A related benefit to being freed from paradigm imprisonment would be a greater readiness for addressing the forest of diversity. Some individuals are so constrained by their dominant paradigm that they can only see their pet dimension and fear that any focus on the forest would diminish attention for their favorite diversity issue. Others are not even aware of the forest. Clearly, for these individuals, any release from their dominant paradigm would greatly enhance their capability to be productive with other dimensions in the forest.

The development of World-Class Diversity Management would facilitate talent management. In a real sense, we are circling back to where we were years ago—talking about the need to get the most from diverse human resources in organizations and communities. About twenty-five years ago, in the wake of the Hudson Institute's *Workforce 2000* report,[1] pioneers in the diversity arena advocated the importance of preparing to manage an increasingly diverse workforce. Now, incredibly, it's possible to engage in discussions and read books about talent management with barely a mention of diversity. Against this backdrop, proponents of world-class diversity can enhance understanding of the importance of taking diversity into account when tapping the potential of a diverse pool of talent, and simultaneously secure a platform for furthering their rationalization agenda. While this reminder might seem unnecessary, apparently, it is. The reality of global talent pools calls for thinking in terms of worldwide best practices in diversity management.

The pursuit of World-Class Diversity Management at this time would take advantage of a growing implicit and explicit awareness of diversity beyond race, gender, and ethnicity in the workforce. President Barack Obama's selection of members for his National Economic Council provided an example of implicit awareness of diversity. The president wanted representation of different schools of thought on the council, in hopes that the variety would better generate solutions for the country's complex economic challenges. Most agreed with him but worried that a group of competent, confident, and assertive people with various views might degenerate into dysfunctional chaos. The implicit concern was that the group might not be able to manage their thought diversity.[2]

With its emphasis on the diversity forest, World-Class Diversity Management would enhance the ability of individuals, organizations and communities to deal with dimensions other than race, gender and ethnicity. Achieving World-Class status would be especially helpful in situations involving diversity of thought.

Finally, taking action now would permit the leveraging of a growing desire for more professionalization and rationalization. For some, this desire is fueled by a perceived decline in the field's status. For others, it comes from a feeling of "being stuck." For still others, the persistence of ongoing diversity challenges creates an urgency to move on to the next level. Whatever the specific reason, the reality is clear. We must move forward as a rationalized professional field.

THIS BOOK

Overall Purpose

In spite of the diversity field's many problems and the belief by many that it is premature to discuss World-Class Diversity Management, the overall purpose of this book is to demonstrate that it is possible to establish and pursue world-class standards. I believe that the Strategic Diversity Management Process (SDMP) and the Four Quadrants Model that form the core of this book meet the requirements for achieving world-class status:

- a framework that can be applied universally
- an approach that allows for ease of comparison, discussion, and analysis across the globe
- an approach that fosters awareness and understanding of the field of diversity and not just its individual dimensions
- an approach grounded in a universal process for addressing any diversity issue

The SDMP provides a set of universal definitions and a decision-making process that can be used with any approach, while the four quadrants collectively offer core diversity management strategies that can be used with any diversity mixture. Together, they provide the wherewithal for establishing and pursuing global standards in diversity.

Content and Organization

Figure I-1 captures the book's content. "World-Class Diversity Management" is positioned at the top of the figure because that is the focus of the book and where this introduction began. The vertical arrows represent the four quadrants, or *core diversity management strategies*, presented in part I, chapters 1–4. They are the paths to world-class status. The strategies are as follows:

1. **Managing workforce representation.** The focus is on attaining the desired numerical workforce profile with respect to race, gender, ethnicity, and other selected demographic dimensions.

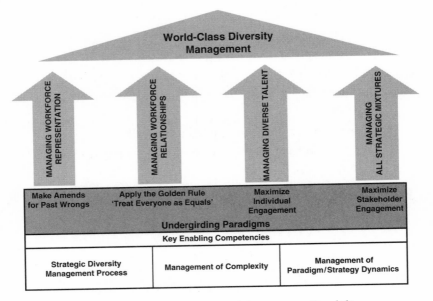

FIGURE I-1. Building World-Class Diversity Management Capability

2. Managing workforce demographic relationships. The focus is on achieving and maintaining harmonious relationships.

3. Managing diverse talent. The focus is on creating an environment that enables leaders and managers to access talent however it comes packaged in terms of race, gender, and ethnicity.

4. Managing all strategic diversity mixtures. The focus is on developing a capability to make quality decisions in the midst of any type of strategic diversity mixture.

These four strategies serve the organization's overarching mission, vision, and strategy, which determine its diversity management aspirations. The words "A Strategic Approach" in the title of this book suggest that the way an organization applies its world-class capability will be a function of its overall strategy.

The horizontal bar beneath the arrows in figure I-1 reflects the paradigms that undergird the strategies. Each diversity paradigm predisposes individuals and organizations to one of the core diversity management strategies. The four paradigms are as follows:

1. Make amends for past wrongs. The focus is on compensating oppressed or disadvantaged groups for past injustices against them. Proponents of this paradigm are predisposed to Managing Workforce Representation.

2. Apply the Golden Rule. The focus is on pursuing harmony and achieving peaceful coexistence among groups. Proponents of this paradigm are predisposed to managing workforce demographic relationships.

3. Maximize individual engagement. The focus is on integrating the talent in the organization and maximizing the engagement of participants in an entity. Proponents of this paradigm are predisposed to Managing Diverse Talent.

4. Maximize stakeholder engagement. The focus is on engaging stakeholders by making quality decisions in the midst of all kinds of diversity. Proponents of this paradigm are predisposed to managing strategic diversity mixtures.

Next figure I-1 reflects the content of part II, chapters 5–7. These chapters discuss the *key enabling competencies* that must be mastered to make possible the implementation (actualization) of the core diversity management strategies: the Strategic Diversity Management Process, the management of complexity, and the management of strategy and paradigm dynamics.

Part III of the book, chapters 8–9, focuses on the application of the various components in the interest of building World-Class Diversity Management capability and taking diversity management to the next level in a corporation. Included here is the composite case study of Jeff Kilt.

My hope is that figure I-1, when combined with an understanding of two other aspects of the book's organization, will allow the reader to easily navigate the discussions that follow, even though that may require negotiating some unfamiliar territory. The two other aspects of the book's organization are:

1. Discussion of the diversity management strategies from an evolutionary perspective. I take this approach in hopes of highlighting how the dynamics of diversity and diversity management have developed over the years.

2. A focus on the United States. I use this focus in an effort to keep the scope of the book manageable, not to minimize diversity work and its evolution in other countries. I also have selected this focus because of my belief that in the United States, diversity and diversity management practices flow from a peculiar legacy of slavery, oppression, civil rights, and social justice. Hopefully, observers familiar with diversity work in other geographical locations will provide an accounting that can be compared to what I report for the United States.

World-Class Diversity Management in Action

As readers move through the book, the principal attributes of World-Class Diversity Management in action will become clearer. At this junction, I offer a glimpse of what might be involved.

As figure I-1 denotes, organizational participants with World-Class Diversity Management capability would be using the four quadrants and would be capable of addressing workforce diversity and *all* other strategic diversity mixtures. Similarly, individuals would be capable of managing *all* diversity mixtures critical to their personal well-being—whether at work, at home, or in the community.

To be able to use the Four Quadrants Model, people individually and collectively would have accomplished the following:

- Developed skill and competency in applying the SDMP in all four quadrants. This is absolutely essential for effective decision making in each area.
- Developed skill and competency in managing complexity. Since diversity generates complexity, working through related complexities becomes a prerequisite for diversity management.
- Developed skill and competency in managing core strategy and paradigm dynamics. To use each core strategy to the appropriate degree, individuals and organizations will need sufficient paradigm flexibility to move among the quadrants. Inflexibility will mean rigid adherence to a core strategy even when using it is dysfunctional.

Overarching this activity would be an ongoing effort to build and maintain sustainable capability. Diversity management would be seen as a tool to be accessed as needed, not as a problem to be solved and pushed aside. Continuous learning and improvement would be paramount considerations.

Audiences

My hope is that this book will engage a number of diverse audiences. Its *primary* intended audience is CEOs, CDOs, and other senior-level general managers who want to know how diversity management can help in ratcheting up their efforts to achieve workforce diversity.

Leaders seeking guidance as to how diversity management can be applied to other managerial issues—such as customer relations, acquisitions and mergers, headquarters and field relations, functional synergy, and innovations—will also find this book useful. In particular, the notions of craft and capability should be of interest. Overall, the book should enhance leaders' ability to develop and implement diversity strategies for their organizations.

Why senior-level leaders? Writing primarily for senior-level leaders highlights that for me diversity management is not an end in and of itself, but, ultimately, a means of achieving the *overall* mission and objectives of an enterprise, responsibilities that fall under the direct purview of senior executives. Also, some of my most productive experiences as a consultant have been working with senior executives who understood diversity management and took care to be operationally involved. As a result, I am convinced that senior management engagement is essential to optimal results.

The book's *secondary* intended audience is diversity professionals, HR leaders, academicians, Equal Employment Opportunity (EEO) officials, and policy makers:

Diversity professionals. This book can serve as a primer for individuals new to the field. It can serve as a context for experienced professionals deciding how to "move to the next level" and for rationalizing diversity efforts across dimensions and locations.

HR leaders. The benefits for diversity professionals apply for HR practitioners, as well. Additionally, the book can foster an enhanced understanding of the differences between diversity management and human resources and provide clarity about how the two fields can complement each other. For example, the book might serve as a reminder of how diversity management can support talent management and help to clarify that diversity management is not an "HR function."

Academicians. Professors who offer an overview of the diversity field should find the book invaluable. In addition, academicians focused on the study and research of diversity in organizations and communities will find that the book provides a framework for mapping new lines of inquiry to advance the field.

EEO officials. The book should foster understanding of how the efforts of EEO officials can coexist or even mesh with diversity efforts. In a very real sense, as the book differentiates among the trees in the forest of diversity, it should affirm the legitimacy of the EEO function.

Policy makers. As political leaders move to diminish dysfunctional divisiveness within the country, policy makers will become more aware of the importance of managing diversity. This, in turn, should increase their desire to learn more about the field. Even experienced policy makers should find the book a useful primer to inform their thinking and deliberations about diversity-related options.

The intended audiences constitute a diverse set of groups. Some have said that this audience diversity presents a significant writing challenge, as the various groups are likely to have different criteria for judging a book as useful. I agree. The intended audiences do have different perspectives, requirements, and preferences, and the writing has been a challenge. Still, individuals within each group share a commonality: a desire to engage in thoughtful dialogue about diversity. It is for these people that the book has been written.

TIPS FOR THE READER

Six tips will help to make reading this book more enjoyable and profitable:

1. **Read the book from the perspective of a craftsperson sharpening his capabilities.** Read not for solutions, but rather for frameworks and processes that might be used to generate solutions.

2. **Think of the book as presenting the "big picture," as a "survey exploration" on diversity.** As any good exploration does, the book will provide a useful way to organize the field. Readers may leave the book wishing more had been said about a given topic, or more had been drawn from certain fields or academic research. In addition, the book's focus on the forest (or whole) of diversity means that individuals' pet dimensions may be covered only to a limited extent—if at all. Similarly, "hot" diversity topics of the day may not be included. My expectation is that greater awareness of the diversity forest and its dynamics will enhance the reader's ability to deal with the trees (dimensions) of their choice.

3. **Read the book with an eye toward determining what is useful, not what is "right or wrong."** My intent is to provide frameworks that can be used for understanding, organizing, and generating solutions and action planning with respect to diversity management, rather than presenting evaluative critiques of different strategies and approaches.

4. **Keep in mind the evolutionary perspective of the book with respect to the core diversity management strategies.** This calls for a discussion of historical context. These discussions are presented not for the sake of history, but for the sake of context. Some of these historical discussions will revolve around issues of civil rights, social justice, and human rights, territory with which many readers are familiar. You will take more from the book by reading for *context* with respect to each diversity management strategy rather than presuming the material is typical of such discussion.

5. Remember that the book is not a review of the academic literature on diversity, but rather one person's reasoning as to what would constitute world class in the field and how that status might be achieved. Although there is substantial and significant diversity academic literature, a review of that literature is beyond the scope of this book. At some point, it would be beneficial to see if a review of the academic literature might lead to similar or different reasoning and projections about World-Class Diversity Management.

6. Although the book is not about "global diversity" as usually discussed, its "universal" projections apply globally. Because I begin my survey with the evolution of diversity in the United States, it might seem as if my universals apply only to the United States. But I don't think that's true. I believe that if another writer were to conduct a survey beginning with the early diversity practices of a different country or set of countries, her universals would be congruent with those coming from this book. I base my belief on the reasoning that unfolds in this book and on my personal exposure to diversity work in other countries. (That is another project that might be beneficial at some point.)

In summary, my intent is that the book will promote the development of a diversity management capability that can be applied to diversity forests anywhere in the world. My hope is that realization of this intent will advance the field's credibility as a global influence.

Discussion

Interestingly, as the book has evolved, I have found myself projecting paths to world-class status not only for individuals and organizations, but for the field of diversity, as well. This, for me, has been an exciting undertaking.

My hope is that the reader will relate some of the many insights I gleaned in writing this book to his own experience and, like me, become more optimistic—indeed, inspired—about the field's future and possibilities. Neither my own nor the reader's optimism will prevent false starts and challenges. Still, the opportunities for contribution are great. I hope that in a small, but significant way this book will encourage the craftsmanship and capability that will be required.

Part I

THE FOUR QUADRANTS MODEL: INTRODUCTION

My consulting colleagues and I have been using the Four Quadrants Model for at least ten years. At first, we spoke of it as a way to capture and differentiate the various approaches to diversity. More recently, we have come to see the four quadrants as representing the four core fundamental diversity management strategies for addressing collective mixtures characterized by differences and similarities, and their related tensions and complexities. I believe that all approaches to diversity fall into one of these core strategies: Managing Workforce Representation, Managing Workforce Relationships, Managing Diverse Talent, and Managing All Strategic Diversity Mixtures.

We have dug more deeply into these core strategies to determine the paradigm or mindset that gave rise to each. This came about as we puzzled over why practitioners did not move easily between the strategies.

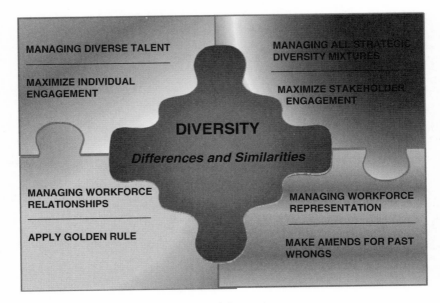

FIGURE PI-1. The Four Quadrants Model

We found the beginnings of a possible answer in the 1987 work of Judith Palmer, in which she argued that loyalty to different diversity paradigms was the basic reason for tensions between practitioners.

Extrapolating from her work, we argued that a different paradigm undergirded each strategy and inhibited movement among them. Further, the different paradigms predisposed individuals to a particular strategy. We, thus far, have set forth four pairings and frequently have presented them as a four-piece puzzle representing the totality of the practice of diversity management. (See figure PI-1.)

In the four chapters in this part of the book, I discuss each core strategy and its undergirding paradigm. For me, these four strategy-paradigm combinations represent the areas of the diversity forest within which one can practice diversity management. I also think of these four core diversity management strategies as paths to World-Class Diversity Management capability. Part II looks at how these strategies may be actualized.

1 MANAGING WORKFORCE REPRESENTATION

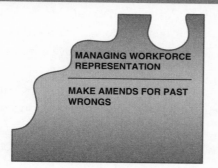

Quadrant I

MANAGING WORKFORCE
REPRESENTATION

MAKE AMENDS FOR PAST
WRONGS

C EOs and other senior executives initiated the Managing Workforce Representation strategy (quadrant) in the 1960s to address the "diversity problem" of mainstreaming African Americans into their organizations. It is one of the two original organizational diversity management efforts—and the one that most people think of when they speak of diversity. The other strategy was Managing Workforce Relationships.

In the spirit of the civil rights laws and the civil rights movement, those senior managers sought to remove barriers to having descendants of slaves involved (represented) in their organizations. They sought this representation not for the sake of diversity or for the benefit of their organizations, but rather to make amends for past injustices.

On the surface, recruiting and hiring African Americans should have been rather straightforward. Yet it wasn't. These leaders encountered an unexpected complication. Though willing, they were unprepared and lacked experience to recruit and select African Americans for professional, managerial, and skilled positions.

Initially, it had been hoped that outlawing employment discrimination would be sufficient to trigger a rush of African American applicants. When that did not happen, all kinds of questions surfaced: Where can we find qualified African Americans? How do we attract them? How do we assess their qualifications? Are there any qualified African Americans? How do we gain a competitive edge in attracting and hiring them?

The disappointing results of desegregation made clear that additional ways were needed to make the mainstreaming of African Americans happen.

This chapter discusses Quadrant 1's attributes and those of its underlying paradigm—Make Amends for Past Wrongs. It also explores the ways a combination of societal, legal, and moral motives and actions interacted with the motives and actions of organizational leaders to give this quadrant its characteristic qualities.

QUADRANT PARAMETERS

Definition of Diversity

A review of the literature of the 1960s and 1970s reveals clearly that mainstreaming African Americans—not achieving diversity— was the initial goal. Over the years, various equal opportunity and antidiscrimination laws and policies for achieving that goal have expanded the population to be mainstreamed to include all "protected groups," and any others who have been missing from the workforce. When talk of diversity and managing diversity emerged in the 1980s, for many, diversity and representation became synonymous. As a result, today, most laypeople speak of diversity as if it means representation. Code for this quadrant is "the numbers," reflecting a concern with the numerical composition of the workforce.

Goal

The original goal of mainstreaming African Americans to increase their presence (representation) in the workforce remains. However, the goal has been expanded to create a workforce that is representative of the broader society by minimizing or eliminating the underrepresentation of multiple groups that have been insufficiently present.

Motives

There are several motives for pursuing representation. One is to comply with antidiscrimination and equal opportunity laws and policies. Another is to pursue social justice and human rights in the spirit of the civil rights movement. Some collapse legal compliance and social justice–human rights–civil rights motives into corporate social responsibility. The premise here is that society expects organizations to have a workforce whose composition reflects the broader community, and that socially responsible companies will pursue this end.

In recent years, others have sought to identify a business motive for advancing representation. For me, corporate social responsibility is the strongest motive for pursuing numerical representation in the workforce. Readers familiar with my early work in *Beyond Race and Gender: Unleashing the Power of Your Workforce by Managing Diversity*[1] may be surprised that I say this, since I then stressed the importance of the business rationale. When doing that, however, I was referring to a motive for managing workforce diversity, not for pursuing representation. I continue to believe that for managing workforce diversity, the business rationale is the stronger motive.

Focus

Historically, the greatest attention has been placed on special efforts to make amends by creating a representative workforce. This focus has translated into a lot of attention on "the numbers," as a key measurement of mainstreaming.

Approaches

Since the 1960s, several approaches have been used to create a representative workforce. Each reflects an ongoing effort to secure sustainable progress with the numbers.

One of the first tools was the Civil Rights Law of 1964. This landmark legislation outlawed racial segregation in schools, public places, and employment. In sum, the law broadly eliminated legal sanctions for segregation. Many advocates for desegregation had hoped that the law would promote racial and gender pluralism. When that did not happen, they turned once more to proactive options—the most prominent manifestation of which has been Affirmative Action.

Affirmative Action in the United States refers to policies that take gender, race, and ethnicity into account to promote equal opportunity. The practice began in 1961 with respect to projects funded with federal funds via President John F. Kennedy's Executive Order 10925. Subsequently, in 1965, President Lyndon Johnson—via Executive Orders 11246 and 11375—expanded Affirmative Action to require that federal contractors and subcontractors "take affirmative action to ensure that 'protected class, underutilized applicants' are employed when available, and that employees are treated without negative discriminatory regard to their protected class status."[2] President Johnson's orders went beyond those of President Kennedy in that they required not just freedom from racial bias in hiring and employment practices, but also steps to ensure the actual employment of the "underutilized protected" class.

Even organizations not covered by those Executive Orders moved to adopt Affirmative Action–type policies, reflecting the relatively widespread acceptance of Affirmative Action that existed until recent years.

As Affirmative Action both gained in acceptance and attracted opponents, advocates used the *benefits of the diversity* that would come from effective Affirmative Action to justify its continuance. The landmark use of this justification occurred in the 1978 case of *Regents of the University of California vs. Bakke*. Writing for the majority of the Supreme Court, Justice Lewis Powell upheld diversity in higher education as a "compelling interest" that justified the use of Affirmative Action on the basis of race.[3]

My view is that by "diversity," Justice Powell meant racial pluralism *and* behavioral variations; further, he assumed that representation (pluralism) would give rise to behavior variations (such as that of thought and problem solving) that would benefit the educational process. For example, he wrote that "the atmosphere of speculation, experiment and creation—so essential to the quality of higher education—is to be promoted by a diverse student body."[4]

In spite of this, Affirmative Action's focus continues to be primarily on achieving numerical profiles and not on behavioral variations. Justice Powell's assumption—despite the arguments of the defendants— was a big leap of faith. Implicit within the assumption was that pluralism and behavioral variations are related.

Experience has demonstrated otherwise. It is quite possible to have racial pluralism without behavioral variations and vice versa. This happens when managers work to screen out possible behavioral variations, or when the representation attributes do not define the individuals in

question. For example, five engineers from an engineering program—
say Georgia Institute of Technology—may be racially pluralistic but
behave similarly because of their engineering training.

Nonetheless, the 1978 decision linked Affirmative Action and diversity and shifted or expanded the rationale for Affirmative Action
from that of solely promoting equal opportunity to also fostering diversity (pluralism *and* behavioral variations). This link strengthened
the tendency to equate Affirmative Action and diversity, even though
fostering diversity was not part of the original concept. It also led to
everything in this quadrant being labeled as diversity.

The benefits argument has advanced from the educational sector
to other arenas. Corporations, for instance, often subscribe to the
"benefits of diversity" school of thought. In a 2003 amicus curiae brief
filed with the Supreme Court, sixty-five corporations maintained that
diversity provided four basic benefits in the area of employment:

1. A diverse group of individuals educated in a cross-cultural environment has the ability to facilitate unique and creative approaches to problem solving arising from the integration of
   different perspectives.
2. Such individuals are better able to develop products and services that appeal to a variety of consumers and to market offerings in ways that appeal to those consumers.
3. A racially diverse group of managers with cross-cultural experience is better able to work with business partners, employees,
   and clientele in the United States and around the world.
4. Individuals who have been educated in a diverse setting are
   likely to contribute to a positive work environment by decreas-
   ing incidents of discrimination and stereotyping.[5]

Once again, these "benefits" presume representation *and* behavioral variations. In practice, this may not hold true, as previous examples suggest.

Another approach or tool has been the *antidiscrimination laws* that came about after the Civil Rights Law and the Affirmative Action executive orders. Illustrative of these laws are the Equal Pay Act, the Age Discrimination in Employment Act (ADEA), the Rehabilitation Act of 1973, and the American Disability Amendments Act of 2008.[6] These laws suggest why compliance is often a motive for this quadrant. Early on, they often motivated corporations and other organizations to *use strategic alliances* to facilitate the recruitment of minorities and women. Corporate executives established these alliances with community groups to receive assistance in identifying possible candidates for employment.

Another tool has been to *establish clear lines of accountability.* Until recently, many diversity programs and strategies did not address this aspect. Some very elaborate and impressive plans lacked accountability—for example, about what happens if the plan is not implemented. As this weakness was recognized, change agents called for tying diversity objectives to managerial incentives. The prevailing sentiment was "If you don't hit them in the pocketbook, you will not get their attention or results."

An approach closely related to the benefits tool is to *connect representation to an organization's bottom line.* These efforts, however, have not been persuasive. This is in part because it is difficult to trace an enterprise's success to one factor—diversity or whatever. In addition, social justice advocates resist the bottom-line approach, fearing that it will distract from the attention required for "injustices" that remain.

Still another approach has been to *secure CEO sponsorships.* Proponents of this tool argue that CEO support is critical—without it little or nothing can be done. In organizations where this thinking prevails, the first question asked is "Does the CEO support this?"

Inclusion, a recently formulated approach, means different things to different people in theory. In practice, it often means representation; so here an "inclusive organization" becomes one that has significant race, ethnic, and gender representation.

Quadrant Accomplishments

Use of the strategy of Managing Workforce Representation has enhanced awareness and acceptance of the notion that representation should exist in all sectors of society, especially with respect to race, gender, and ethnicity. This signifies an important change from the mid-1960s, when law and custom reflected a view that not everyone *should* be in the mainstream.

Our country and its organizations are much more representative than ever before. So much so, that in April, 2009, deliberations regarding the continuation of the Voting Rights Act of 1965, Supreme Court Chief Justice Anthony M. Kennedy acknowledged "that the provision has been successful in rooting out discrimination in voting over the past 44 years. But times have changed."[7] Despite that view, the Supreme Court declined to eliminate critical parts of the act. The discussion of the quadrant's challenges that follows suggests possible reasons for that.

Quadrant Challenges

Sustainability is a major challenge to this quadrant. Corporations cyclically make progress with the numbers only to experience a retreat. One CEO described his company's diversity work over the past fifteen years and concluded by saying, "We go through frustrating five-year cycles of 'special efforts' to fill our pipeline with minority talent and set high expectations for their advancement—only to see them leave. Then we start over." In particular, he was referring to the difficulties of retaining minorities and achieving proportionate representation throughout the hierarchy.

Some call this the *revolving door* challenge, in which members of targeted groups enter an organization but do not stay. One year a company emphasizes minority hiring, for example, and experiences significant numerical gains, only to find three or four years later that its "progress" has left through the revolving door.

Glass ceilings and premature plateauing are related challenges that result in members of targeted groups being disproportionately clustered at the bottom of the organizational pyramid. *Glass ceiling* refers to the invisible barriers that block upward mobility of a particular group of individuals, while *premature plateauing* references the failure of members of a group to realize their full potential. The two can be connected. Glass ceilings can cause premature plateauing.

One cause of a glass ceiling for women might be an unspoken belief that women for whatever reason cannot perform certain roles. One corporation, for example, had unwritten policies that women could not serve in executive roles requiring late hours because of family responsibilities. Eventually, a woman succeeded a senior male manager who routinely worked from eight in the morning to ten in the evening. This woman not only performed in an outstanding fashion; she left at 5 p.m. When her predecessor was asked why he had stayed so late, he responded, "I hung around in case the CEO needed me."

Another challenge is the *tension between the original mainstreaming–social justice motive for pursuing representation and the benefits-of-representation motive.* Those who subscribe to the justice motive fear that a focus on the benefits of diversity (representation) will lead to decreased emphasis on African Americans and the need for social justice in general. Instead, they contend, all kinds of representation will be sought for reasons other than justice. This split allegiance creates divisiveness about rationales for representation and about the definition of progress.

A challenge dating back to the 1960s is that of *assuring harmony* among workforce participants. Demographic tension—the stress and strain that can come from coexisting with people who have different physical and ethnic attributes—can threaten workforce harmony.

Do we have demographic tension today? We do. Between men and women: "She should not be here because she is preventing a man from working." Between whites and Mexicans: "They're everywhere; they're taking over." Between African Americans and Hispanics: "When Hispanics become the largest minority in this community, we'll be in trouble."

Often, but not always, racism and other "isms" are the cause of tension. Many have a strong desire to move beyond this challenge. This aspiration is reflected in the hope that the election of an African American president of the United States signals enormous progress in eliminating the "isms." While progress undoubtedly has been made, considerable evidence suggests that much remains to be done.

UNDERGIRDING PARADIGM: MAKE AMENDS FOR PAST WRONGS

The Managing Workforce Representation quadrant is best viewed within the context of its undergirding paradigm: Make Amends for Past Wrongs. Regardless of the discussion, at the core of Quadrant 1 is the *desire* to make amends for past wrongs. Sometimes this is explicit; at other times it is implicit. But in whatever form, it is not far away.

The reality is that the paradigm—as you will soon read—in no way identifies diversity as a goal. Even when the focus is on the benefits of diversity, representation is *not* defined as diversity. The tone of the dialogue tends toward *justifying* the real task—to make amends for past wrongs.

This was reiterated in recent remarks by Rev. Dr. Joseph Lowery in a 2009 meeting of Civil Rights activists. Dr. Lowery, after listening to a discussion about diversity, forcefully reminded the audience that the desired end of the civil rights movement was never diversity but rather justice.[8] For Dr. Lowery, the issue was and is not a matter of achieving demographic variations for the sake of diversity, but rather of realizing the numbers at the entry levels and throughout the organizations in the pursuit of this justice.

This paradigm sprung forth as the civil rights movement reached its peak in 1964 and produced the Civil Rights Act of 1964 and the Voting Rights Act a year later. Subsequently, a wide variety of antidiscrimination laws emerged around age, disability, equal compensation, ethnicity, pregnancy, religion, retaliation, and sexual harassment. Race and sex were covered in the Civil Rights Act of 1964.

As can be seen, both rhetoric and accomplishments reflect the moral and legal nature of this paradigm and the reality that it is not positioned around diversity. The paradigm's parameters further demonstrate this reality. These include its goals and focus, definition of diversity, principal vehicles, principal undergirding assumptions, key obstacles, key facilitators, approach tendency, desired results, and global relevancy.

PARADIGM PARAMETERS

Definition of Diversity

As a consequence of the paradigm's initial focus on racial and ethnic minorities and women, those who hold this paradigm define diversity as the inclusion of individuals who are different from white males—in particular, African Americans, other minorities, and women.

Goals and Focus

The founding intent of the civil rights movement was to make amends to African Americans for the "sins" of slavery and discrimination. The goal has expanded over time to include women and other minorities who have been oppressed or disadvantaged by practices now considered illegal and undesirable.

The second goal has been to mainstream African Americans, other minorities, and women into and at all levels of the country's society and organizations, in the interest of justice. The aspiration has been representation, not diversity.

Principal Vehicles

Two vehicles have characterized this paradigm's efforts to foster the making of amends to African Americans. The passage of laws banning segregation and discrimination served as the initial vehicle. High expectations and considerable fanfare accompanied the passage of those laws, along with predictions that change had finally arrived. When those legal developments did not generate the desired increase in the involvement of African Americans in the workforce, proponents of making amends looked for a more direct vehicle.

Outreach became that vehicle. It often manifested itself as corporate responsibility, which gave rise to affirmative outreach—the most prominent form of which has been Affirmative Action, which was designed to promote the recruitment, selection, and retention of qualified persons who otherwise might not be included.

As Affirmative Action grew in use, it attracted challenges. Going forward, the issue will be whether politically acceptable reasons can be found for continuing Affirmative Action[9] or for developing new forms of acceptable affirmative outreach.

Also, corporate social responsibility gave rise to community involvement efforts in minority communities. This support, for example, took the forms of financial contributions to community nonprofit entities, board memberships, executives on temporary assignment with nonprofits, and other creative involvements. Offices often were established to coordinate these efforts, all of which have proven to be more politically acceptable for making amends than Affirmative Action.

It should be noted that amends in the form of "reparations," or under that label, have been even less acceptable than Affirmative Action. Requests for reparations have not been warmly received by the public.[10] (More will be said about reparations in the next section.)

Principal Undergirding Assumptions

This paradigm placed four critical assumptions on the table. The first was that making amends would be achieved by fostering equal opportunity in ways congruent with the country's values. The congruency requirement prohibits Affirmative Action from granting preferences on the basis of race, gender, ethnicity, or other demographic variables. In other words, the country will not discriminate illegally to make amends for past discrimination.[11]

Implicit in that first assumption was the notion that reparations for past sins would not be in the form of money. In the past, that view has been challenged, but proponents of financial reparations have been largely dismissed. However, Douglas A. Blackmon's recent Pulitzer Prize–winning book *Slavery by Another Name: The Re-Enslavement of Black Americans from the Civil War to World War II*[12] might reenergize the reparations debate.

Blackmon documents that despite the official ending of slavery in 1862, law officials and corporate representatives often conspired through trumped-up charges to "legally" imprison African American men until the 1940s. Specifically, he describes a widespread scenario in which an impoverished black male would be arrested on a frivolous charge, taken before a makeshift court, and fined an amount he could not pay. A corporate official would then pay the fine in exchange for the individual working off his indebtedness. Unfortunately, years—indeed, lifetimes—could expire before the debt was paid. Blackmon's documentation of such practices reaffirmed the argument of reparations advocates that many economic enterprises thrived on the backs of blacks, either as slaves or as victims of "slavery by another name."

A second assumption of the "make amends" paradigm has been that making amends for past wrongs is a moral, social justice–human rights–civil rights issue. This reflects a view that slavery and the related subsequent discrimination were morally wrong.

A third assumption has been that the mainstreams of society should reflect the racial, gender, and ethnic makeup of the general population. This assumption undergirds societal expectations that the workforce of our organizations and government agencies should reflect the racial, gender and ethnic make-up of the broader society. That is the mainstreaming aspiration.

Finally, this paradigm assumed that new entrants into the workforce would assimilate (fit in). Logically, this made sense. If people want to be mainstreamed, they must like what they see and try to fit in so as to participate to the fullest. The "on boarding" responsibility of welcoming managers was to assimilate these new entrants. Books and courses were made readily available to assist in the assimilating process. This assimilation expectation is another critical piece of evidence that representation, not diversity, has been the goal of this quadrant.[13]

Key Obstacles

The paradigm Make Amends for Past Wrongs has been popularly held, but there have been obstacles to acting upon it. A critical one has been the legacy of slavery, segregation, and discrimination. On the one hand, individuals and groups have the scars of discrimination: cultures characterized by poor education, limited workplace experience, and esteem issues. On the other hand, organizations and the broader society have been characterized by cultures and parameters designed by and for white males, and, indeed, often built on the premise that minorities and women were to be excluded or their presence minimized.

The tendency to think that slavery and discrimination are part of the United States' "long ago," not its recent history, has been a barrier, as well. Yet *Slavery by Another Name* argues in well-documented fashion that slavery continued under another guise far beyond its official ending. The practices giving rise to this challenging legacy may be more recent than typically thought. As such, the legacy questions may be more difficult than we might expect.

One aspect of this legacy has been a lingering set of discriminatory beliefs and practices that hinder building environments for pluralistic populations. Although a lack of readiness for pluralistic change might exist without racism, lingering racism is one of its driving forces.

Because of the legacy, there has been a backlash or resistance to the presumption of debt owed to minorities and women. Those offering the resistance have insisted that very few slaves—if any—are living now; therefore, the victims of injustice are not around to receive the amend. However, the *Slavery by Another Name* argument may mitigate this position.

Another obstacle has been our society's many affinity subcommunities based on race, ethnicity, or gender. The existence of such subcommunities has often made it difficult to have pluralism within organizations. As one senior executive of a large corporation commented, "How can I create a pluralistic environment internally when society is still focused on maintaining a white male dominant environment with homogenous racial and ethnic subcommunities?"

To complicate matters further, members of the white male communities and the affinity subcommunities often have little understanding of each other and poor communications between them. Their relationships frequently reflect parochialism and defensiveness about their perceived turfs—characteristics that discourage pluralism.

Key Facilitators

Juxtaposed with the obstacles have been three powerful facilitators fostering action on the basis of this paradigm. *First and foremost, society desires the mainstreaming.* Society values a mainstream pluralism characterized by harmony and unity. What the civil rights movement fought for has become by and large the aspiration of the land.

Further, this mainstreaming has been viewed as a moral imperative. This is why when I talk about a business rationale for diversity, someone frequently says, "And it is the right thing to do." They are saying representation is a moral imperative—a social justice, human rights, moral imperative matter.

Backing up society's aspirations around this moral imperative is a significant body of laws and administrative policies. These laws and policies put legal and governmental teeth behind representation.

Desired Results

The goal of this paradigm has been proportionate representation of minorities and women in all sectors and at all levels of organizations and society in pursuit of justice. While there is straightforward agreement about this aspiration, some question how serious community and organizational leaders are about achieving it.

Strategic Predisposition

Proponents of the Make Amends for Past Wrongs paradigm favor the Managing Workforce Representation strategy to achieve their goals. This strategy, serving as a filter of perceptions, channels all thought and actions toward the numbers as the mechanism for promoting social justice, human rights, and civil rights and mainstreaming African Americans, other minorities, and women.

Global Perspective

This chapter, perhaps more than the others, is U.S. centric. Given my foci on the *origin* and *evolution* of each diversity management strategy, this is appropriate. Yet I have long recognized that the United States is not unique in having to make diversity decisions—decisions about who will become a citizen and on what grounds—or in experiencing racial and ethnic tensions. While the specifics of this chapter and its discussion of Quadrant I are oriented toward the United States' experiences, every country and its organizations have grappled with the core dynamics reflected in this discussion. This is not to say that every country has experienced the U.S. history of enslavement and oppression, but simply that each has had to determine who can become a citizen and on what grounds. This is not a uniquely U.S. discussion.[14]

DISCUSSION

Several observations emerged as I reflected on this chapter. The first is that the Managing Workforce Representation Quadrant and its undergirding paradigm Make Amends for Past Wrongs have—paradoxically, given the paradigm's position against financial reparations—had a largely undiscussed role in facilitating such reparations. As such, they may comprise the basic components of a reparations approach to diversity.

That is because as our society has resisted the idea of reparations per se, it actually has been going about the business of reparations. For example, Managing Workforce Representation can be thought of as a form of financial reparation, since it enhances financial opportunities for African Americans. Further, recent apologies for slavery offered by governmental and other entities illustrate a reparation spirit in the midst of resistance.[15]

It seems as if despite the distaste for the word *reparations*, our actions as a society have been somewhat accepting of the notion. It will be interesting to see how *Slavery by Another Name* influences the discussion, as well as our practice, of reparations.

My second observation is that the dynamics around "Making Amends" can help us appreciate how this initial paradigm has affected the development of the diversity field. The centrality of the paradigm explains, for example, why when Justice Powell talked of diversity as pluralism *and* behavioral variations, paradigm subscribers heard "Diversity is synonymous with Affirmative Action." This happened even though Affirmative Action has *never* focused on behavioral variations, but rather has focused on the numbers. The paradigm filter prevented recognition of the inconsistency.

Similarly, this paradigm has allowed its advocates to avoid scrutinizing Justice Powell's assumptions that pluralism generates behavioral variations and that these variations can be beneficial. What subscribers have heard is that if these assumptions are true, we can take race into account as one of several factors when making selection decisions—that is, we can continue our desegregation, antidiscrimination, Affirmative Action, mainstreaming along racial and ethnic lines.

This is unfortunate. Without the "Make Amends" paradigm, the following questions would also be part of the bottom line of the *Bakke* case:

- Under what circumstance does pluralism generate behavioral variations?

- If necessary, what has to be done to foster behavioral variations?
- How do we ensure that these variations are beneficial, and not harmful? Or are these variations always inherently positive?

The "Make Amends" paradigm has allowed subscribers to stay focused on pluralism and the numbers. But this consistency has had its costs. It may also have blocked explorations that in all likelihood would have advanced the field of diversity without compromising Quadrant I.

The dynamics around this process demonstrate very well how paradigms encourage the holder to pour new wine into old bottles. On the one hand, this minimizes distractions, but on the other, it inhibits exploration, creativity, and innovation that might bring progress.

A related, third observation is that by encouraging the pouring of new wine into old bottles, the "Make Amends" paradigm has contributed to "diversity fatigue"—at least the version where people grow weary of talking about the same thing over and over, as in "How can we get the numbers required for pluralism?" By attempting to "fit" new ideas into "old" paradigms instead of other diversity paradigms that would be more compatible, the "Make Amends" paradigm has hindered the development of the field.

My fourth observation is that—as is true of all the quadrants—neither this quadrant nor its underlying paradigm has within itself the capability to address its challenges, especially those of the revolving door, glass ceiling, and premature plateauing. Because of the emphasis on pluralism and the numbers, relatively little attention is allocated to creating environments that will promote greater utilization and retention of new entrants to the workforce. As a result, the "Make Amends" assumption of a willingness to assimilate on the part of newcomers remains a critical obstacle to achieving the paradigm's goals.

Despite the prominence of the "Make Amends" paradigm in the diversity arena and its successful undergirding of progress with representation, its net impact on the field's evolution may very well be negative.

SOME TAKE-AWAYS

CEOs and other senior leaders have used the strategy of Managing Workforce Representation to solve the "diversity problem" of mainstreaming African Americans, other minorities, and women. To sum up:

1. Historically, the driving motive has been the pursuit of justice, and operationally this has meant a focus on "the numbers."
2. Considerable progress has been made, but sustainability has been an issue.
3. Representation (mainstreaming) and diversity management are not the same.
4. The undergirding paradigm for this strategy is Make Amends for Past Wrongs.

2 MANAGING WORKFORCE RELATIONSHIPS

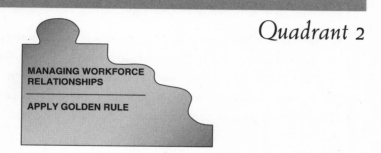

Quadrant 2

MANAGING WORKFORCE
RELATIONSHIPS

APPLY GOLDEN RULE

CEOs activated the Managing Workforce Relationships strategy in the 1960s shortly after initiating the strategy of Managing Workforce Representation. In doing that, they sought to address the diversity problems of helping a pluralistic group of employees "get along" and fostering relationships conducive to efficiency and effectiveness. Attempts to mainstream African Americans quickly brought CEOs once again face to face with the complexity of diversity—this time, with respect to relationships. Corporate executives soon determined that they could not bring African Americans and Caucasians together and expect that productive relationships would naturally evolve.

Among the complexities in play were (1) the legacy of slavery and oppression, (2) a history of acrimonious relationships between the two races even after slavery, (3) a history of Caucasians as the dominant group, (4) a history of African Americans as the subordinate group, (5) and the legacy of recent hostilities related to the civil rights movement.

These complexities made getting along more complicated than CEOs had anticipated. Given that African Americans had been agitating to be included, many executives had felt that they would come in and not "stir up trouble" in appreciation for being mainstreamed.

Despite these complexities, in the 1960s the desire for workplace harmony remained strong and resulted from several factors:

1. The United States society now aspired to racial harmony—in part, to avoid repeats of earlier race riots and also to promote the healing needed to minimize racism, discrimination, and other remnants of slavery. People advocating for racial healing were quick to see signs of racial harmony as indications of progress and to use them as building blocks.

2. Just as the broader society looked for signs of progress, African Americans whose ancestors had been enslaved were doing the same. They consciously and unconsciously pursued affirmation that "things have really changed," and that they were being viewed as full and equal human beings. They also sought evidence that they were accepted, understood, and valued, and they were vigilant for signs that apparent change was not genuine. This motivated society and organizations to make great efforts to demonstrate authenticity as they worked to provide equal opportunity and quality relationships among "equals." CEOs of the 1960s were not able to take for granted that their good intentions and goodwill would be apparent and viewed as "real."

3. Productivity required a certain amount of harmony. Companies thinking about locating to a community with a history of racial strife often included a demand for racial harmony as a condition for doing so. They knew that harmony within and outside the plant was essential to creating optimal conditions for productivity.

4. As the "benefits of diversity" perspective flourished, accepting, understanding, and valuing new workforce entrants began to be seen as essential to reaping gains from the differences and similarities. Behind this view was an assumption that the better relationships were, the greater the potential for gleaning positives from diversity.

These factors and others have helped to make the Managing Workforce Relationships strategy as popular as Managing Workforce Representation. Like the first approach, this strategy is not about diversity per se, but rather about furthering racial pluralism and representation.

QUADRANT PARAMETERS

Definition of Diversity

As in Quadrant 1, diversity in Quadrant 2 first meant African Americans, other minorities, and women and gradually expanded to include other dimensions of pluralism without taking into account behavioral variations. In the 1960s, this approach—synonymous with efforts to enhance racial representation—focused on minimizing racism and improving relations between blacks and whites.

Goals

This strategy has three goals:

1. Achieve harmony by accepting, understanding, and valuing new entrants and their differences and similarities into the workforce, thereby minimizing representation tensions.

2. Establish a workplace and workforce that affirms everyone as equals so that people can come to work and feel accepted, understood, and valued as human beings.

3. Create a workforce climate free of disruptions caused by demographic tension, in the expectation that such an environment fosters productivity. The reasoning is straightforward: If people are not fussing and fighting about their pluralistic differences, productivity gains will follow.

Motives

Supporters of this strategy were motivated by a desire to do the following:

- Minimize tension in the midst of demographic diversity. Particularly during the early years, advocates of good race relations viewed racial tension as symptomatic of racism and sought to squash it in pursuit of harmony.
- Promote effective problem solving in the midst of racial tension. The city of Atlanta, Georgia, for a long time enjoyed a reputation as "the city too busy to hate." In reality, Atlanta was not too busy to hate, but it was too focused on economic vitality to let racial tension prevent effective problem solving and collaboration. As a result, Atlanta has become the economic and transportation hub of the Southeast.
- Foster a climate conducive to optimal productivity. Corporate managers early on used this strategy to ensure that demographic tension did not compromise productivity. Unlike the first motive where the desired *end* was to foster relationships per se, advocates saw this strategy as a vehicle for maintaining productivity. In this context, the quadrant becomes the flip side of represen-

tation: "If you are going to mix the races in the workplace, you had better make certain they get along." This perspective implicitly recognizes that tensions and complexities come with diversity.

- Affirm that new entrants to the workforce are viewed and treated as full human beings and equals of everyone else. As difficult as it may be to believe today, during the 1960s, some individuals did not see African Americans as full human beings.

For some time, I did not see the last item as a priority motive. Two experiences convinced me otherwise.

After a presentation, an African American man approached me and said, "What you say about managing diverse talent makes sense, but I'm not moving until somebody tells me they are sorry." He was saying that significant relationship issues had to be addressed before he would feel whole and willing to expand his perspective.

In the midst of another discussion of managing diverse talent, an African American woman abruptly shouted, "They don't *value* us." Her vehemence said to me that this was not just about benefits for the viability of the business. It was also about helping corporations develop a capability to see African Americans as worthy of respect as human beings and not as "less than" descendants of slaves.

The tragedy for this man and woman as well as for their employer was that neither could focus fully on contributing their talents toward meeting their assigned responsibilities because of their parallel personal agendas to turn their organization from its racist ways. The incongruence between their agendas and those of their organizations compromised their efforts to be viewed as productive associates, even though they very well may have been. Both incidents highlighted for me how critical this motive and need for affirmation continues to be.

The affirmation motive is not something that employees and employers can easily speak about, and where it exists confusion often reins. While consulting with one people-of-color affinity group, I listened as members described how things had not changed and how much remained to be accomplished. Yet their membership had increased at least tenfold. How could they have such an increase and contend that progress had been minimal? As the discussions continued, they determined that they were complaining about still feeling *as if* they were "less than," despite their numbers. Progress had been made with representation, but not with relationships.

Focus

Attention historically has been on accepting, understanding, respecting, and valuing pluralistic differences and similarities—all in pursuit of harmony. Initially, this began with respect to race, gender, and ethnicity. It gradually expanded to include other dimensions along which a workforce can be pluralistic: age, geographic origin, tenure, sexual orientation, and functional background.

Also, the focal point of this quadrant has been "awareness," with relatively little attention to action. Earlier practitioners, in particular, assumed that if people become sensitized to their prejudices, they would self-correct. In the past decade or so, however, more attention has been paid to action.

Approaches

In the sixties, *racism seminars* were a major tool for enhancing workforce harmony. These seminars sought to help white males and minorities explore the dynamics of racism in corporations. A successful seminar would generate awareness of how individuals experienced racism, and that awareness would allow managers and associates to behave more sensitively and to minimize racism and representation tension. This tool is not used as often today as in the past, but many argue that it should be.

A related and more recent tool has been *sensitivity training*. The formal version of this enables a relatively small group of people to openly and confrontationally explore issues around interpersonal relationships. Typically, the exploration is limited to "real-time" interactions in the group. Participants and facilitators often exchange candid observations about behavior. For people not prepared for the experience, or in the absence of a professional facilitator, this "sensitizing" can be psychologically challenging, even damaging. However, if it is properly conducted and participants are prepared, they can glean valuable learnings about their "isms" and interpersonal behavior.

Another version of sensitivity training that has been around a while takes place in larger groups of fifty to one hundred people. In a very confrontational fashion, the lead facilitator offers a variety of experiences that put participants in touch with their feelings around sensitive issues like racism and sexism. The major goal, again, is increasing awareness. When successful, participants frequently report having many eye-opening experiences.

An additional approach is the *personal development seminar for minorities and women*. This tool dates back to the late 1960s and the 1970s and continues today. In groups that are homogenous with respect to race, ethnicity, or gender, individuals explore requirements for success in their organizations and examine issues that might be unique to their group. The goal is to empower minorities and women to be successful where they have not been the historically dominant group. When successful, participants gain insights and networking relationships that can promote individual and collective success.

Valuing differences, a popular approach dating back to the 1980s, has advocated not only accepting and respecting differences, but valuing them, as well. This approach alerts white males to ways their behavior can be disrespectful to minorities and women. As such, it has been useful in fostering the affirmation of minorities and women as "equal" organizational and community citizens.

The *cultural competency*, or *understanding differences*, approach focuses on promoting understanding of the cultures of the different racial, ethnic, and gender groups, under the assumption that greater understanding will enhance communications and relationships. Here the emphasis is on raising the cultural competency of members of all groups, not just white males.

Seminars on understanding and valuing differences and developing cultural competency set the stage for *leveraging differences*. Once differences are understood and valued, a next logical step is to ask if and how those differences might be used to benefit the organization. To the extent that they can be leveraged, their acceptance and value increases, so leveraging and valuing reinforce one another.

Political correctness is the action side of the awareness that comes with accepting, respecting, understanding, and valuing differences. The expectation is that when people are aware of how their actions might be inappropriate with respect to race, ethnicity, gender, and other pluralistic dimensions, they will behave more sensitively—referred to as being politically correct.

Finally, *inclusion*, when defined as ensuring that all feel that they belong, contribute as a part of the organization, and provide value, can serve as a useful tool in this quadrant. Here the goal is to ensure that all experience feelings of belonging and being valued.

Quadrant Accomplishments

By and large, the Managing Workforce Relationships strategy has generated civility within organizations, and, presently, civility does serve as the norm in most entities. Further, friendship and communication exist across racial and ethnic lines and suggest progress with accepting, understanding, and valuing differences across demographic differences.

Unfortunately, this progress with relationships has not solved the challenge of the revolving doors, glass ceilings, and premature plateaus for racial and ethnic minorities. White women appear to have made greater progress. Still, conversations with them reveal dissatisfaction with the price they perceive they've paid in terms of work-life issues.

As organizations have progressed in accepting, understanding, and valuing demographic differences, it has become clearer how unprepared organizations are to manage the resulting behavior diversity that can generate the "benefits of diversity." Remember the example of President Obama and his National Economic Council. Observers feared that the council might become too diverse and descend into gridlocked, divisive chaos. That is, the panel might have difficulty making quality decisions in the midst of their differences.

In the broader United States society, relationships across differences have become increasingly more tense—not just across race and ethnic lines, but across differences in general. Because of this phenomenon, talk about the divisiveness of our society is common; talk even exists about "culture wars." Indeed, President Obama campaigned on the theme of bringing the country together.

While there is no consensus about the extent of this divisiveness, there is growing sentiment about the need to curb tensions across differences. The extent of the turmoil raises questions about what we are teaching our youth about managing differences. In sum, we have done better within organizations than in society.

Why? In part, the potential for being fired for uncivil behavior acts to foster civility in the workplace. Also, organizations have focused on managing differences and valuing differences more than society in general has. Further, in the United States, society tends to be more protective of individual constitutional rights such as freedom of speech than organizations are. For example, what society might consider a legitimate practice of free speech an organization might ban as disruptive, divisive, and unacceptable. In general, society has a higher tolerance for controversy than a corporation with requirements for cooperation in pursuit of organizational objectives. As a result, society experiences more overt expressions of tensions than organizations do.

Quadrant Challenges

Several challenges come with this quadrant. *The notion of harmony is one.* As we mature with the concepts of demographic and behavioral diversity, as well as demographic tension, it becomes clear that tension is a given, and only so much harmony is possible. Further, it is clear that in this quadrant, the real tasks will be making quality decisions in the midst of demographic tension and becoming comfortable with this tension. It is not that harmony is unimportant or undesirable, but rather that it must be viewed within the dynamics of demographic diversity.

Those who see harmony as an indicator that they are affirmed as equals will have to become clear that *insensitivities that cause discomfort may not necessarily indicate a lack of respecting, understanding, and valuing.* They may, instead, be a reflection of the tension that comes with demographic diversity. Efforts should continue to minimize insensitivities, but their presence cannot be automatically viewed as evidence that an organization lacks a welcoming culture. Organizations and individuals will have to become more sophisticated about tensions and harmony in the context of pluralism and diversity.

A corollary challenge is created by *linking harmonious relationships and assimilation.* While many might embrace harmony, there has been considerable backlash against assimilation. Three examples illustrate this point. First, in the 1950s, William Whyte, in his book *The Organization Man,* cautioned that "groupthink" and conformity would dampen the individual's spirit and freedom.[1] His warning resonated far beyond the 1950s.

Second, in the late 1960s and early 1970s, within the black community, several thrusts appeared advocating the empowerment of blacks. One was the Black Power movement, which emphasized racial pride and the creation of black political and cultural institutions to nurture and promote black collective interests, advance black values, and secure black autonomy.[2]

Another thrust of the black empowerment surge was the Black Is Beautiful movement which, as an article in Wikipedia notes, was intended "to make African Americans totally and irreversibly proud of their racial and cultural heritage."[3]

Consistent with this thrust was one of the anthems of the Black Power movement, James Brown's 1968 recording, "Say It Loud—I'm Black and I'm Proud." This recording and another by James Brown, "I Don't Want Nobody to Give Me Nothing (Open Up the Door, I'll Get It Myself)," addressed prejudice toward blacks and the need for black empowerment.[4]

So paralleling this strategy's unfolding, and juxtapositioned with its emphasis on harmony and accepting, understanding, respecting, and valuing differences, was a black empowerment thrust that stressed self-reliance. As a result, African Americans, new to the corporate mainstream, had the task of maintaining their black identity and pride while assimilating and acculturating as needed.

The difficulty of this task was reflected in the divisiveness generated by Brown's recordings. In his autobiography, he reports losing his crossover audience after "Say It Loud—I'm Black and I'm Proud," noting that from that point forward, his concert crowds were mostly black.[5]

Ironically, a third challenge to the requirement of assimilation came from the success of this strategy in promoting acceptance of differences. As the general population become more aware that "being different" was not necessarily a negative, people became more comfortable being different. This, in turn, enhanced the backlash against assimilation and generated more differences and behavioral diversity—which made achieving harmony more problematic. The initial thinking that harmony could be achieved through assimilation had been compromised.

A *related organizational challenge has been balancing the desire for harmony and the need for diversity.* Pluralism (demographic diversity) has the potential to generate behavioral variations. However, an undue emphasis on harmony can stifle the possibility that this will happen. Organizations that desire the benefits of the behavioral variations that flow from demographic diversity would be wise not to eliminate or even minimize their associated representation tension. Instead, they will wish to see quality decision making *in spite of* the tension.

Because this strategy in part addresses individual beliefs, attitudes, and interpersonal skills, a further—and significant—challenge is to *make certain that progress with this "personal work" does not generate risky psychological trauma.* Only professional, well-qualified facilitators should be doing this work.

As in Quadrant 1, *diversity fatigue can be a challenge,* as well. This fatigue—the weariness that individuals sometimes express with respect to political correctness—is not uncommon.[6] People who experience it often ask such things as "Why do *they* have to be so sensitive?"

What complainers of fatigue miss are that the "different people" are not necessarily overly sensitive, but are navigating a culture that evolved without them in mind. The culture evolved under the assumptions of a homogeneous population of the dominant group. Unless members of that group change the culture so that it takes into account the emerging heterogeneity of the population, they will have to compensate for the culture. This will require being sensitive ("political correct") to where the environment does not work for those who are not members of the dominant group. Political correctness will become unnecessary only when organizational and societal cultures have been changed so that they work for everyone.

Another kind of fatigue has become an issue, as well. Diversity practitioners increasingly express fatigue over having to repeatedly plow the same ground with limited positive results. This tiredness becomes especially frustrating when they do not know how to get further traction in their work.

The potential for stereotyping is another challenge. Our increasing efforts to understand the different groups in the workforce, or other mixtures, can lead us to generalize unduly from the group to the individual—that is, to engage in stereotypical thinking, whether positive or negative.

Thomas Kochman and Jean Mavrelis address this challenge in their book *Corporate Tribalism: White Men/White Women and Cultural Diversity at Work.* The authors write of "cultural archetypes" that are "scientifically generated through the ethnographic process."[7] Their basic premise is that these cultural archetypes, defined as "a shared value, pattern, or attitude that *insiders* [italics added] would accept as representative of a significant number of members of their group,"[8] can help both corporate leaders and participants understand their own and others' beliefs and behaviors. Their discussion of cultural archetypes and stereotypes convinced me that care must be taken in applying a cultural archetype. Even statistically generated and "insider"-sanctioned items can be viewed only as a starting point in relating to members of a given group. It still is risky to *assume* that they hold true for a particular member.

The reality of multiple identities presents another reason for care with cultural archetypes—or generalizations. Consider, for example, a white male who identifies as a white male, an engineering professional, an alumnus of his alma mater, a member of his religious affiliation, and a member of his social fraternity. A cultural archetype based on his white male status would be less accurate for him as an individual if his dominant identification is with his religion. The utility of cultural archetypes depends on the extent to which they reference an individual's *dominant* affinity group—that is, the affinity group that most significantly influences that person's behavior.

A final challenge is that *accepting, understanding, respecting, and valuing differences has not resolved problems with revolving doors, glass ceilings, and premature plateauing.* This led in the 1980s to considerable rethinking of some basic assumptions of both Quadrants 1 and 2.

A major question regarding Quadrant 1 became "Can Affirmative Action produce sustainable progress?" Many advocates of Affirmative Action spiraled into frustration and doubt. Champions of Quadrant 2, with their agendas of eliminating racism and promoting harmony as the means to progress, also faced some tough questions, such as: "If we've been sensitized, and if we've minimized racism and sexism, why do we still have glass ceilings, revolving doors, and premature plateauing? Are there other forces at play? If so, what are they?"

Proponents of assimilation struggled to be clear about how to compensate for a declining willingness to assimilate. With less assimilation, would chaos emerge? Does "multiculturalism" mean multiple cultures in an organization? If so, how could this multiplicity be managed?

Facilitating Factors

Four facilitators are currently in play. A central one is that people are weary of perceived societal divisiveness. Their desire for less divisiveness surfaced during the 2008 presidential election in the United States. Also, we're becoming clearer that the prescription for "bringing us together" remains to be developed—that ending divisiveness is easier said than done. Such awareness should encourage greater focus on this challenge.

The growing sophistication of the diversity field also offers hope. Initially, diversity practitioners—internal and external—often were social justice and human rights advocates. Moral indignation and the righteousness of their cause provided fuel for their efforts, and, make no mistake, these individuals did achieve much and made a significant difference.

Now, however, a need for consolidation and systemic development of the practice *and* theory of diversity work is emerging. This is not a negative reflection on the pioneering advocates; indeed, if anything, it is a tribute to their work. Consolidation and systemic development are what one would expect in the natural order of a field's evolution and will build on the work of early practice pioneers.

As the diversity field's evolution moves forward, we will be learning more about diversity per se and will pay greater attention to the forest, or whole picture, of diversity. We'll also exert more effort on developing and extending concepts, paradigms, and frameworks. And, as this happens, we, individually and collectively, will learn more about how simultaneously to minimize dysfunctional divisiveness and foster acceptance, understanding, and respecting of differences—even intense ones.

Finally, the recognition of the cost of poor relationships across racial and ethnic lines—and for that matter, across other differences, as well—likely and hopefully will prompt progress. The United States cannot afford a continuing escalation of tensions across demographic differences. An inability to master the integration challenge in the midst of increasingly pronounced differences would threaten the connectedness of our societal fabric. The country has little choice but to make progress in this regard.

Global Perspective

The content of the previous section suggests a pattern for the evolution of diversity work. I suspect that—in all cultures—diversity work begins locally, oriented to the specific needs of a given situation in a country. Advocates driven by moral imperatives lead. The advocates' commitment and success attracts others, some of whom desire consolidation and systemic development, and expansion of theory *and* practice. The greater the consolidation and systemic development of theory, the more universal and global prescriptions become.

At that point, the task becomes one of consolidating universals derived from different geographical locations into one set of global-based universals. This chapter and its discussions about demographic relationships are an important first step toward the global universals that will benefit all.

UNDERGIRDING PARADIGM: APPLY THE GOLDEN RULE

The paradigm of the Managing Workplace Relationships strategy, Apply the Golden Rule, is the twin of the one undergirding the Quadrant 1 strategy, Make Amends for Past Wrongs. The two are fraternal, not identical, twins in that both are about different aspects of mainstreaming. Make Amends for Past Wrongs focuses on ensuring the *physical* presence of those who have been denied access to the mainstream because of slavery or discriminatory practices, while Apply the Golden Rule targets *relationship* mainstreaming.

To appreciate the Golden Rule paradigm, you must understand the context that gave rise to its popularity with respect to demographic diversity. During the early to middle 1960s, as the country experienced racial turmoil and the creation of civil rights–related laws, several questions were in the air: "Are blacks and whites truly equals?" "Can blacks and whites get along in the workplace?" "Do whites really want change?" "Can whites respect blacks as equals?" "Can blacks respect whites?" "Would blacks truly forgive?" Treating others as you would like to be treated promised encouraging answers to these questions.

Several features made this paradigm attractive in the midst of turmoil. First, it promoted harmony. Just on the surface, treating each other as you would like to be treated would seem to encourage harmony—assuming that new entrants wished to be treated as traditional participants did.

Second, it reinforced the notion that blacks and whites are equals. For whites to assume that blacks wanted to be treated as they like to be treated and to agree to treat them in this way would represent the essence of the equality of the two races—at least, on the surface. For descendants of slaveholders to agree to treat descendents of slaves in such a fashion reflected a strong signal of major change.

Third, it had a "moral imperative" feel about it—in part, because in one form or another, the Golden Rule can be traced to various religions (e.g., Buddhism, Baha'i Faith, Christianity, contrarianism, Hinduism, Islam, Jainism, Judaism, Sikhism, and Taoism) and philosophers (e.g., Pittacus, Confucius, Thales, Sextus the Pythagorean, Isocrates, and Epicurus).[9] This moral feel was appropriate, given that the issues on the table were related to slavery and discrimination.

Fourth, the Golden Rule possessed a healing or peacemaking aura. You can easily envision a playground scenario where a teacher asks little Johnnie, who is agitating little Billie, "Would you like Billie to treat you like you are treating him?" After Johnnie replied, "No," the teacher then would affirm the Golden Rule for both disputants.

Fifth, it implied reciprocity and a sense of fairness. Johnnie and Billie would likely leave this peace-making session thinking, "If I treat him like I want to be treated, he will treat me as I want to be treated." This reciprocity feature generates a win-win sentiment that is difficult to dispute.

Indeed, the Golden Rule's ethic of reciprocity explains why initial tools related to this paradigm focused primarily on awareness. Given the assumption of reciprocity, it was reasonable to believe that if individuals learn that their behavior is offensive, they will discontinue that behavior because they would not want to be treated that way.[10]

Finally, this paradigm is simple and straightforward—misleadingly so, as will be discussed later. Nevertheless, in the midst of racial turmoil, the Golden Rule was welcomed as a calming influence and a foundation for relationship mainstreaming. The paradigm also meshed well with efforts to foster racial healing and harmony. Even today, you can see its influence as this quadrant-paradigm combination continues to evolve.

PARADIGM PARAMETERS

Definition of Diversity

Like paradigm 1, paradigm 2 initially referred to racial and ethnic minorities and women. In practice, this meant defining diversity as *individuals who were different from white males*. In recent years, its focus has evolved to include other dimensions of demographic diversity: age, geographic origin, religion, educational background, and sexual orientation.

Goals

In the spirit of the civil rights movement, the intent of this paradigm was to foster relationship mainstreaming—to infuse blacks into the relationship mainstream of whites. Behind this overriding goal were three subgoals:

1. To encourage civility and racial peace. Against a backdrop of protests and riots, minimizing civil disturbance became a priority.

2. To foster harmony beyond peaceful coexistence through mutual acceptance, understanding, and respect. The civil peace thus achieved would aid in achieving social justice, human rights, and civil rights. Simply getting along was not enough.

3. To affirm the equality of all individuals. Initially, advocates intended to minimize any lingering doubt that the descendants of slaves were in any way less than the descendants of slaveholders.

The belief was that if these goals were achieved, whites and blacks not only would physically be part of a mixture, they would experience quality, authentic relationships across the races, as well. Some in the 1960s called this highly complex goal integration.

Motives

Why would subscribers to this paradigm accept its goal and subgoals? They wished to ensure that the equality and equal opportunity aspirations of the civil rights movement became reality. Like those in the United States desiring to end divisiveness today, advocates of this paradigm wanted to end the racial strife of the era of the civil rights movement. The paradigm became a major vehicle for achieving that end.

Many were motivated by the desire for social justice. Considerable consensus existed about the existence of injustices, particularly against African Americans. The Golden Rule offered a mindset for addressing those injustices and moving beyond them.

Principal Vehicles

By and large, the practice of the Golden Rule, which was supported by assimilation, acculturation, and the elimination of racism, was the principal vehicle for achieving the paradigm's goals. In the 1960s, 1970s, and early 1980s, this vehicle and its supporting processes played major roles in the evolution of this quadrant. Because of the apparent simplicity of applying the Golden Rule, most people who perceived those with racial and ethnic differences as equals saw the rule as a "gold standard" for fairness.

The Golden Rule approach was also attractive because it allowed individuals, organizations, and communities to work toward eliminating racism passively and proactively. Human Relations and Race Relations Councils, for example, used a passive approach when they addressed real issues in a problem-solving fashion. A major assumption in these settings was that the more the races interacted with each other, the more they would come to accept, understand, and respect each other—despite their "superficial" differences. Engagement with each other was key.

When I first came to Atlanta as a student, a biracial group of civic leaders routinely met to discuss problems as they arose. Many credited this group with ushering Atlanta through periods of racial turmoil. As I learned more about these leaders, I found that genuine relationships grounded in trust and respect *did* emerge among them. These individuals could come together and talk candidly about the city and its challenges. Tensions existed, but a concern for Atlanta and good intentions allowed quality problem solving in the midst of those tensions.

In some cities, demographically diverse leadership development groups continue to bring young leaders together to experience their community and its challenges. A major purpose of these programs is to foster cross-racial, cross-ethnic, and cross-gender networking based on trust and respect grounded in a genuine love for the participants' community.

A more proactive approach toward eliminating racism has been hard-hitting sessions aimed specifically at exploring racism in the community. In contrast to the passive approach, which sought engagement through problem solving and did not necessarily tackle racism, the emphasis here is on engagement through the exploration of the specific nature and magnitude of racism in the community or organization.

In corporations, a facilitator might convene blacks and whites for the purpose of exploring racism in their particular organizational environments. Key would be having black participants able and willing to present the perspective of their group's members. Such sessions have typically brought to the surface "racist" issues of which whites often professed to be unaware. In the best of circumstances, whites and blacks have left with a foundation for building problem solving. In other instances, some whites have left with an awareness that influenced their behavior, while others, both black and white, have left with a lack of clarity about what they should do with their learnings or, worse still, with cynicism.

The Golden Rule paradigm undergirded and has been supported by implicit and explicit requirements for acculturation and assimilation. *Acculturation*, the first level of integration, requires *only* "appropriate" behavior and is the most easily achieved of the various degrees of "fitting in." Success within the organization or community, for example, might require attendance at a Christmas party even though you might not personally celebrate Christmas. Mentoring, coaching, affinity groups, and acculturation workshops supported new entrants' efforts to acculturate.

Corporations, for example, frequently provided workshops for minorities and women around acculturation requirements. These sessions offered a wide range of prescriptions for fitting into a company's culture—ranging from how to decorate your office to how to position yourself for upward mobility.

Assimilation, the second level of integration, is more difficult. It requires greater commitment to organizational or community mores that may differ from your own. While acculturation might require that you attend the annual holiday party, assimilation demands that you convert to the religious beliefs behind the party. Acculturation might require that you be willing to relocate as necessary, while assimilation might call for a "company first" posture as you consider a transfer— even if it means being away from family for an extended time.

Acculturated individuals conform, while assimilated persons conform *and* believe. They do not just go through the motions.[11]

Today, the principal vehicle associated with this paradigm remains the practice of the Golden Rule, supported by the elimination of racism, acculturation, and assimilation. However, a couple of significant changes have occurred. First, as differences have become more acceptable, the desire to eliminate racism has expanded to include the desire to minimize bias against *any* groups characterized by differences of *any* kind in both minority and majority populations. I say "desire" because most would agree that much remains to be done in this area.

Second, the supporting vehicles have broadened their aspirations to include acculturation and assimilation on the part of communities and organizations, as well as individuals. The word "aspirations" suggests that this development may be more talk than reality. Organizational representatives speak of a willingness to make cultural changes with respect to diversity; however, anecdotal evidence and my personal experiences suggest that while cultures may have been tweaked to become more sensitive to minorities and women, they remain oriented to and dominated by white males. That means that although it may be politically incorrect to target minorities and women specifically and formally for acculturation and assimilation—as was done in the past—leaders and managers still expect these individuals to do most of the adapting to ensure a good individual-organization fit.

Principal Undergirding Assumptions

A critical assumption undergirding this paradigm has been that demographic diversity alone is not enough. Dr. Martin Luther King, Jr., articulated this in a speech entitled "The Ethical Demands for Integration."[12] He contended that desegregation and the resulting pluralism were not sufficient. He defined integration as "the positive acceptance of desegregation and the welcomed participation of Negroes into the total range of human activities." Integration was "genuine intergroup, interpersonal doing" and was not a means to an end but rather an ultimate goal in and of itself.[13] What Dr. King referred to as integration equates to what we have discussed as harmony, or what has been referred to in this chapter as relationship mainstreaming.

In this context, integration and harmony refer to a comprehensive cohesiveness with respect to relationships. This differs from racial pluralism, where the emphasis is on achieving racial representation with little attention to relationships.

While Dr. King saw integration as an end in and of itself, managers in this paradigm assumed that harmony was a requirement for optimal productivity. Lack of harmony would hinder overall productivity and the pursuit of organizational objectives.

A related and supporting assumption was that all individuals should be treated as "equals." Dr. King argued that integration (harmony) was needed because "Everybody is somebody."[14] Because the initial focus of this paradigm was on relationships between descendants of slaves and slaveholders, the treatment of all as "equals" and the acceptance that everybody is somebody became more challenging than it might otherwise have been.

That accepting, respecting, and valuing differences was a moral—social justice—human rights issue was another assumption. Dr. King felt that this harmony or integration was required by the fact that "We are all one and created by the same Creator."[15] This moral assumption is reflected in a description of the Golden Rule provided by a Wikipedia article entitled "Ethic of Reciprocity":

> The Golden Rule is an ethical code that states one has a right to just treatment, and a responsibility to ensure justice for others. It is also called the ethic of reciprocity. It is arguably the most essential basis for the modern concept of human rights. . . . A key element of the Golden Rule is that a person attempting to live by the rule treats all people, not just members of his or her in-group, with consideration.[16]

Still another assumption has been that differences are challenging, or that being different can be difficult. So much is said today about differences being good that it's easy to forget that a few years back no one wanted to be different. Being different meant "less than" or "lacking in some respect"—especially in the context of slaveholders and slaves.

A corollary here is the implicit or explicit assumption that everyone aspired to be as white and as male as possible—or, stated differently, as "normal" as possible. This was why whites could talk about inserting blacks into their mainstream. Also, this was in keeping with the civil rights movement's claim that with the exception of color, we were all the same. We all bled red when cut.

Finally, another important assumption was that blacks would be willing to acculturate and to assimilate. Given the challenges of being different, it seemed reasonable to expect that people who were different would be open to acculturation and assimilation, especially if their differences related to their ancestors having been slaves. And, in fact, many leaders and managers assumed that blacks would leave their "blackness" at the door and seek to fit in as much as possible.

These are the basic assumptions that have undergirded the evolution of this paradigm. Some have challenged these assumptions and suggested modifications, but that does not change the reality that they are the "roots" of this quadrant.

Key Obstacles

A critical obstacle to treating everyone as an "equal" and with respect has been the legacy of slavery and discrimination. I think that fundamentally we have overestimated the ease with which this could be achieved. More specifically, we underestimated the difficulty with which an organizational or communal culture evolved by and for a homogeneous dominant group could become one that respects members of all groups.

Members of the dominant group likely would struggle to do only as much as absolutely necessary as they considered cultural changes, while members of subordinate groups would be vigilant to ensure that apparent respect was real and meaningful. This, of course, has led to very stressful debates about when enough is enough with regard to political correctness.

Much (not all) racial discord in our organizations and communities appears to be less about racism (malicious action against a person because of his or her race) than about a perceived lack of respect, in part because of bigotry and prejudices. This raises the questions of how we show authentic respect to each other, and, also, whether one can be too sensitive about alleged acts of disrespect.

Another obstacle has been the reality of demographic tension. This obstacle has come into play as organizations and communities have pursued harmony and have realized that demographic tension comes with demographic diversity (representation). This reality conflicts with the legacy of the civil rights movement's tendency to focus on similarities and not differences. The concept of demographic tensions says that regardless of how similar you might be, if you have demographic diversity, you will have demographic tension.

Another challenging obstacle has been a changing attitude about differences. Contrary to the initial assumption undergirding this paradigm, that differences are problematic at best, many now see differences as good and as something to be embraced. This emerging perspective not only legitimizes being different, but also raises doubt about the wisdom of acculturation and assimilation. As such, it can make getting along more challenging and complex as differences become more acceptable and prevalent. (Remember, demographic diversity generates demographic tension.) Without a doubt, this change in attitude presents a major challenge for this paradigm.

Initially, this paradigm argued for acceptance and tolerance of differences on the one hand and acculturation and assimilation on the other. This facilitated harmony. However, the compromise opened the door wide for demographic diversity and demographic tension, and ultimately for skepticism about the usefulness of acculturation and assimilation for dealing with differences.

Acculturation and assimilation have become less attractive as the need to escape being different has diminished. In the process, across-the-board, indiscriminate use of acculturation and assimilation is now seen as inappropriate. Obviously, roles exist for acculturation and assimilation. The issue becomes when and how to use these options.

While the general population has become less enthusiastic about across-the-board acculturation and assimilation, blacks, in particular, tend to find it unacceptable. That is because the notion of integrating blacks into the white mainstream does not support thinking of blacks and whites as equals. It is true, as I stated earlier, that the essence of the Golden Rule supports the equality of the races. It is also true that for whites to agree to treat blacks as they (whites) would like to be treated can be interpreted as acknowledgment that the races are equal. On the other hand, if blacks and whites are equal, why not construct a new mainstream that reflects the attributes and requirements of blacks *and* whites, instead of integrating blacks into the existing white mainstream?

"New" would not have to mean "totally different," but rather could mean a white mainstream modified to reflect black *and* white realities. The supporting processes of assimilation and acculturation made it clear, however, that constructing a new mainstream or modifying the existing one—designed by and maintained for whites—was not an option.

A final obstacle for this paradigm has been the failure of the United States society to make significant progress with integration. In *Someone Else's House: America's Unfinished Struggle for Integration*, Tamar Jacoby notes the decline of integration as a goal:

> Integration is in decline as a goal not as much because we do not believe in it but because we've failed to get there. The means haven't

worked, or have made the problem worse, and when one road after another leads to a dead end, it's natural to start believing we can't get there from here. Devising new strategies will not be easy; but history can guide us, if we know how to listen.[17]

To sum up: The challenge has been to achieve integration (relationship mainstreaming) in the midst of growing awareness and acceptance of demographic diversity and the corresponding demographic tensions. To date, we have not done well. We have sown the seeds of accepting, understanding, and respecting demographic diversity; however, we have not evolved integration mechanisms that will work in the midst of expanding diversity and related tensions. This societal failure spills over into the country's organizations and dampens their internal efforts to achieve integration.

Key Facilators

Among the facilitators is the tendency of many to see the Golden Rule and integration (harmony) as moral issues. "Do the right thing" is the mantra for these individuals. The morality perspective drives this group to continue seeking a way to achieve integration in the midst of demographic diversity.

Further, as stated previously, people are tired of strife. They want to move beyond the divisiveness that characterizes identity group conflict. They demonstrated this in the last U.S. presidential election. Many of the electorate sought someone to "bring us together."

Finally, the horses are out of the barn. Differences now more than ever are a part of the country's landscape. Unless we learn to achieve integration in the midst of these differences, the United States faces an increasingly complex dynamic of demographic diversity, identity group politics, and demographic diversity tensions. Without progress with integration, divisiveness likely will hold sway and make us increasingly dysfunctional as the country struggles with complex issues.

Desired Results

Initially, this paradigm sought to mainstream African Americans into the dominant white male relationship culture. This was before diversity and the acceptance of differences. Now it is unclear what the goals of this paradigm and its related quadrant are. Do we still envision continuing a white male relationship culture, with others assimilating and acculturating as required? Are we aspiring to a new relationship culture that can encompass all groups without one being dominant? Or do we envision muddling through divisiveness with band-aids and "making do" with the status quo?

Clearly, we desperately need more discussion, dialogue, and debate about our alternatives and their pros and cons. We need to think deeply about how to achieve integration in the midst of demographic diversity and identity groups. More specifically, we need to determine how to accept, understand, and respect differences while pursuing integration. In short, we need to learn to advocate and celebrate demographic diversity while simultaneously pursuing integration. I think that World-Class Diversity Management can be helpful in this regard, once we are clear about what we want to do. World-Class Diversity Management can help us build a culture that works for multiple groups in the absence of a dominant group.

Strategic Predisposition

The strategy most associated with the Apply the Golden Rule paradigm has been Managing Workforce Relationships. While diversity does compromise the Golden Rule, making it less simple, its implicit tenets of accepting, understanding, respecting, and valuing differences have held sway over efforts to achieve integration in the workforce.

Most of the professed consternation about demographic diversity tends to be about the numbers. *However, I believe that much of the difficulty in sustaining representation gains can be traced to relationship issues around the accepting, understanding, respecting, and valuing of differences.* Further progress with this quadrant should result in more success with Quadrant 1's numeric goals.

Some Critical Questions

Although I have talked about this quadrant for a number of years, rarely have I discussed it as being about integration. Nor have I heard many practitioners describe their work as being about what we traditionally have called integration. Whether this says something about the work we are doing or our understanding of the word *integration*, I do not know. I *am* clear, however, that this quadrant-paradigm combination is about fostering traditional integration (relationship mainstreaming). As such, its role in fostering and supporting success in Quadrant 1 is significant.

Below is an exploration of a few questions based on the earlier discussion of Quadrant 2 and its supporting paradigm. These explorations will provide a transition to Quadrant 3.

Question 1: *Will the Platinum Rule ("Treat others the way they want to be treated"*[18]) *replace the Golden Rule as the undergirding paradigm for this quadrant?*

I do not think so. While the basic assumptions that made the Golden Rule effective as the undergirding for this quadrant have been compromised, it is still useful. Among its pluses are its grounding in religious and philosophical cornerstones, its implicit assumption of equality, its ethic of reciprocity, and its implicit endorsement of accepting differences.

Its negatives are significant. Not the least of these are the complexities of differences and demographic diversity. Further, the compromising of acculturation and assimilation as supporting vehicles makes the Golden Rule more difficult to apply.

I think that in the midst of demographic diversity, the Golden Rule is inadequate as a guide for personal interactions. But as a tool for establishing a values framework or a climate context—for this quadrant and its pursuit of integration—I believe it remains credible and effective. To me, the Platinum Rule does not offer sufficient added value to merit replacing the Golden Rule. As we gain more experience with the Platinum Rule, replacement may make more sense.

Question 2: *Do we need integration (harmony)?*

This is a fair question, given the limited attention to integration per se. Even in organizations where considerable integration activity is under way, this activity is not held in high esteem. Organizational associates not only discount integration activities; they often carry them out with low expectations. Rather than expecting significant progress and accountability with integration, leaders, managers, and individual contributors settle for civility and getting along. Two factors may account for this: The first is ambivalence about integration; the second is an inadequate understanding of how to achieve it even when it is desired.

Achieving desirable and sustainable levels of civility and peace is not a mean feat and is not to be dismissed lightly. Indeed, in the midst of a growing amount of demographic and behavioral diversity and the resulting diversity tensions, it can be quite an accomplishment.

So, do we need integration? I think we do. At issue is what kind and how much. Although carried out in a very different context, the work of Paul Lawrence and Jay Lorsch in *Organization and Environ-*

ment around the concepts of differentiation and integration seems relevant.[19] Lorsch, in a subsequent work, *Managing Diversity and Interdependence: An Organizational Study of Multidimensional Firms*, provides a summary review of his pioneering work with Lawrence and offers the following definitions of differentiation and integration:[20]

> Differentiation . . . was defined as the differences in behavioral, cognitive, and emotional orientations, and ways of organizing work which develop among managers in different organizational units as each of these units copes with its part of the organization's total environment . . . [21]
>
> Integration was defined as the quality of collaboration which exists among departments required to achieve unity of effort by the environment.[22]

As Lawrence and Lorsch studied functional departments, they found that "the more differentiated any two interdependent units were, the more difficulty they encountered in achieving integration."[23] From the perspective of organizational design, the work of Lawrence and Lorsch suggests that in the context of an organization's task environments, managers seeking to analyze and diagnose their organizational structures should ask four questions:

1. How much and what kind of functional differentiation is required?
2. How much and what kind of functional integration is required?
3. What kind of mechanisms will be required to achieve the required amount of differentiation?
4. What kind of mechanisms will be required to achieve the required amount of integration?

If this framework is applied to race relations (specifically, black-white relations), the key finding about the paradoxical relationship between functional differentiation and integration can be restated as follows: "The more different any two interdependent racial groups become, the more difficulty they will encounter in achieving integration (relationship mainstreaming)." And the four organizational design questions become the following:

1. How much and what kind of differentiation (differences) are organizations and their employees required to allow between whites and blacks?
2. What kind of mechanisms will be required to achieve and sustain this necessary differentiation between whites and blacks?
3. How much and what kind of integration is optimal between whites and blacks?
4. What kind of mechanisms will be required to achieve and sustain the optimal amount of integration between whites and blacks?

This framework is useful in examining black-white relations in our society, as well. It helps to explain why claims of accepting, understanding, respecting, and valuing differences have compromised integration issues and generated an increase in pronounced diversity. The more you accept, understand, respect, and value demographic differences, the more demographic tensions you will have. Also, the greater the tensions, the greater the challenge of integration. This racial differentiation-integration tension has been exacerbated by an assumption that racial differences imply inequality among the races. In light of African Americans' requirement of affirmation as "equals," this assumption has worked further against integration.

In addition, a look at the four design questions as they apply to white-black relations reveals that these inquiries have not been addressed. With respect to integration, for example, we have assumed a "We want it all" response as to how much integration is required. Truth be told, there are degrees of racial integration. What is appropriate depends on the situation. It is not true that "as much as possible" fits every situation. That premise is useful *only* if we assume that racial differences (differentiation) suggest inequality and we are trying to demonstrate racial equality. Under that assumption, "We want it all" is valuable—especially when we are trying to eliminate differences (read inequalities).

So back to the question "Do we need integration?" As stated earlier, the issue is what kind and how much. Chart 2-1 presents descriptions of three prototypical levels of integration. The optimal degree of integration depends on the situation. For example, if there is a high level of interdependence between the races, or a high need for affirmation of "equals," a high level of integration is needed. In addition, if an organization is seeking to raise the level of engagement across the board, a high level of racial integration is essential.

The point is that although we think we want as much integration as possible, it might not be desirable because if we achieve that aspiration, we might not get the degree of differentiation needed. It is also a matter of readiness. We may need a high level of integration ultimately but not be ready, or able, to pull it off.

If, on the other hand, for whatever reason, a low level of interdependence exists between blacks and whites (perhaps blacks are clustered in a self-contained department), there is not likely to be a pressing need for integration. In addition, if the blacks in the organization are clear about being equals and don't require affirmation, the demand for integration might be low.

Once you are clear about the optimal level of integration and differentiation, you must decide which mechanisms will allow you to achieve that level. This may not be easy. Given that we have been working on relationship integration for over forty years and that racial blow-ups are often about respect and sensitivity issues rather than outright, overt, racial hostility, existing mechanisms appear to be inadequate. We need to assess these systems, refine them in innovative ways, and extend them. We may even need to replace them with a new set of mechanisms.

In any event, we as individuals, organizations, and a nation have not addressed explicitly these four questions about racial differentiation. We

CHART 2-1. Prototypical Workforce Racial Integration Levels

Analytical Variable	Low	Moderate	High
Racial Identity	• High, visible • Strong affinity groups	• Moderate, visible • Weak affinity groups	• Not visible • No affinity groups
Racial Relations	• Civil • Low level of trust • Separate at lunch and after work • Separate social networks • Racial missteps met by great surprise and dismay	• Civil • Emerging trust • Separate and homogenous groupings at lunch and after work • Some overlapping of social networks • Racial missteps met with surprise and dismay	• Civil • High level of trust • Rarely see racially homogenous groups at lunch • Cross-racial socializing after work • Social networks racially heterogeneous • Racial missteps treated as natural by-products of diversity and met with professional problem solving
Working Relations	• Little routine cross-racial problem solving (low interdependence)	• Routine cross-racial problem solving not uncommon	• Cross-racial problem solving *and* collaboration are common and critical
Commitment to Company	• Low level of engagement • Associates refer to company as "they" • Company seen primarily as source of paycheck • Acculturation low	• Moderate level of engagement • Associates tend to refer to company as "we" • Beginning to identify with company's mission and vision • Acculturation moderate	• High level of engagement • Associates refer to company as "we" • High level of identification with company

are long overdue for that discussion—especially in light of the embracing of differences and diversity. As part of that discussion, we might benefit from reviewing what has been said in the Complex Organizations literature about differentiation and integration.

Question 3: *When will we be able to stop worrying about being politically correct? Or when will the United States be post-racial?*

In the context of racial integration, political correctness refers to the efforts of both majority and minority individuals to behave in ways that foster cohesive relationships across races. This typically means behaving in ways that are out of the norm and often inconvenient. This, in turn, means that political correctness requires a lot of tiptoeing around, as if walking on eggshells. It can be tiring for all parties.

When will political correctness no longer be needed? I'm not expecting that any time soon. Only two conditions would make it prudent. The first is if we abandon the integration goal (and that seems unlikely). The second is if all parties were to agree and declare that integration has been achieved. Accepting either condition would be foolhardy unless or until we first understand what we are seeking.

Presently, the country seems ambivalent about integration. We have been pursuing it since the 1960s. Currently, few talk about it. Those who do often express weariness about political correctness. Yet I believe that we will continue our integration efforts—in part, because our collective preference is an integrated populace. We as a country have never said that we wanted diversity. What we *have* said is that our country will be welcoming to a broad array of people as long as they become members of our mainstream. This is what we have said about African Americans. Specifically, we desire a mainstream populated by diverse people defined not by their diversity but by their commitment, acculturation, and assimilation to the United States' mainstream.

This suggests that a large part of the challenge is about more than just relationships. It also involves creating a mainstream that works for people defined in significant part by their diversity. Such a mainstream would allow them to commit to the new dominant, all-embracing culture while retaining their diverse affinities. This conflicts with the "melting pot" aspiration of our society. We will need to develop new mindsets and aspirations if we are to achieve such a culture.

Question 4: *What should we do about "eggshell" situations?*

With respect to racial integration, it is important to understand and accept eggshell situations for what they are—signs of evolving change—while at the same time realizing that by their nature they can be taxing. This realization is the first step in responding to the resulting stress.

A key aid in handling eggshell situations is to know yourself. A good practice is to monitor your response to determine if you are over- or underreacting. Another good practice is to check the lens you are using to view the situation. Are you seeing it as one of race relations, of class relations, or of diversity, to name a few possibilities?

As I was writing this chapter, an African American male university professor experienced an encounter with a local, white male policeman in Cambridge, Massachusetts. The professor and his African American driver had difficulty opening the front door to his home. A neighbor saw the two black males struggling with the door and called the police to report a burglary in progress. By the time the policeman arrived, the two men had gained entry to the professor's home. The policeman entered the house and asked for identification. From this point, scenarios differ.

The professor contended that the policeman was rude and disrespectful, while the policeman argued that the professor was rude and disorderly. The policeman arrested the professor, who was subsequently released after disorderly conduct charges were dropped. The incident received national visibility and various citations as a case of racial profiling; the professor demanded an apology, which the policeman refused to give. Ultimately, the president of the United States invited the two of them for a beer.[24]

It didn't have to happen the way it did, though. If both men had realized that they were in an eggshell situation of the first magnitude, they could have dialed down their behavior to avoid provoking the other and walked away from the encounter. That is, they might have chosen to be politically correct.

They also could have checked the lens through which they were seeing their situation. If they were using a race relations lens, as apparently they were, the professor possibly saw in front of him a white policeman reflecting all he had learned and heard about improper police behavior toward African Americans The policeman possibly saw the stereotype of an uppity African American man refusing to accept the legitimate authority of a white male. This racial relations lens probably is the most volatile of possibilities.

A city-university lens would have suggested to both men that racial dynamics were not necessarily the issue. The encounter could be seen as reflecting the traditional tensions between the city and the university. Here the professor might have viewed the policeman as the personification of an unreasonable city government, while the policeman might have seen the professor as representative of high-brow academic circles. This scenario likely would have been less volatile than that seen through the racial dynamics lens.

Another lens possibility would be that of class relations. Here each man would have seen the other as reflecting a particular class of society, and that would have been the crux of their conflict. Indeed, for the policeman and the professor, that, too, might have been an intense situation.

Whatever the lens they were using, mutual self-awareness and the ability to step back and use multiple lenses could have helped to ratchet down a tense situation. Overreacting or underreacting can be dangerous in eggshell situations. Essentially, Quadrant 2 is about managing eggshell situations and reducing their occurrence. As long as race-relations eggshell situations are plentiful, political correctness will be around.

Question 5: *Within corporations and throughout United States society, diversity practitioners are frequently viewed as low persons in the hierarchy—whether they work internally or externally. Why are diversity practitioners often held in low esteem?*

A possible reason is our society's ambivalence about diversity. We have always welcomed the idea of diversity as long as it molded into the mainstream without racial and ethnic identities. This was the color-blind ideal.

The need of blacks for affirmation as equals led organizations to claim that they valued diversity—or for some, differences—as a way of assuring blacks they were equal and welcomed. This affirmation of blacks' equal status—despite their history of enslavement—opened the door for diversity of all kinds and challenged the notion that being different was undesirable. Few anticipated that mainstreaming blacks would compromise the color-blind, melting-pot ideal. Jacoby describes the prevailing sentiment about mainstreaming blacks:

> The common White assumption, so widely held that it was rarely discussed, posited that Blacks, like other migrant groups, would simply assimilate into the mainstream. "The early definition of integration," James Farmer noted years later, "said forget you're Black, forget that you're a Negro. Just think of yourself as an American. All you need is a little learning and you'll do fine." Once Jim Crow barriers had been removed, it was assumed Blacks would naturally and inevitably move into the system, climbing the familiar ladder—public education, on the job training, mom-and-pop entrepreneurship, and ward politics—into the middle class and beyond. What Blacks needed from Whites was simply access to the ladder, and beyond that they would require no further help . . . [25]

Jacoby's comments capture well the thinking that blacks would fit into the mainstream and offer minimum diversity, that after the removal of Jim Crow barriers everything would be fine. Further, her discussion suggests that the ease of integrating descendants of slaves and slaveholders was underestimated. The need to work on relationships was not anticipated.

That means that diversity practitioners have two strikes against them. They are advocating and facilitating something that goes against the United States grain—partially acculturated and assimilated diversity. Additionally, they are engaged in what was not anticipated—working on relationship integration between blacks and whites.

Not anticipating having to work on black-white relationships was reasonable. Given that blacks had been enslaved and discriminated against as less than human, surely they would be grateful for inclusion and an opportunity to fit into the mainstream. Why would they have difficulty getting along with their benefactors?

Global Perspective

Individuals reading this chapter may have noted that I have not included the experiences of other minorities and women. That is true. My purpose has been to explore the origin of this diversity management strategy and its initial evolution, not to give a full accounting of its ongoing development. A major implication, however, is that the United States' approach to demographic relationships has been driven by its experiences with African Americans.

Given that reality, is there any relevancy of this approach for countries other than the United States? I think so.

All countries must decide who is to be allowed in the midst, and to what degree, and how those individuals are to be integrated. How much differentiation and integration are desired? What mechanisms would be required?

In sum, specifics of this chapter may be United States–centric, but the core dynamics are global in nature. The issues of integration and differentiation are not unique to the United States.

DISCUSSION

For me, a major learning in this chapter has been the realization that the United States now has more visible and celebrated differences than its leaders ever anticipated. Further, the country's vehicles for dealing with differences—assimilation and acculturation—have been compromised.

This in part explains the current divisiveness that citizens increasingly desire to get around. In the absence of effective mechanisms for producing the required integration, even as differences increase in quantity and significance, the result predictably will be intensified demographic tensions. These differences and their corresponding diversity had not been a part of the country's vision. Instead, the United Sates desired *acculturated* diversity.

Our current situation presses for development of an enhanced capability to manage diversity—not just in our organizations, but also in our broader society. Without this capability, our racial, ethnic, and gender differentiation may outstrip our integration efforts.

SOME TAKE-AWAYS

1. CEOs engage the strategy of Managing Workforce Relationships to deal with the diversity issues that come with the mainstreaming of African Americans, other minorities, and women.

2. The strategy's driving motive has been a search for justice, which in terms of relationships has meant, operationally, the accepting, respecting, and valuing of differences.

3. Operationally, this strategy can also be viewed as being about the integration of nontraditional workers into the relationship mainstream of traditional white male workers.

4. Progress has been made in fostering the accepting, respecting, and valuing of differences, which in turn has compromised integration efforts. (The greater the acceptance of differences, the greater the degree of difficulty becomes in achieving the desired level of integration.)

5. The desired degree of integration can vary across situations.

6. Relationship integration does not necessarily mean talent integration.

7. The undergirding paradigm is Apply the Golden Rule, which incidentally is not totally compatible with accepting, respecting, and valuing differences.

3 MANAGING DIVERSE TALENT

MANAGING DIVERSE TALENT

MAXIMIZE INDIVIDUAL ENGAGEMENT

Quadrant 3

The Managing Diverse Talent Quadrant emerged when the earlier two strategies did not resolve a seemingly intractable problem. As CEOs made progress with creating a representative workforce and promoting productive relationships, they struggled with the persistent and ongoing challenge of retaining nontraditional workers. They concluded in the mid-1980s that part of the problem was their inability to fully utilize the capabilities of African Americans. Recruiting them and accepting, respecting, and valuing their differences had not led to full utilization of their talent and to their retention. The revolving doors, glass ceilings, and premature plateaus continued. So management began to embrace this strategy in hopes of enhancing utilization and thereby, retention of African Americans. Later, this strategy was extended to women and other minorities. However, as in previous chapters, from an evolutionary perspective, I will focus on the situation vis-à-vis African Americans.

In attempting to address the diversity problem, CEOs again encountered the complexity of diversity—this time with respect to fully utilizing the talent of *all* organizational employees. In the mid-1980s, a prevailing managerial philosophy was that "the cream would rise to the top." But CEOs found that this relatively uncomplicated approach to people development was not working: The cream of African Americans in particular was not rising to the top. Complexities engulfed this diversity problem. A few are mentioned below:

1. No consensus existed as to what was causing the problem. One school of thought argued that African Americans simply were not qualified, not necessarily through any fault of their own—but nevertheless, unqualified. Some who expressed this view believed that "employing unqualified African Americans was now a cost of doing business."

A second school of thought asserted that corporations did not know how to engage a heterogeneous workforce—that their culture and systems were all geared around a homogeneous white male workforce. The school of business dean of a historically black school routinely responded when asked whether his students were ready for corporate America, "Is corporate America ready for our students?"

2. Many—indeed, most—organizational managers were not managing anyone. Most were outstanding "doers" of the work on the lookout for any rising cream that might be of help. "People managers" or "managers good with people" were rare. Racial diversity further complicated the task of managing for those managers who were already ill prepared.

3. Efforts to facilitate full utilization often created a stigma.[1] Such efforts, often known as "leveling the playing field" drew mixed reviews.

Some saw them as needed and welcomed them. Others viewed them as giving opportunity to unqualified African Americans and hurting qualified white males. As a result, individuals who benefited from the leveling process were often stigmatized.

African Americans differed in their opinions of these efforts. Some wanted to avoid the stigma. Others felt that the playing field was not level and welcomed any corrective measures. Still others welcomed corrective measures if they materialized, but also were prepared to succeed without them—even if it meant working longer and harder than white males who were playing on a level playing field.[2]

4. The legacy of slavery remained in play and generated questions like these:

- Can African Americans *really* learn?
- Can African Americans *really* produce? How do we know they are not fully utilized at their current low levels of productivity?
- If they were *really* qualified, would they not naturally rise to the top?

Finally, it was becoming clear that organizational cultures and systems must change if corporations and other enterprises were to achieve full utilization of all employees. This complexity remains a challenge today.

In the midst of these complexities, CEOs embarked on this core diversity management strategy by attempting to create an environment that empowered everyone to contribute to their full potential. I initially called this strategy Managing Diversity and then later Managing Workforce Diversity. I now refer to it as Managing Diverse Talent to highlight the role of this strategy implicit in talent management. I believe that it is impossible to engage a diverse talent pool without a Managing Diverse Talent capability.[3]

As noted above, this belief and the strategy that developed from it grew out of the continuing frustration of organizational leaders, who were unable to realize sufficient representation and relationship integration to create the desired degree of sustainability with demographic diversity. When I entered the diversity field in the mid-1980s, executives and managers frequently puzzled over this failure. Manager after manager described a frustrating cycle characterized by successful recruitment of minorities—African Americans again, in particular—only to be followed by a disappointing loss of gains and periods of dormancy.

I developed this strategy in response to the question "Will managers be able to continue using the same approaches they employed to engage a homogeneous workforce with respect to race, gender, and ethnicity, or will they need to do things differently to fully engage a body of diverse individuals?"[4] I believed that something more would be needed. As a result, this chapter emphasizes what organizations can do to engage a diverse workforce once they have created it and ensured at least the beginnings of appropriate cross-ethnic and cross-racial relationships.

This engagement is urgent because it is impossible to achieve a high level of demographic integration without it. The effectiveness with which an organization engages a diverse workforce ultimately will determine its success in managing diversity relationships and, indeed, maintaining its representation gains. Engagement with the organization here becomes part of the ties that bind (integrate) people cohesively with each other in pursuit of organizational objectives. As a result, it is nearly impossible to achieve full utilization of diverse talent without maximum engagement.

As I wrote in *Beyond Race and Gender: Unleashing the Power of Your Total Workforce by Managing Diversity*,[5] achieving this engagement requires that organizations and their managers define managing as "creating an environment that allows the people being managed to reach their full potential and to act accordingly." At its best, this means eliciting from employees not only everything the organization has a right to expect, but everything they have to offer.[6]

Specifically, this approach's perspective is anchored in Empowerment Management, which appeared in the mid-1980s, reached its peak popularity in the mid-1990s, and is now resurging as high-involvement management in the context of talent management.[7] I contrasted Empowerment Management with the Doer Model of management in *Beyond Race and Gender*.[8] Doer managers see employees as extensions of themselves, as opposed to assets to be empowered. Empowerment Managers view employees as assets to be engaged or enabled in pursuit of organizational objectives.

A cornerstone of this strategy is the differentiation between *creating, celebrating* or *embracing*, and *engaging* workforce diversity. Unlike Quadrants 1 and 2, in which achieving representation goals and establishing quality relationships initially were essentially ends in themselves, Quadrant 3 seeks to establish conditions that allow a diverse workforce to contribute to the full extent possible in pursuit of organizational objectives.

A corollary cornerstone of this approach has been the importance of organizational culture. This was the first strategy to suggest that organizational cultural change might be required if internal environments were to enable managers to access talent however it comes packaged. Key to this idea was the question "Will a culture designed by and for white males allow the full accessing of everyone's talent, or will it be necessary to implement cultural change in pursuit of full utilization of available talent?"[9]

Also differentiating Quadrant 3 from the previous two quadrants was the definition of diversity as demographic *and* behavioral diversity along *all* workforce dimensions—as opposed to primarily the dimensions of race, ethnicity, and gender. A further difference was that this quadrant clearly specified white males as diverse, so references to the diverse work force included *all* participants—not just racial and ethnic minorities and women.

QUADRANT PARAMETERS

Diversity

In contrast to Quadrants 1 and 2, this core strategy defines diversity as the differences and similarities that can exist among the members of a workforce. While Quadrants 1 and 2 have focused on the demographic attribute dimensions of diversity, Quadrant 3 expands the focus to include behavioral dimensions such as work practices and thought. It further acknowledges that these differences and similarities generate tensions and complexities. With this definition, *any* new member joining the workforce brings differences or similarities of some sort. Accordingly, everyone is considered to be diverse—including white males.

Goals

Quadrant 3 seeks to achieve full engagement of the talents of *all* members of a diverse workforce. It is not enough simply to elicit compliance with a manager's directives. Organizations must create an environment that encourages a directed and nondirected flow of capabilities in pursuit of the organization's goals. Here associates connect with a company's mission, vision, strategy, and culture and freely look for opportunities (including and going beyond those pointed out by managers) to advance the well-being of the enterprise. Empowered individuals share a commitment to determine and pursue what is in the organization's best interest—in part because they are simultaneously serving their own interest.

Obviously, empowerment is an ideal, but to the extent people are engaged, they not only bind with the organization, they also bind with each other.

FIGURE 3-1. Three-Legged Stool Requirements for Full Workforce Utilization

This strategy is the third leg of a three-legged stool whose legs represent the requirements for fully utilizing the talents of a diverse pool—namely, (1) creating a diverse workforce, (2) fostering quality relations along *all* dimensions of demographic diversity, and (3) creating managerial systems that engage and empower a demographic *and* behaviorally diverse talent pool. (See figure 3-1.) If you use only the first leg, you will have a demographic pool of talent without integration. If you use legs one and two, you will have a demographically diverse pool of talent with integration to the extent possible. In either of these situations, neither sustained progress with demographic diversity nor full utilization is possible because the "managerial strategy" has not been put in place.

The third leg embraces and relies on the first two. It presumes at least minimum effectiveness with the first two. Full utilization of talent truly is a three-legged stool.

I've been asked if the legs must be implemented in a particular sequence. Typically, the question is "Thomas, can you learn how to manage African Americans before you recruit some to your workforce?"

The answer is "No, you cannot learn to manage *African Americans* before you employ some." You can, however, learn how to manage *diversity* before African Americans arrive. You develop this capability by practicing on the diversity you do have. If you do not have racial diversity, perhaps you have diversity of age or tenure with the organization. Regardless of the dimensions on which you develop a diversity management capability, you can always transfer it to any other dimension.

You cannot, of course, learn to manage diversity before you have at least *some* diversity. Practically speaking, however, I know of no actual workforce without diversity of some kind. So sequencing is not an issue.

Regardless of your sequencing, all three legs are required for effective management of any dimension.

Motives

To enhance competitive advantage in pursuit of organizational objections by eliminating the revolving door, premature plateau, and glass ceiling limitations of the earlier two quadrants has been the driving force behind this quadrant. Because this central motive emphasizes engaging talent in pursuit of an enterprise's viability, many refer to it as the business rationale. Some refer to it as the competitive advantage motive.

Leaders, managers, and practitioners can and do come to Quadrant 3 with a social justice–civil rights–human rights motive. These individuals understand that without a managerial environment that engages all, they will be unable to realize maximum or sustained progress with Quadrants 1 and 2.

Focus

By far, the major focus of this quadrant is *managerial capability*. It raises the question of whether organizations have the capability to manage a demographically and behaviorally diverse pool of talent. *By stressing Empowerment Management, this quadrant implicitly says that traditional "doer" managerial practices do not work for a diverse workforce.*

The doer management model sees the manager as having two responsibilities: (1) managing the business and (2) managing people. *In Beyond Race and Gender,* I wrote the following:

> Typically they [doer managers] see their job as two-dimensional: They must manage the business and manage people. . . . And they fail to integrate the two. Typically, they talk of "people" and "business" issues as if they were unrelated. Furthermore, they see "doing" as their major task and taking care of people as secondary. They cherish the "real work" of doing (accounting, for example) and minimize "managing people" activity. Any hint of a "people challenge" is referred immediately to the human resources department.[10]

The doer manager sees himself as the center of the action, the "chief doer," if you will. From his perspective, the organization promoted him because of his doer capabilities and expects that he will continue to *do*; therefore, in his view, his primary focus should be on doing. Further, people are assigned to him not as assets to be empowered, but rather as assets to serve as extensions of him, to expand his capability to engage in doing. In essence, managing people (diverse or not) is not a legitimate priority for the doer manager.[11]

I expressed these sentiments in 1991, but the tendencies they describe continue. Indeed, people management responsibilities in sizable enterprises have by and large been given formally or informally to a talent management or human resource department, thereby freeing up the manager to do even more "doing."

The same is true for managing diversity. Today, in large, and not so large, organizations, senior line management has delegated diversity issues to a diversity department headed up by a chief diversity officer.

My concern isn't the expansion and enhanced professionalization of human resources and diversity departments. It is about separating people management and diversity management from line managers. Ultimately, line management must manage both people *and* diversity—albeit assisted by human resources and diversity professionals.

As such, line managers must be proficient in Empowerment Management. This model sees no duality between managing people and "doing" the business. The empowerment manager's principal responsibility is to enable her people to do the work. The model directly links empowerment of people to business objectives. So, for example, accountants who become empowerment managers are agreeing to give up doing accounting work and to focus on enabling others to do accounting in pursuit of business objectives. Accountants who love the process of accounting may—and often do—have difficulty giving up doing accounting and focusing on empowering others. Because this is true, of course, for practitioners in multiple arenas, it has been difficult for individuals and organizations to let go of the doer model. Refusing to do so, however, has multiple organizational and social costs.

The Doer Management model is particularly inappropriate for achieving the goals of Quadrant 3. First, it discourages acceptance of diversity. Doer managers seek people who can predictably clone their behavior. They aren't interested in the ways differences can enhance corporate profits. Second, doer managers don't see managing people as a legitimate activity. They will always have difficulty managing a diverse workforce because they place no priority on managing people in general.[12]

Managing Diverse Talent requires that all aspects of management be examined to ensure that they are in tune with Empowerment Management and work to engage all. These include the organization's mission, vision, strategy, culture, recruitment practices, selection criteria, measurement systems, performance appraisal process, promotional practices, planning processes, and compensation. In practice, most organizations tweak these parameters and adjust them only when they prove problematic for a diverse pool of talent. Managing Diverse Talent prescribes a more proactive approach—one that anticipates that traditional practices will be insufficient for a diverse workforce.

For example, organizations that wish to continue traditional practices must explore ways they can be carried out in nontraditional ways. Consider the case of mentoring within organizations. Traditionally, the mentor and mentee share commonalities of gender, race, and so forth. Indeed, they are often paired for their perceived compatibility. In a diverse environment, however, this process more appropriately would work to identify and nurture talent in individuals who differ from their mentors in significant ways.

Managing Diverse Talent differs from Quadrants 1 and 2 by focusing not just on managers, but also on the individual associate as actor. In Quadrants 1 and 2, the focus is on what the organization can do through its managers to foster workforce representation and quality demographic diversity relationships. An implicit and sometimes explicit assumption can be that racial and ethnic minorities and women have been suffering victims, and it is up to white male organizational leaders to fix matters.

Managing Diverse Talent and the attendant Empowerment Management philosophy, on the other hand, broaden responsibility for the company's success with Managing Diverse Talent by prescribing that every individual—regardless of organizational position—has managing diversity responsibility. All are called upon to make quality decisions in the midst of differences, similarities, tensions, and complexities along all dimensions of workforce diversity. This quadrant offers the Strategic Diversity Management Process as a structure and guide to facilitate such decision making.[13]

I explored the complexity of this decision making in *Building a House of Diversity: How a Fable about a Giraffe and an Elephant Offers New Strategies for Today's Workforce.*[14] The fable goes as follows:

A giraffe builds a house for himself and his family. It is a great house, designed to accommodate the giraffe's uniqueness. He enjoys his house so much that he puts his woodcrafting business in the basement so that he can work without leaving his home. As the business grows, he must seek help.

The giraffe knows and respects the woodcrafting skills of a local elephant and invites him to join the business. The elephant agrees to come on board. Once in the business, however, the elephant experiences the challenges one would anticipate in a house built for a giraffe—high, narrow door frames and steep, narrow steps. A major point of the discussion in the fable is what the giraffe should do. After exploring the giraffe's options, attention turns to the elephant's alternatives. The point is that *both* the giraffe and the elephant must manage diversity.

Just as the giraffe must decide when—if ever—and how she will change her house, the elephant must decide whether he would—or could, or should—change his physical parameters so that he can fit in, or just resign from the business. Both have critical decisions to make.

In real life, elephants don't always appreciate their options and, indeed, are not always prepared to accept their responsibility to "manage" diversity. Giraffes, too, aren't always aware or appreciative of the elephant's call to manage diversity. They are preoccupied with their decisions and obligations as the dominant players in the situation.

A final focus of Managing Diverse Talent has been organizational culture. Quadrant 3 defines an organization's culture as the fundamental assumptions that drive the organization and the manifestations that flow from those assumptions. Its basic premise is that those fundamental assumptions constrain what an organization can do. Little of lasting consequence will endure if incongruent with those assumptions. To ensure sustained success with diversity aspirations, organizations must examine their organizational culture to determine its congruence with the diversity agenda. What is incongruent must be changed.[15]

Once again, this is a major shift from the previous quadrants. Both assumed that minorities and women would make the adjustments and that organizations and their cultures would remain intact. For organizations, the prospect of culture change—not as an accommodation to minorities and women but as a way to equip managers for accessing talent, regardless of how it comes packaged—is a major challenge, one that I have defined as analogous to personality change.

Assume for a minute that after interacting with you for a while, I suggest that you appear to need a personality change. I inform you that I can help with the process.

Now, given that you have had your personality for much of your life, your initial response likely would be not a rush to get on with the modification, but rather a cautious attitude: "Do we really need to do this?" "Can we just wait, and the need will pass?" Organizations respond similarly. They do not rush to tamper with their culture. So this quadrant's prescription of cultural change where needed differs enormously from the invitations of other quadrants to fit everyone in.

In practice, most organizations prefer to modify the manifestations and to leave the driving assumptions alone. There are two key reasons for this: (1) the magnitude and complexity of the task of changing assumptions is daunting; (2) few managers possess the experience and expertise to pull off a cultural change around assumptions *and* manifestations. This is, in fact, why many diversity initiatives do not succeed. Modifying manifestations is intended to change behaviors. New behaviors that do not fit an organization's basic assumptions don't "take hold."

Approaches

Adding leg three of the three-legged stool does not mean that the approaches of Quadrants 1 and 2 are no longer available. Those approaches explicitly and implicitly contribute to the vitality of Quadrant

3, and the approaches of Quadrant 3 complement those of the other two strategies. One approach differentiating this strategy from the other two is its reliance on *cultural change*, where culture is defined as the basic assumptions that drive an organization and also the manifestations that flow from them.[16] This is also the first strategy to propose that a diverse workforce may require a different organizational culture from that which was appropriate for a homogenous workforce.

Successful culture change is an arduous process. Organizational leaders must do the following:

- Identify their diversity aspirations.
- Identify driving assumptions and manifestations.
- Determine whether the identified culture is compatible with diversity aspirations. (If it is, no cultural change is required.)
- Determine what assumptions *and* manifestations would support their diversity aspirations.
- Compare the current organizational culture with that needed for their diversity aspirations. The resulting gap represents the nature and amount of cultural change required.
- Prepare a change plan for closing the gap—for transitioning the culture to the newly identified desired state.
- Implement the plan.
- Institutionalize the changes (lock them in place).[17]

These steps require a temperament and skills that few managers possess. They also require patience and persistence. Some cultures have been in place for decades; as such, modifications often will require multiple years for full implementation and institutionalization.

Cultural change is one of the most misunderstood and poorly implemented aspects of the diversity arena. Some of the most common errors are these:

- Confusing the organizational culture with organizational climate. In an online article, Mitch McCrimmon compares culture to one's personality and climate to an individual's mood.[18] Mood is more temporary than personality and easier to change. Organizations often gather information on climate and call it culture, but that ignores the driving assumptions and perhaps some manifestations.

- Failing to get at the driving assumptions. This error springs from the previous one. Driving assumptions are analogous to the roots of a tree—out of sight, underground, but controlling what the tree can and cannot become. A tree with peach roots cannot easily become an apple tree. If an organization's roots do not support diversity, its aspirations are doomed. For example, if an organization has a root labeled "We ought to behave as if we are family" that sees family membership as a prerequisite for organizational participation, but minorities and other nontraditional employees would find it difficult to qualify as part of a white male family, diversity is not encouraged. Similarly, if one of an enterprise's roots is the Doer Model of management, diversity will be thwarted. Without a change in or replacement of these roots, no amount of effort will bring sustainable progress with diversity.

- Lack of a clear definition of diversity.

- Failure to specify diversity aspirations. This error springs from the previous one. Without clarity as to what should be achieved, it is difficult to assess the compatibility of the current culture. Culture can only be evaluated in context. Yet managers frequently speak of a good or bad culture without specifying the objective being served.

- Failure to specify the desired culture. If the existing culture is inadequate, what culture would be appropriate? Again, clarity about what is hoped for is essential to determining the parameters of the desired culture. Managers often imply what they want from the new culture by criticizing the existing one. They neglect to state explicitly what they are aiming for.

- Failure to plan carefully before implementing cultural change. This is a big trap. Implementation cannot be shortchanged. Yet many managers appear to run out of gas after careful and effective analyses of the existing and desired cultures. Sometimes they don't understand the magnitude and complexity of changing driving assumptions. Often, multiyear plans are needed in this arena, where managers have relatively little expertise and even shorter time frames. Managers who lack a multiyear perspective may be tempted to act as if identifying and understanding the need for cultural change equate to implementation.

- Failure to institutionalize (lock in) cultural change is a major error. In the rare cases where the earlier errors have been avoided, change agents often fail to institutionalize change. This involves knitting the new assumptions into the fabric of the enterprise, and it can take several years to accomplish. Here, once again, the obstacle may be the manager's short time frame.

I often hear managers talking about having changed their organization's culture relatively quickly—within the past year, say, or even the past three years. This relatively short time period suggests in and of itself that the desired cultural change was not properly and fully implemented.

Changing cultural assumptions is very difficult, and many prefer instead to devote strenuous effort to bringing about desired behaviors. However, if those behaviors are incompatible with the driving assumptions, it is only a matter of time before the assumptions signal, "I'm still here," and stifle the newly instituted and incompatible behaviors.

In sum, in the area of diversity, managers have not mastered the tool of cultural change. They may "talk" and "think" the game, but they still have difficulty "walking" their talk and thoughts.

Cultural change, though essential, is not enough. *Cultural manifestations*—systems, policies, and practices—must be altered to reflect the change. This, too, can be a challenge.

CDOs often report that their organization's cross-ethnic, cross-racial, and cross-gender relations are good, as are their numbers. They express concern, however, that promotions (upward-mobility opportunities) are not proportionately distributed across their demographically diverse workforce. These managers worry about how to get the attention of senior management, which perceives no issue.

These CDOs have some work ahead of them. Once they secure their senior colleagues' endorsement to address this challenge, they will have to dismantle and analyze their upward-mobility process brick by brick. The goal: to determine why it is not generating opportunities proportionate to the ethnic, racial, and gender representation in the workforce.

Many if not most diversity officers attempt to address manifestations before looking at culture. Theoretically, this could work, but *only* if it is part of a roundabout way of getting to culture. Usually what happens is that managers determine what the problems are and identify corrective behaviors. They then "backtrack" to ensure that the organization's culture is compatible with the planned corrections. If the culture is not congruent, they seek a set of corrections that will be compatible, change the culture, or undertake some combination of those options. A tempting and ill-fated trap is to put the corrections in even without compatibility with the driving assumptions. Experience demonstrates that that is a prescription for failure.

In today's environment, making the business case for managing diversity is a significant approach (for the government and nonprofit sectors, viability corresponds to the "business case" for the business sector). Organizations rarely undertake major culture changes or substantial modifications in systems, policies, and practices without a strong sense that the changes will enhance the organization's viability. If managers are to make the business case for managing diversity with respect to diverse talent, their organizations must first view talent as strategic. They often do not. When I have made this assertion in a discussion with various groups of senior executives, more than one key executive has said, "I'm not sure that I even think people are strategic." The low priority that organizations often place on people matters explains in part why advocates for diversity management have difficulty making a compelling business case.

Another reason for this difficulty is that advocates often try to make the business case for diversity while referring to representation or demographic diversity, as defined in Quadrants 1 and 2. The strongest rationale for these two quadrants (strategies) may be not a business case, but rather one that relates to social justice, civil rights, or human rights. Advocates can, however, make a strong business case for Managing Diverse Talent and its prescriptions for cultural and systems changes where needed. Here the potential gains in terms of enterprise objectives are clear. As a result, the business case for managing diversity is considerably more compelling than the business case for demographic diversity or quality relationships.

When defined as I define Managing Diverse Talent, *managing inclusion* can be a tool for this quadrant. However, I also have heard it defined as I define Managing Workforce Representation and Managing Workforce Relationships. I even have heard it used when the user had no idea what it meant. One CDO spoke proudly and convincingly about his firm's work with diversity and inclusion. "Diversity and inclusion" was spread throughout his conversation. So convincing were his statements that I was inspired to learn more about what he meant by inclusion. When I asked, he burst out laughing and said, "That's what we are trying to determine."

I personally do not refer to inclusion—primarily, because however I have heard or seen it defined, it falls within the confines of what I have called Managing Workforce Representation, Managing Workforce Relationships, and Managing Diverse Talent. Since I was using this terminology or some variants before "inclusion" came into vogue, for me, the potential value added is not significant enough to merit change.

Also, "inclusion" belies the reality that effective management of diversity can call for exclusion, as will be seen in my discussion of the Strategic Diversity Management Process in chapter 5. So minimization of confusion is another reason I don't use inclusion phraseology.

I do, however, recommend that CEOs and their colleagues, as well as others, use the terminology that they find useful, and that they do not get caught up in semantic games. What matters is that they are secure about the meanings behind the terminology they employ and how their terminology differs from alternatives. I hope that the inclusive nature of the Four Quadrants will help with that clarification process.

I also argue that regardless of whatever nomenclature you use, the essence of the three-legged stool will be required for full utilization of workforce potential. Keep the stool in mind.

Quadrant Accomplishments

So much talk abounds about "managing workforce diversity" that it is hard to believe so little has been accomplished. The achievements of this quadrant by and large remain to be realized. That's not to say that much good work has not been done under the rubric of managing workforce diversity; it has. However, it has tended to relate to legs one and two of the three-legged stool.

The biggest accomplishment to date is that this strategy now is on the radar screen of most diversity practitioners, even though they may be unclear about what it is and what it requires. Stated differently, many are recognizing the need for a three-legged stool to achieve full utilization of talent. Being visible on the radar screen is a significant and substantial achievement, but it is only a first step. Actualizing this strategy remains to be accomplished.

Quadrant Challenges

As with earlier quadrants, some important challenges work against applying this approach effectively. *Perhaps the most significant challenge is the illegitimacy of management.* In many organizations, this illegitimacy is the Achilles' heel of Quadrant 3, which is often called the "managerial quadrant." Individuals frequently want to be managers but do not desire to function as empowerment managers. They prefer the Doer Model of management, which allows them to continue to "do" the work. Because Empowerment Management is one of the quadrant's cornerstones, that preference hampers the adaptation of this approach.

It is true that Empowerment Management is a popular concept in many circles, even though confusion remains as to what it is. It is frequently used in conjunction with engagement and other managerial thrusts such as High-Involvement Management,[19] Six Sigma,[20] and Total Quality.[21] Yet the continuing prevalence of the Doer Management model indicates that the concept has not moved into large-scale practice.

The difficulty of cultural change presents another obstacle. While the need for such change can be apparent, and it is easy to talk cultural change, as noted earlier in this chapter, effective implementation eludes many.

Conceptual confusion between managing diversity and civil rights creates another obstacle. This confusion is a problem because the mindsets behind each are so different—the pursuit of managerial effectiveness and efficiencies in the midst of workforce similarities and differences on the one hand, and the pursuit of sustainable justice on the other.

This is not to say the two concepts are incompatible. If, in the name of social justice and civil rights, organizations assemble a diverse workforce and encourage harmonious relationships, they cannot sustain these gains without the ability to engage this diverse talent in pursuit of their enterprise objectives. Managing diversity complements civil rights.

Because we have ignored their ability to complement each other, the notion persists that the two strategies are in conflict. Interestingly, organizations' failure to reconcile these strategies can be seen as a diversity challenge that involves a mixture of two methodologies. It can further be seen to reflect the inadequacy of a developing managing diversity capability. Unless organizations grow in this capability, they will be unable to reconcile the two. Unless reconciliation takes place, their diversity capability will remain stifled. This presents a challenging stalemate.[22]

Facilitating Factors

A critical facilitating factor is that integration of talent (Managing Diverse Talent) is essential to stabilizing representation and relationships gains. Organizations that recruit a diverse pool of employees and integrate them into the enterprise's relationship networks but fail to access and integrate their talent will see that talent leave.

By the same token, organizations that recruit a diverse pool of employees and access and integrate their talent but fail to integrate then into relationship networks will also see significant departures. Full utilization of the workforce requires the three legs of the stool: representation, relationships, and empowerment.

A second facilitating factor is that in today's economic climate, few corporations can afford to underutilize human assets. Full utilization of human resources was once an ideal; today, it is rapidly becoming a necessity.

Finally, while the creation of representative and diverse workforces cannot be taken for granted, we've made enough progress to permit raising the question "Now that we have a diverse workforce, how do we manage it to secure realization of its full potential?" Up to this point, managers have been so preoccupied with creating a diverse pool of talent that they could not focus on the managerial questions.

While few in number, these facilitating factors represent major shifts that will encourage organizations to embrace the Managing Diverse Talent strategy.

Global Perspectives

Fundamentally, the Managing Diverse Talent strategy focuses on effective management of human resources characterized by demographic and behavioral diversity. While the specifies may vary, corporations across the globe are dealing with this issue. In that lies this chapter's global applicability.

UNDERGIRDING PARADIGM: MAXIMIZE INDIVIDUAL ENGAGEMENT

The Maximize Individual Engagement paradigm was a logical follow-up to the Make Amends for Past Wrongs and Apply the Golden Rule paradigms because it addresses a key reality: It is not enough to have a diverse workforce that gets along. Managers must also be able to tap the potential of *all* of their employees in pursuit of organizational objectives. This task became more pressing as both the new entrants and traditional white males became less inclined toward assimilation.

If individuals had remained willing to assimilate across a broad range of variables, their demographic diversity would not necessarily have resulted in behavior diversity, and traditional managerial practices more likely would have been effective. However, in the midst of a declining willingness to assimilate and the continuing reality of glass ceilings, revolving doors, and premature plateaus, the managerial question of the day became "Are organizational managers prepared for a diverse talent pool?" Many were concerned that they were not.

The need for a better way led to the Maximize Individual Engagement paradigm, which incorporates two subcomponents: Empowerment Management and organizational cultural change. I talked earlier about why Empowerment Management gained favor with respect to diversity over traditional Doer Model practices, but I should make one other point.

The value of the Empowerment Management component, which had its seeds in the 1950s but became more widely accepted in the 1980s, is made clear in Ed Lawler's description of High-Involvement Management, the most recent incarnation of Empowerment Management. He writes,

> The high-involvement approach places a great emphasis on the nature of work that individuals do. It argues for work that allows individuals to make decisions, gives them feedback about the effectiveness of their performance, and challenges them to develop and use their skills and abilities. It also emphasizes the importance of having employees who have the ability to self-manage, are well trained, and can reasonably expect to have careers with the organization.[23]

This contrasts significantly with the Doer Management model, which relies on hierarchy and compliance. A workplace that employs High-Involvement Management holds the promise of engaging *all* employees by conveying to *all* associates that they are viewed as "equals" and welcoming their potential to contribute on their own. As such, it suits tumultuous times and offers a solution to unsolved management problems.

The second subcomponent of the Maximize Individual Engagement paradigm, organizational cultural change, also helps to create an environment that works for all associates. In the mid-1980s, as this paradigm was evolving, the works of Deal and Kennedy,[24] Peters and Waterman,[25] and Schein[26] were noting the importance of organizational culture in influencing behavior. I particularly found Schein's definition of culture as "the basic assumptions and beliefs that are shared by members of an organization"[27] to be insightful. These assumptions give rise to manifestations such as values, vision strategy, myths, rites, rituals, network processes and systems, structure, and traditions.[28]

In *Beyond Race and Gender*, I conceptualized the organization as a tree, with its roots being Schein's driving assumptions and its branches being their manifestations. A critical point is that the roots (assumptions) are out of sight and out of awareness. At that time, enterprises struggled with revolving doors, glass ceilings, and premature plateaus with respect to minorities and women. I believed that a major issue was whether organizational cultures (driving assumptions and manifestations) meshed with their diversity aspirations. So I wrote about the importance of culture and cultural audits, a research process designed to unearth and assess these driving assumptions to see whether or how they support the organization in successfully managing diversity.[29]

In many instances, the inability to integrate organizational talent remains, and I still believe that the process of finding what in the organization's culture does and does not support its diversity aspirations is critical for successful diversity management.

PARADIGM PARAMETERS

Definition of Diversity

This paradigm defines diversity not as people or as elements of a collective mixture, but rather as *the differences, similarities, and related tensions and complexities that can exist among the components of the mixture.* A diverse mixture, therefore, becomes one characterized by differences, similarities, and related tensions and complexities. Every member of the mixture contributes to its diversity in some fashion.

That means that *all* members of the workforce are included in the concept of a diverse workforce. A "diverse hire," therefore, refers to any qualified, breathing individual. With respect to any given diversity dimension, each individual brings differences or similarities, or both.

A member of the workforce might, for example, consider herself to be an early baby boomer and have similarities with others in the baby boomer category, but because she is an "early boomer" as opposed to a "late boomer," she would bring similarities and differences with respect to the dimension of age.

I suspect this is true for most—if not all—categorizations. Years ago, I conducted research on the experiences of ethnic groups such as African Americans, Hispanics, Asians, Pacific Islanders, and Native Americans. To my surprise, I found an enormous number of subgroupings under each categorization. It was as if the larger designations were intended to minimize the need to deal with the diversity of each.

I have long held this paradigm's definition of workforce diversity as being more than race and gender. Indeed, the title of my first book—*Beyond Race and Gender*[30]—mirrors this claim. In that book I wrote,

> Diversity includes everyone; it is not something that is defined by race or gender. It extends to age, personal and corporate background, education, function, and personality. It includes life-style, sexual preference, geographic origin, tenure with the organization, exempt or nonexempt status, and management or non-management. It also shows up clearly with companies involved in acquisitions and mergers. In this expanded context, white males are as diverse as their colleagues. A commitment to diversity is a commitment to all employees, not an attempt at preferential treatment.[31]

This paradigm also defines diversity as demographic and behavioral diversity (thinking and interpersonal styles, for example). Even twenty years later, this inclusion of behavioral diversity remains significant and represents a departure from the previous two strategy-paradigm combinations. My thinking, as I contributed to formulating this paradigm-approach option, was that one reason glass ceilings, revolving doors, and premature plateaus persisted was the often unrecognized and unaddressed reality of behavioral diversity. Simply stated, individuals operating out of the previous two strategies have acted as if assimilation and acculturation were working.

Goals

Accessing talent regardless of how it is packaged is, without a doubt, this paradigm's overarching goal. This aspiration recognizes that although talent can come in packages that are similar, it can also arrive in some very dissimilar combinations of attributes. It further acknowledges that as late as the mid-1990s, managers had done an uneven job of accessing talent contained in disparate packaging. These recognitions, implicit in this paradigm, resulted from the following realities: (1) global markets were becoming more attractive and competitive; (2) the makeup of the U.S. workforce was changing significantly, toward more demographic diversity; and (3) individuals were stepping up their resistance to assimilation and acculturation.[32]

Supporting the overarching goal have been two subgoals. One has been integration of talent. In her "Personal Diversity Paradigm: A Tool for Exploring Your Orientation to Diversity," Elizabeth Holmes states that one of that paradigm's goals was to "foster unity of purpose and cohesiveness among workforce or other group members and to integrate all talent into the mainstream."[33] This statement suggests that two integration processes were under way: (1) developing unity and cohesiveness among individuals (the explicit purpose of Quadrant 2 and a secondary purpose of Quadrant 3), and (2) accessing and inserting the talents of all into the talent mainstream. While the integration of people does facilitate the integration of talent, the two are different tasks. Failure to integrate talent shows up when managers underutilize people.

In one setting, for example, many fast-track white males talked fondly about an African American male who had "taught them the ropes" and started their climb up the hierarchy. All spoke highly of him, his talent, and his willingness to teach; yet he remained at the bottom of the pyramid—presumably because no one knew he wanted to be promoted.

Here an individual participates in the organization's relationship mainstream, in that he is accepted, respected, valued, and beloved. However, he is not included in the talent mainstream—even though he prepares white males for their upward mobility within the mainstream. Undoubtedly, his managers have not accessed his talent fully and included it in the talent mainstream. He is part of the "people" but not the talent mainstream. This integration subgoal explains why empowering work environments are so important to fostering the mainstreaming of talent.

Lawler's description of a contemporary version of Empowerment Management (High-Involvement Management) captures its potential for fostering talent integration:

> Perhaps the defining feature of high-involvement organizations is that they value a long-term loyalty relationship with their workforce and make a major effort to demonstrate the commitment of the organization and a sense of community in the organization. They also emphasize a commitment to high job and financial performance. This is usually done in the context of building commitment to the organization and creating a win-win relationship with employees.[34]

Motive

This paradigm's motive is competitive advantage. A CEO, trying to understand why his corporation needed to embrace this paradigm and its corresponding strategy, Managing Diverse Talent, captured the motive as follows: "Let me see if I get this. If I am in a fight and my opponent has all of his faculties, and I am fighting with one arm tied behind my back, I'm at a competitive disadvantage. Managing Diverse Talent frees my arm and levels the playing field. Is that right?" "Yes," I replied.

A corollary is that if both opponents are fighting with one arm tied behind their back, the first to figure out how to free his limb will have a competitive advantage. The corporation that pioneers with Managing Diverse Talent will gain a competitive edge over those who wait on the sidelines.

Principal Vehicles

At least four vehicles have played major roles in pursuing the aspirations of the paradigm Maximize Individual Engagement. Theoretically, at least for me, as I have contributed to this paradigm's development, the *Complex Organizations theory* has been a principal vehicle—especially the works of Paul R. Lawrence and Jay W. Lorsch.[35] Their emphasis on differentiation, integration, and related mechanisms has supported my thinking on the integration of people *and* talent in the midst of demographic diversity *and* behavioral diversity. It also has made it easier to think beyond race and gender and to focus on differences *and* similarities.

Diversity defined broadly has been another vehicle. Although I have used "defined broadly" many, many times in writings and presentations, I really do not believe you have the option of defining diversity narrowly or broadly. The definition is what it is. You, do, however, have options as to how broadly you wish to focus on diversity. So, here, a more accurate statement would be "This paradigm has adopted an inclusive diversity definition that embraces all possible dimensions. While still acknowledging and addressing race and gender dimensions, it takes into account other variables as well."

Because it explicitly placed on the table that organizational parameters (culture, systems, policies, and practices) might have to be changed to develop a capability for accessing talent, *organizational culture* has been a critical vehicle. Given the nature and magnitude of culture change, the potential enormity of the task of engaging diverse talent became clearer through discussion and analyses of organizational cultures. This clarity empowered some; it frightened and essentially immobilized others.

Those who were frightened either went with a watered-down version of organizational culture change or concluded that it was too great a challenge for them to address. So, for many, organizational culture has become something people know should be assessed and possibly changed, but few feel prepared to attempt that.

A fourth major vehicle has been *Empowerment Management*. Indeed, maximizing individual engagement cannot happen without Empowerment Management. This managerial option explicitly and implicitly incorporates the notion of a diverse workforce.

Principal Undergirding Assumptions

Several assumptions differentiate this paradigm from the previous ones.

One, managers *and* associates are jointly responsible for developing individual performance. This assumption differs from more traditional ones such as "The cream will rise to the top naturally" and "The individual is responsible for her development." In each of these two instances, neither the organization nor its managers do any adapting; they place the burden solely on the individual.

The challenge with the traditional assumptions is that the "one-way adaptation" approach does not help managers who seek to convey to nontraditional workforce entrants that they are welcomed and are equals. This is especially true in the context of slavery and discrimination. Asking those whose ancestors have been enslaved or discriminated against by white males to fit into an environment developed for, managed by, and maintained for white males does not communicate equality.

Two, the manager's role in the two-way adaptation process is to create an environment that facilitates accessing *all* talent. Within this discussion, this may appear to be obvious, but it is not necessarily so. Many managers do not accept this as their role, or at best they give lip service to the proposition. They often feel that associates are there to serve as extensions of them and to enhance their (the managers') ability to do the work.

In a research setting, associates reporting to one manager finally accused him of plagiarism. They would submit reports to him, and if he liked and agreed with their work, he would literally remove their names and place his on the cover sheet as author. When challenged, he expressed great surprise, for he had seen the associates as extensions of himself. He felt that he had been made a manager and assigned associates so that his capability to research would be expanded. Instead of having one set of hands with which to conduct research, he had additional sets equal to the number of people assigned to him. He had no inkling that his job was no longer to do research, but rather to create an environment where his associates could do research and reach *their* full potential.

Three, Empowerment Management is necessary for integrating (or accessing) the talents of all diverse people—including white males. In a climate where people are cautious about assimilation and acculturation, it will be impossible to integrate all talent without both Empowerment Management and the development of a new mainstream—one different from that dominated by white males. Managers must design a talent mainstream that engages and embraces all talent—including white males—regardless of how it comes packaged.

Not everyone agrees with these propositions. The critics respond by saying things like this:

- "Our country and its organizations have done well with the white male–dominated talent mainstream, so we need to be careful with change here."
- "Really sounds like white male bashing to me."
- "So what do you gain by replacing a white male–dominated talent mainstream with one dominated by minorities and women?"
- "So now we want to punish white males?"

The comments are reasonable and need to be addressed. However, what is being proposed is not the bashing or punishing of white males, or the establishment of talent mainstreams dominated by minorities and women. Rather, it is the development of mainstreams that embrace *all* talent, regardless of how it is packaged. Failing to develop such a mainstream means that we as a society are prepared to continue accepting the costs of revolving doors, glass ceilings, and premature plateaus that we have experienced in Quadrants 1 and 2. Empowerment Management is the key to eliminating these costs.

How do we know such underutilization of minorities and women exists? Is it not possible that we have tapped all they have to offer? One down-to-earth senior executive addressed these questions: "Hell, I don't need sophisticated evidence that we are underutilizing minorities and women. We're running around saying we need more and more leadership; yet we have people in our corporation who are leading all kinds of organizations in the community but are sitting on their hands in corners within the company. Why can we not tap that obvious talent?"

Can we afford not to tap fully the potential of all employees? In today's economic times of uncertainty and intense competition, organizations can ill afford to underutilize *any* talent. Wasted talent translates into lost efficiency and effectiveness and lost competitive standing. No enterprise can stand consistent, systemic underutilization of any segment of its workforce without paying a significant price.

Four, an environment that presumes conformity and assimilation may be inappropriate for a diverse workforce (including white males). The changing attitude toward being different and resistance to across-the-board assimilation have compromised the effectiveness of traditional managerial environments. Such environments may not work for all employees because of their implicit message about the inequality of associates.

Five, the ability to access and integrate talent is a business (viability) issue. I made this point in *Beyond Race and Gender* with respect to corporations. Two decades later, the message still seems appropriate:

> It is not necessary here to document the battering that U.S. companies have taken from overseas and domestic competitors, or to describe the climate of competitiveness that drives so many major corporate decisions. This competition is not going to go away; it is only going to increase, as American companies continue their scramble to markets.
>
> The point for us to remember is that, at the same time, they are scrambling for the best talent they can find. And searching for ways to get the best from the employees they now have. That is at the core of the business rationale for thinking about diversity. Managers must be clear about this.[36]

The fact that integration of talent is a business issue does not mean that it is not a civil rights–human rights–social justice issue, as well. Diversity practitioners and other change agents can select the rationale they believe will be effective in their given situation. Most enterprises (businesses and others) find it difficult to embrace Empowerment Management and entertain culture changes where required, unless its leaders are convinced of the business (viability) rationale for talent integration. Where the viability case cannot be made, it will be difficult to generate sustainable change.

Key Obstacles

Proponents of this paradigm face a number of obstacles. First, the two cornerstones of the paradigm, Empowerment Management and organizational cultural change, have yet to become the norm. While I see efforts to be more empowering, the Doer Model remains the fundamental assumption and preferred option for managers. This is true even in organizations where managers talk about the desirability of Empowerment Management.

That doesn't mean that nothing has changed. Twenty-five years ago, when my colleagues and I began conducting cultural audits, we found overwhelming indications that managers paid relatively little attention to people management and, indeed, were not really rewarded for addressing people issues. Interview and survey respondents spoke as if people and work issues were separate.

More recent cultural audit research data suggest that managers—especially supervisors—do appear to be delegating more around specific job tasks. Even so, managing people still receives less priority than doing the work. This is especially true for senior managers and executives. As a result, developing people ranks among the lowest items in terms of attention received.

The slowness to embrace Empowerment Management, which has morphed first into Engagement Management and subsequently into High-Involvement Management, is in significant part due to the complexity of implementing it. The philosophy cannot be implemented without adequate preparation. Where managers lack readiness to practice Empowerment Management, or employees lack readiness to be empowered, the result has been confusion and a perception that "anything goes." It has become clear that Empowerment Management is not a panacea, nor is it an option for all situations.[37]

All of this has contributed to this cornerstone of the paradigm becoming problematic. The fact that it continues to be reincarnated provides testimony that its potential is real. A major issue is implementation.

The challenge of organizational culture change comprises the second cornerstone of this paradigm. Often, widespread agreement will exist that cultural change is needed to foster effective managing of diversity. However, the translation of that consensus into successful change management has remained elusive. Managers either stop short of actual cultural change, or they simply cannot bring about lasting modifications.

Second, the legacies of organizational environments that originated in the days of segregation and discriminatory practices present additional obstacles. These barriers can be overt and pronounced or subtle.

One overt example is when the disproportionate presence of minorities at the bottom of the pyramid is taken as the natural and acceptable order. In one corporation, a senior manager recently hired from another company was unresponsive to all the talk about the need for greater mobility for minorities. "Is there a problem?" he asked. "I see minorities all through the halls." When told that the bulk of them worked at low levels, he replied, "Well, at least they're here. You should see the halls of the company I came from. There were very few there." Clearly, this manger had difficulty seeing the urgency for action.

A large nonprofit provides a more subtle example. As part of a celebration of a major anniversary of its founding, the organization produced a commemorative booklet. Although the enterprise had a very demographically diverse population and clientele, no people of color appeared in the booklet. When confronted by this reality, a spokesman for the organization first wondered why anyone would be counting and then replied that the count must be incorrect. He reasoned that because the organization's mantra was "People are our greatest assets," they could not have produced a whites-only booklet. A review confirmed that indeed people of color did not appear on any pages. As far as the mantra was concerned, "people" at the time of the organization's founding meant "white males." They had neglected to expand the definition of "people" to reflect the demographics of the staff and clientele.

Third, traditional thinking that equates "managing" with "controlling" offers another obstacle. Some people have as much difficulty with the word "managing" as with the word "diversity" in "managing diversity." When I first started talking about managing diversity in the mid-1980s, I inevitably would be asked, "Why do we have to *manage* (control) diversity?" The individuals asking that question lacked awareness of Empowerment Management.

Fourth, conceptual confusion about the meaning of diversity constitutes another obstacle. Many people continue to exclude white males in their definition. Another sign of conceptual confusion with diversity has been an inability to understand why it must be considered. One senior manager recently noted, "We're doing fine with our numbers, and we're treating people fairly. Why do we need to talk about diversity?" For him, they were doing it all. Apparently, he and his colleagues deemed their level of engagement with minorities satisfactory. He also might have been influenced by the negative baggage that diversity has picked up in some circles.

Fifth, the difficulty of making a compelling business (viability) case has been a major obstacle and in many instances has been a deal breaker. I talked about this challenge earlier in the chapter. For some, particularly those who subscribe to social justice–civil rights–human rights rationales, this challenge has not been a direct problem. However, those individuals often run out of gas with the moral motive alone. Organizations simply are reluctant to make changes of the magnitude described in this quadrant without a clear understanding of the benefits for their viability. In other words, individuals relying primarily on moral motivation also have been affected by the difficulty of making a compelling business case—even though it is not their primary motive.

Facilitators

Countering the barriers are some significant facilitating factors. One is the increasing demographic and behavioral diversity of the workforce. This domestic trend is exacerbated by the diversity implicit in globalism. Indeed, between domestic and global forces, only the rare organization is not experiencing the reality of an increasingly diverse workforce. Two, economic uncertainties and challenges make it extremely risky for organizations to underutilize any segment of their workforce. More than ever, failure to fully engage can exact a steep price. Finally, growing awareness exists that continuing traditional managerial practices may not work for a workforce that is diverse in race, gender, and ethnicity.

Desired Results

Simply stated, those who embrace this paradigm aspire to achieve a fully engaged, diverse workforce. They are working to empower managers and associates to make decisions that will result in accessing the talent of *all* members of the diverse pool.

DISCUSSION

This strategy-paradigm combination pivots around questions about the role of the manager: What is the role of the manager? Does it make any difference whether the manager is managing someone like himself or managing someone who differs from him with respect to race, ethnicity, or gender?

The answers to these questions are still evolving. Still, I am convinced that the prudent choice is to come down on the side of Empowerment Management as the managerial role required in the midst of diversity, and to answer in the affirmative as to whether it matters that the workforce is diverse in terms of race, gender, ethnicity, and other demographic dimensions.

The driving force for this strategy-paradigm combination continues to be the perception that minorities and women are underutilized. With white women, perceptions may suggest greater success in avoiding glass ceilings and premature plateaus. However, in-depth conversations with these women often reveal managerial issues grounded in not accepting and respecting gender differences—that is, not taking them into account in the design of organizational cultures, systems, policies, and practices. So, while it can be argued that organizations have made more progress with white women, underutilization also exists with this segment of the workforce. As long as the perception and reality of underutilization persist, white women also will work to foster enhanced capability with this quadrant.

Enhancing implementation of Empowerment Management and cultural change would be a major step in advancing this quadrant. I am not certain how rapidly we'll make progress in that direction, but surely the economic challenges of today will prompt faster movement along those lines. When that happens, organizations will have all three of the legs required for the three-legged stool.

Some Take-Aways

1. CEOs engage this core diversity management strategy as a way to address the diversity problem of achieving full utilization of a diverse workforce.

2. The driving motive has been a desire for enhanced competitive advantage.

3. This strategy can be called the "managerial strategy." It also can be described as the strategy for mainstreaming the talents of traditional *and* nontraditional associates.

4. Its cornerstones are the Empowerment Management model and cultural change.

5. Managing Diverse Talent represents the third leg of a three-legged stool required for fully utilizing a diverse workforce: (1) representation, (2) relationships, and (3) empowerment.

6. Relatively little progress has been made with this strategy. Most workforce diversity accomplishments relate to Managing Workforce Representation and Managing Workforce Relationships. Managing Diverse Talent, as defined in this chapter, is just appearing on the radar screen of senior executives.

7. The undergirding paradigm for this strategy is Maximize Individual Engagement.

4 MANAGING ALL STRATEGIC DIVERSITY MIXTURES

MANAGING ALL STRATEGIC
DIVERSITY MIXTURES

MAXIMIZE STAKEHOLDER
ENGAGEMENT

Quadrant 4

Quadrant 4, Managing All Strategic Diversity Mixtures, is less well known than the earlier quadrants. But it is not unknown. CEOs and other organizational leaders who define *work-force* diversity as "the differences and similarities that can exist among the elements of a workforce mixture" are increasingly aware of and beginning to gravitate toward this quadrant. As a rule, they do so gradually.

Having begun to view workforce diversity with a broader perspective, CEOs and other organizational leaders start to think about *non-workforce* differences and similarities that may be hampering productivity. Once they do, many of these executives come to believe that organizations must address more than workforce diversity. They see more clearly that an infinite number of diversity mixtures exist and, in one form or another, demand daily attention. They begin to view this quadrant as the "universal strategy."

A key attraction of a diversity strategy that can manage non-workforce issues is that these issues frequently relate to challenges that unquestionably are critical to the bottom line: achieving functional synergy, implementing an acquisition or merger, managing a product portfolio, fostering innovations, promoting effective field and head-quarters relationships, and coordinating global expansion. Because many senior executives see their personal stock as leaders rise and fall on how such issues turn out, such a strategy possesses face validity as something they can legitimately sink their teeth into.

Because this quadrant's definition of diversity resonates with many senior leaders, chief diversity officers (CDOs) and other diversity champions find it an effective window through which the business, or viability, case for diversity management can be made. This is espe-cially important where a relatively low ranking has been assigned to the importance of people. By focusing beyond people diversity, these champions have been able to provide ample evidence for the strategic advantage of diversity management. Consider the example of a diver-sity council below.

The council first rolled out its business case for managing diversity, only to have it resoundingly rejected. It was not compelling. When members went back to the drawing board, they were still unable to make a compelling business case for managing *workforce* diversity. A cochair wondered, "Is there another area where we could begin with managing diversity and more easily make a business case?"

Someone responded, "In our strategic plan, we said that we needed more synergy between two functions—which incidentally constitute a diversity mixture. But they still bicker constantly. We could start there."

Another observed, "Our plan calls for us to grow through acquisi-tions and mergers, and we are well on our way. We did not explicitly think of this move as involving diversity, but we did *implicitly* assume that we could deal with the consequent diversity. This would be an interesting place to introduce managing diversity."

Another individual said, "Don't forget our efforts to grow by going global! We are already experiencing diversity issues as we plan to step up our move in that direction. This will become more and more important for the company. It should be an easy arena in which to make a compelling business case for managing diversity."

The presiding cochair recommended that they develop business cases for all of those settings and return to the workforce issues after selling the company on the need to manage critical non-workforce diversity. At that point, they could also argue convincingly for the benefits that capability could generate. He reasoned that regardless of where diversity management skills are learned, they can subsequently be applied wherever they are needed. His council colleagues agreed.

As the example indicates, paralleling a need for greater proficiency in making the business case has been an increasing understanding that the diversity dimensions of the workforce are not the only mixture of concern. Yet most diversity frameworks are still oriented toward workforce diversity.

When I was lunching recently with a CDO, a line manager came by and said that he now understood offshoring to be a diversity issue. The CDO welcomed that awareness and viewed it as evidence that her colleagues were finally "getting it." I sensed, however, that she was not prepared to assist with offshore diversity but simply hoped that the enhanced awareness would promote greater understanding of workforce diversity. She had encouraged awareness of non-workforce issues as a way to facilitate management of workforce diversity.

Still, as the implications of non-workforce diversity have become more evident, demand has grown for guidance on how to manage diversity beyond the workforce and beyond race and gender. In many instances, rank-and-file line managers have pushed for help with non-workforce diversity even when their CDOs were not ready to move in that direction.

In one organization, I discussed the various types of diversity dimensions during an executive briefing. Shortly afterward, an executive who had been in the audience called me. He reported that his division and another in the organization were forming a strategic alliance that had an enormous upside for the company's future and that he anticipated significant diversity issues. He asked if my colleagues and I could help with the process.

Excited about a possibility that would lend credibility to the embryonic diversity effort in the organization, I immediately called my client contact and relayed the news about the opportunity. I also said that we were lucky to see such an application possibility so early in the process and that it should provide great leverage for getting traction.

To my surprise, my contact immediately said, "No, we cannot do it." My contact felt that the individual who had asked for help was getting ahead of the process. However, the real obstacle, in my view, was that the contact's organizational hierarchal context was race, gender, and the workforce. It simply would not allow him to move forward with this innovative possibility—even if he wanted to.

For me, the forces represented by these examples came together years ago in a meeting of supporters of the American Institute for Managing Diversity. As we talked about the institute's work, one person said to me and my colleagues at the time, "You keep saying this is more than race and gender, but all your examples are about race and gender in the workforce." This challenge prompted my initial serious thinking about generalizing or universalizing what we were doing with respect to workforce diversity.

Also, that challenging comment led me to write my second book, *Redefining Diversity*.[1] That book includes chapters on diversity with respect to color, lifestyle, function, nation, and strategy. It also offers a set of "action options" that can be used with those types of diversity and others. This was my first formal effort to offer a universal framework. Since 1996, my thinking about a framework for addressing *any* type of diversity mixture has continued to evolve. This discussion of Quadrant 4 reflects my current thinking on a universal strategy.

QUADRANT PARAMETERS

Definition of Diversity

This quadrant defines diversity as the differences and similarities and related tensions and complexities that can exist among the elements of any mixture. In *Redefining Diversity*, I informally adopted the practice of using *diversity management* to refer to the managing of both workforce *and* other mixtures. So *managing diversity* meant managing *workforce* diversity, and *diversity management* referred to the management of *any* diverse mixture.[2]

Goals

The overarching goal of Quadrant 4 is effective management of *all strategic* diversity mixtures. The "strategic" criterion differentiates between mixtures critically relevant to an organization's mission and those that are less important. This differentiation minimizes the likelihood that practitioners will be overwhelmed and ensures that the most critical mixtures will be addressed.

A secondary goal is greater understanding of diversity and its benefits for a particular organization. Increasingly, managers explore non-workforce mixtures as a means of learning more about diversity in general.

Motives

Those who subscribe to the overarching goal are generally motivated by a desire for organizational or personal strategic gain. For organizations, strategic means something that will give competitive advantage; for individuals, it means something that is critical to the success of their personal agendas. People with this motive typically possess a greater understanding of diversity and have had sufficient experience with diversity management to whet their appetites for broader applications.

They understand that achieving their goals will require even greater understanding of diversity and diversity management and the benefits for their organizations. They believe that non-workforce diversity experience will help them to be more effective with the traditional people dimensions of race and gender. In addition, these individuals often hope to enhance their ability to make the business case for Managing Diverse Talent.

Some individuals with this motive are also aware of which mixtures in their personal lives need attention. At a book signing, for example, a man asked me, "Do you ever talk about diversity in families?" When I said that I did, he reported that he had four sons who had married four very different women. As a result, his sons now led different lives and were not as close as they once were. In his words, they "had accepted the diversity of their wives and lives, but were not managing it well." As family patriarch, he wanted them to regain the closeness they had as younger men before their marriages. He planned to share my book with them.

Later, this same man reappeared and asked, "Do you ever talk about diversity in the context of religion?" When I again said yes, he told me about his church and his desire to share my thinking with his fellow members.

This man was surveying his life and identifying where diversity might be better managed. He was not defining diversity, but rather deciding what kind he wished or needed to focus on. This is prototypical Quadrant 4 behavior.

Primary Focus

Quadrant 4 focuses primarily on developing a universal organizational, managerial, and individual capability for addressing strategic diversity of any kind. It seeks universality through *one* strategy that can be adapted to *any* diversity mixture. Implicit in this option is a heavy emphasis on diversity—the forest, if you will, as opposed to the trees (different types of diversity).

This quadrant focuses more on diversity *management* than on diversity per se. More specifically, it focuses on developing a "diversity management capability." For example, rarely is there talk about diversity being "good"; instead, the emphasis is on making quality decisions in the midst of any kind of diversity. This tone reflects the emphasis on a business, or viability, rationale as opposed to one of social justice, human rights, or civil rights. Because it encompasses both people and non-people issues, it goes beyond Quadrant 3, as well.

The word *capability* departs from the ambiguous awareness focus of Quadrants 1 and 2. *Capability* implies more vigor. In fact, in *Building on the Promise of Diversity* I wrote of the *craft* of strategic diversity managing.[3] The analogy of hitting a baseball can be used to illustrate the relationship between process, craft, and capability.

Say a boy aspires to be a great baseball hitter. Toward that end, he not only plays Little League ball, but also devours all the educational material he can find. He discovers that hitting is quite a process, with concepts, principles, requirements for practice and continuous improvement, performance standards, characteristics of art, and specific discrete subskills. That is, he comes to understand that hitting is a craft requiring significant preparation and development. He applies himself to the craft and eventually becomes a hitting craftsman—one who understands and has mastered the process of hitting. By mastering the craft, he develops a *capability* for hitting.

It is possible to excel at a craft without mastering it. An example of this is the batter who *naturally* performs well but has no awareness or understanding of hitting as a process or a craft. He simply steps up to the plate and hits the ball. This person cannot train other hitters, for he has no idea of what he does as a hitter or what makes him successful at hitting.

Although both players can hit the ball well, because the first hitter understands and has mastered hitting as a craft, he has the ability to analyze and correct emerging errors and to coach others on how to hit, as well.

Quadrant 4, along with Quadrant 3, presumes that while some naturally excel at diversity management, most of us must prepare deliberately and apply what we know consistently to achieve excellence with this process. Many managers do not share this perspective and would have difficulty describing diversity management as a craft or capability. This quadrant, however, focuses precisely on the building of that capability.

Approaches

This strategy relies on four basic approaches: the *generalized* approaches of each of the three previously discussed quadrants and the Strategic Diversity Management Process. Generalized, these quadrants morph as follows:

Managing Workforce Representation ⟶ **Managing Representation**
Managing Workforce Relationships ⟶ **Managing Relationships**
Managing Diverse Talent ⟶ **Managing Empowerment**

The critical questions and focus for Managing Representation are who or what should be included in any mixture and how to ensure the necessary representation. The Quadrant 4, or generalized, approach must focus on the attribute profile of the mixture *and* also its behavioral variations. To do that, two sets of questions must be addressed:

Attribute Variations

1. Do we want to have attribute pluralism?
2. If so, what kind?
3. If so, how much?
4. If so, how do we go about assembling the desired profile?
5. If so, what will be the managerial implications?[4]

Behavioral Variations

1. Do we want to have behavioral variations?
2. If so, what kind?
3. If so, how much?
4. If so, how do we go about assembling the desired variations?[5]

In contrast to Managing Workforce Representation, which relates *only* to attribute representation, the Quadrant 4 (generalized or universal) version approaches behavioral variations directly. It does not treat them as an incidental by-product of efforts to achieve an attribute profile. The generalized approach specifically and deliberately targets behavioral variation aspirations, a significant distinction from the workforce representation experience.

For Managing Relationships, the central, generalized (Quadrant 4) question is, "What relationships are required among the mixture's elements to ensure optimal productivity and achievement of organizational objectives?" The two fundamental subquestions that frame the answer to the relationship question are these:

1. To ensure achievement of organizational objectives, how much *differentiation* is required between the mixture's elements?

2. To ensure achievement of organizational objectives, how much *integration* is required between the mixture's elements?

Without the answers to these two questions, it's difficult to achieve the necessary degree of integration and differentiation.

Finally, for Managing Empowerment, the central, generalized question becomes "How do we empower or engage each element's individual and collective potential for contribution?" The supporting subquestions are these:

1. What type of environment is required to promote the required integration and differentiation?
2. What managerial model is required for this purpose?
3. What type of organizational culture is required for this purpose?

To see how generalization in pursuit of a universal system might work, let's apply these questions to the non-people, nonanimate mixture of products. The case below is disguised.

A Fortune 1000 company has built a growing, business-to-business enterprise around essentially one piece of equipment. For the next several years, prospects look positive; however, strategic scans of likely future scenarios reveal technological advancements that would make the company's flagship product obsolete, health concerns that would threaten the bread-and-butter product, and also environmental issues that would affect the principal product's viability. Further, larger corporations with significant financial resources appear poised to enter the industry.

Because of these potential threats, company executives are exploring the possibility of expanding their product offerings. In the language of diversity management, they are considering offering a diverse mixture of products. The managers, as a first step in this process, must decide how much product diversity they desire. That is, in the language of Managing Representation, they must ask the attribute and behavioral variations questions.

These might include the following:

Attribute Variations

1. How much differentiation do we want among the new products?
2. Do we want them to be derivatives of the flagship offering?
3. Do we want them to be in a separate but related industry? Separate and unrelated industry?
4. Do we want them to have financial investment requirements similar to those for the flagship product? Less than? Greater than?
5. Do we want them to have managerial requirements similar to those for the flagship product?

As these differentiation questions and their answers are addressed, they provide implicit answers and questions about integration.

Behavioral Variations

1. How much differentiation do we wish with respect to behavioral variations? The answer "none" would say that regardless of attribute variations, we want a behaviorally homogenous set of products. Any answer other than none would signal a desire for some behavioral diversity. (Examples of product behavioral diversity would be life cycles, niches served, pioneers in new market, extension or refinement of existing products, growth rates, or degree of reliance on technological advances.)
2. Economically, do we wish the products to have life cycles similar to those of the flagship product?
3. With respect to growth, do we wish the products to have rates similar to those of the flagship? Less than? Greater than?

4. Do we wish new products to attract similar consumers even if in different industries?

Managing Relationships

Generalized, overarching questions translate into specifics around products by asking the following questions:

1. Should we be concerned if the new products cannibalize the flagship, or is that part of the natural life cycles of products?
2. Should the products share the flagship brand? Yes? Somewhat? Not at all?
3. Do we want the new products to ride the coattails of the flagship?

As an aside, note that answers to the Managing Relationships questions are determined in part by answers to the Managing Representation inquiries. Similarly, responses to the Managing Representation and Managing Relationship questions provide a determining context for the Managing Engagement questions:

1. Are the flagship products and the new offering so different that they require separate organizational cultures? Structures? Managerial models?
2. Or are they sufficiently similar that economies of scale are possible?
3. If different arrangements are required for the flagship product and the new products, how much integration will be required?
4. What mechanisms will be used to achieve the necessary integration?

What the above discussion of generalized approaches and the related example means is that the three-legged stool applies to *all* mixtures of

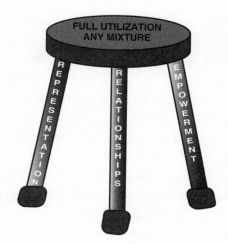

FIGURE 4-1. Universal Three-Legged Stool Requirements for Full Utilization

any kind. With *every* mixture, questions of representation, relationships, and empowerment must be addressed. *The three-legged stool is universal.* (See figure 4-1.)

Quadrant Accomplishments

The quadrant's accomplishments lie ahead, as this is an embryonic strategy. At present, I see no widespread use of a diversity framework to address non-workforce issues. What I do see that can be construed as some progress are situations where diversity champions refer to non-workforce issues as part of the diversity arena. Even then, however, I have not seen application of a diversity framework to these areas.

Quadrant Challenges

One challenge is that this quadrant requires at least an awareness and understanding of Quadrants 1, 2, and 3, since it represents a generalization of those quadrants. It is difficult to generalize that with which we are unfamiliar.

It is possible, however, to come effectively to Quadrant 4 independent of Quadrants 1–3. Doing so requires viewing Quadrant 4 not through the lens of the earlier quadrants, but rather in terms of the requirements of the "universal option." Indeed, approaching Quadrant 4 as the universal quadrant likely will help with some of the challenges experienced with the earlier quadrants.

The quadrant's focus on diversity management (Empowerment Management) creates another challenge. Most managers still prefer to talk about diversity and "doing diversity" rather than diversity management or even managing diversity. This is a challenge to a universal approach to diversity management because even though *all* strategic mixtures are covered in this quadrant, Empowerment Management remains the prescription for engaging and enabling. For new products, for example, the Empowerment Management challenge becomes "How can we create an environment that will allow new products to reach their full potential?"

As with Quadrant 3, the perception of a conflict with the civil rights–social justice–human rights agenda presents a significant obstacle. Some don't believe they should have to talk about diversity if their numbers are okay and they are not discriminating. Others have an either-or attitude and cannot conceive that both the civil rights–social justice–human rights and the diversity management agendas offer benefits and can be complementary.

The thinking that diversity refers only to the workforce is still another obstacle. Individuals with this view see no point in discussing a universal approach that addresses workforce issues *and* any of an infinite number of other possibilities. For them, this quadrant makes no sense.

Others can conceptualize a universal approach and a wide variety of diversity mixtures but fear that moving to those arenas before fully resolving workforce issues would be to abandon the traditional issues of race and gender within organizations. These individuals also exhibit an either-or perspective and cannot see how the universal approach might help in addressing workforce matters.

Frameworks specific to race, gender, and the workforce constitute another substantial obstacle. Until now, neither hardware nor software has existed to support a universal approach. Even when non-workforce mixtures such as products, functions, and acquisitions or mergers are recognized as diversity issues, they are rarely approached through a diversity management framework. In part, this has been because of the lack of an *appropriate* framework. My hope is that the SDMP will help to fill this void.

Finally, perceived and real complexity offers a challenge. The word *universal* simply shouts complexity and scares many people. "How," they wonder, "can we talk about dealing with universal diversity when we cannot deal with two dimensions—race and gender—of the workforce?" Some believe, further, that race and gender are the most difficult challenges and that, therefore, resolving them will enable success with other diversity dimensions. Some even claim that no significant progress with other dimensions can be made without first putting race and gender to bed.

In any event, most of us do not wake up saying, "I just do not have enough complexity in my life. I need more!" Thus, the threat of complexity remains a challenge.

Facilitating Factors

The most compelling factor in pushing us toward the Quadrant 4 approach is what might be called "diversity gridlock." In a real sense, this is a version of the workforce integration challenges discussed in chapter 2 and to some degree in chapter 3.

By "diversity gridlock," I mean those situations where an inability to deal effectively with diversity stifles our ability to make decisions in the midst of differences, similarities, and related tensions and complexities; hampers change; and, by default, further entrenches the status quo.

A good example is the 2009–2010 health care debate in the United States. In the summer of 2009, across the country, a number of "town hall meetings" on health care reform erupted into boisterous, volatile confrontations. An *Atlanta Journal-Constitution* story reflected the intransigence demonstrated by many in those meetings. The article chronicled the views of three dozen people in and around Atlanta about medical coverage. The story was entitled "On Medical Coverage, Many Agree to Disagree."[6]

What is troubling about many agreeing to disagree is that it constitutes an admission that we do not know how to get beyond our differences and tensions—even when, as the writer reports, "everyone agreed: We need some sort of reform."[7] "Agree to disagree" becomes a vote for the status quo in the midst of diverse views, even when consensus exists about the need for change.

Part of the problem is a lack of wherewithal to work through tensions, especially where they are intense. Indeed, the greater the intensity and volatility, the more likely—it appears—agreement will be reached to disagree.

A challenge in the United States is that dialogue and problem solving now mean in-your-face debate without civility. In many instances, the strategy appears to be "If I cannot win by reason, I can do so by shouting you down." This offers few if any prescriptions for how to make quality decisions in the midst of divisiveness. That is, it offers no suggestions for creating a diversity management capability.

Interestingly, this circumstance is rarely approached as a diversity issue. This may be due to a lack of understanding of diversity, or possibly to perceptions about the field's low status. I believe, however, that "diversity gridlock" with respect to public policy and other arenas eventually will push us toward exploring and using this quadrant to minimize "diversity logjams."

Global Perspective

This quadrant has the potential to significantly advance diversity and diversity management across the globe. U.S. companies often go abroad with a desire to perpetuate a strong commitment to diversity—typically defined as involving or including those who have been unjustly excluded. By pushing this perspective, they hope to demonstrate for their home constituencies the strength of their commitment to diversity by their willingness to insist on it abroad. Predictably, host countries and their organizations resent this practice.

The irony here is that while touting diversity, these corporations find it difficult to accept the reality that a given country might have different views about social justice. Quadrant 4 makes it possible to push "diversity" and "diversity management" in a manner that meshes with both the culture of a given country and the strong values of the United States enterprises.

Instead of arriving with a social justice–human rights view of workforce diversity, corporations would express a willingness to foster quality decision making *wherever* differences and similarities exist. They would come advocating to address *all* kinds of diversity issues and also would be armed with World-Class Diversity Management as a *capability* for generating solutions as needed. Leaders of the United States companies and of their host companies could then work collaboratively to develop solutions, beginning where they jointly perceived a need. Later, their learnings and efforts could be applied to the workforce.

This approach would allow companies to demonstrate their commitment to diversity without alienating their host country counterparts. Further, it would result in a broader utilization of diversity management and also quite likely to more commitment to the process.

UNDERGIRDING PARADIGM: MAXIMIZE STAKEHOLDER ENGAGEMENT

This paradigm emerged in the 1990s as a result of the need to address non-workforce diversity mixtures—mixtures characterized by differences, similarities, and related tensions and complexities. Still in its early stage of development, it draws from two sources: stakeholder theory and Empowerment Management.

Stakeholder theory challenges the traditional theory of the firm in which only the needs and wishes of investors, employees, suppliers, and customers are addressed. Under stakeholder theory prescriptions, other parties are involved: government bodies, political groups, trade associations, trade unions, communities, associated corporations, prospective employees, prospective customers, and the public at large.[8] This paradigm argues that organizational leaders must manage the diverse mixture of stakeholders individually and collectively.

The combined stakeholders and the individual stakeholders constitute a diverse mixture that must be managed. Government bodies, for example, contribute to the diversity of the collective mixture of stakeholders but also independently constitute a mixture of elements characterized by differences and similarities. A government body mixture, for example, may contain twenty diverse government agencies. The appropriate executive representatives of the organization would have to deal with those twenty entities. Similarly, the government bodies' collective mixture along with—say, thirty other stakeholders—constitutes the stakeholder mixture that company representatives must also address.

Stakeholder theory further claims that all stakeholder interests are legitimate and require simultaneous attention. As a result, organizational leaders must address each diversity mixture both individually and as a part of the collective mixture.[9]

The Maximize Stakeholder Engagement paradigm goes further than stakeholder theory, which deals exclusively with people and collective mixtures of people. Maximize Stakeholder Engagement includes inanimate mixtures, such as strategies and products. An example would be the case cited earlier in which a company seeks to develop a diversified portfolio of products. This quadrant operates in the spirit of stakeholder theory but with a broader array of entities in the mix.

The same can be said for Empowerment Management, which I discussed in detail in chapter 3. Fundamentally, it represents a model for fully engaging people individually and collectively. *Maximize Stakeholder Engagement prescribes that this empowerment purpose be carried out with nonanimate elements, as well.* Senior product managers, for example, must develop strategies that will facilitate realization of the individual and collective potential of the products in their portfolio and must empower or engage all products to reach their full potential.

PARADIGM PARAMETERS

Definition of Diversity

This paradigm defines diversity as differences and similarities that can exist within *any* strategic stakeholder mixture. As noted earlier, "strategic" ensures that mixtures most critical to an organization's viability are addressed.

Motive

Achieving competitive advantage has been the dominant motive for this paradigm from the beginning. In contrast to workforce mixtures, in which organizational participants find it difficult to see a compelling business rationale, for some strategic mixtures, the potential for competitive edge is so clear that making a "business case" is not necessary.

Principal Vehicles

Several factors contribute to the emerging viability of this paradigm. *Universalization has been one.* By focusing on developing a framework that can be applied to *any* tree from the diversity forest, this paradigm can be relevant where a narrower prescription might not be. This relevancy fosters credibility and a readiness for opportunistic application as diversity is understood. Senior executives, in particular, quickly see the potential benefits of Managing All Strategic Mixtures and often are eager to institutionalize the framework in their organization. Universalization can be key.

Another contributing vehicle can be the generalization of Quadrants 1, 2, and 3. Because this quadrant builds on the approaches of the three preceding workforce quadrants, the possession of at least a rudimentary grasp of those quadrants can facilitate universalization.

General management capability can also be a driving vehicle. Managers thoughtfully engaged in general management can see the big picture and the relevancy of stakeholder theory to their strategic diversity management responsibility, as well as the potential for competitive gain. Indeed, they frequently see their opportunities with diversity management better through a general management lens than through a human resources one.

Finally, *universal strategic diversity management capability is the principal vehicle* prescribed by this paradigm for achieving the goal of quality decision making in the midst of all kinds of diversity. This universal capability is what makes success possible in this quadrant. The Strategic Diversity Management Process, discussed in the next chapter, can be thought of as a decision-making process for each leg of the three-legged stool.

Principal Undergirding Assumptions

A key critical assumption is that *a diverse workforce is only one critical mixture individuals and organizations must deal with*. When offered opportunities to identify their strategic mixtures that require attention, many executive groups and diversity councils find that they have great opportunity for strategic gain in several areas. This is true even for those who earlier were focused on workforce diversity. Not uncommonly, they have to be reminded that they cannot abandon workforce issues—those, too, must be addressed.

Before going through the exercise of identifying their critical mixtures, leaders sometimes ask whether race and gender are the most critical diversity dimensions across all organizations. When I respond, "Not necessarily," I often see looks of disbelief. However, once they complete their own self-assessment of diversity issues, they realize that workforce mixtures represent only one type requiring their attention and diversity management capability.

Interestingly, individuals who go through this self-discovery seldom ask, "How will this help our viability?" A good example is the case of acquisitions and mergers. Once it becomes clear that an organization can address those activities as diversity mixtures, no one questions the possibility of competitive gain. Because this potential is so transparent, we routinely suggest that organizations struggling to make the business case for managing workforce diversity begin with a strategic self-examination. It typically results in an eye-opening experience.

If "strategic" is expanded to include personal mixtures, the impact can be even greater. For many individuals, personal mixtures—in families, communities, and religious groups, for example—can be very revealing. Individuals often experience profound learnings when they apply diversity management to their lives.

One father shared his learnings with his daughter, who was coming out of a short-lived marriage with a divorce. Shortly thereafter he called and said, "Roosevelt, my daughter wants to talk with you. She believes her marriage failed because of poor diversity management. She is thinking about starting a marriage consulting business based on diversity management."

Another workshop participant reported retreating to a room in his house away from his wife, with whom he had been having a heated debate. He then went through a "diversity management analysis" and developed a win-win strategy for himself and his wife. He happily shared that it worked.

That *common patterns and dynamics operate across all kinds of diversity mixtures* constitutes another undergirding assumption. This assumption basically says that while all the individual trees (types of diversity) in the diversity forest differ significantly, they also share some substantial commonalities. Frequently, this is a difficult proposition to sell.

This difficulty accounts for why many individuals discount anything said about diversity that does not refer to their specific dimension of interest. They are unaware that lessons about diversity in general can inform the management of specific types of diversity.

One African American woman's body language and facial expression conveyed continuous frustration with a presentation I was making. When I reached the point about commonalities across diversity dimensions, she could not contain herself. She stood and asked loudly, "You mean to tell me that what I experience when I'm discriminated against at work is comparable to what some white male experiences as a result of frustrations across functions? I don't think so!" Given that this challenge came very early in my diversity work, I have found it memorable. At the time, its force intimidated me.

But I responded by saying, "One person's trivial diversity challenge may be another's mountain of an issue." My challenger made clear that she was unimpressed by my response.

This assumption, that common patterns and dynamics operate across all kinds of diversity mixtures, is, nevertheless, a very important assumption. It is what makes generalization and universalization possible. Without it, it is necessary to address each diversity dimension as if starting from scratch.

Some avoid this challenge by simply dealing with one type of diversity. They are unaware that their work might inform the efforts of others in different diversity arenas. Truth be told, many practitioners do not even acknowledge arenas other than their own. But this prevents learning across the trees in the forest. As I said in the introduction to this book, at core, this book is about the forest of diversity and, indeed, about learning and generalizations we can gain across the various kinds of diversity.

The third and final undergirding assumption—that *it is critical to develop diversity management skills and diversity maturity that can be applied universally*—flows from the previous two. If multiple types of diversity require attention, and if they share certain commonalities, it follows that diversity management skills reflecting those realities are needed.

Over the past twenty-five years, the need for a universal approach has moved from a nice-to-have discussion to an urgent one. Many now hope that such an approach will break some of the stalemates faced by the field and society around race and gender. More specifically, they hope that the universal will inform the specific.

Without the development of a universal approach, the ability to "manage all strategic diversity mixtures" will remain dormant. My thinking and hope are that what I have called the Strategic Diversity Management Process will be a major step in this direction. More will be said about this decision-making process.

Key Obstacles

Four obstacles must be addressed and overcome: (1) paradigm confinement, (2) a lack of universal frameworks, (3) a preference for tactics, and (4) the baggage carried by the term *diversity*.

Paradigm confinement is the inability to expand the diversity paradigm to which you subscribe or to adopt two or more paradigms simultaneously. This is, in a very real sense, a diversity management challenge—that of making quality decisions in the midst of two or more paradigms characterized by differences, similarities, and related tensions and complexities.

This confinement hinders moving to universal thinking about diversity. In the United States, the dominant paradigms—Making Amends for Past Wrongs and Applying the Golden Rule—relate to social justice, civil rights, and human rights. Subscribers to those paradigms find it difficult to embrace other diversity mindsets. Their resistance to other paradigms is a major obstacle.

Another major obstacle is the *lack of universal frameworks*. This lack limits us to celebrating the recognition that other mixtures exist. Without the necessary frameworks for addressing them, not much more can be done.

This is the proverbial chicken-or-egg conundrum. It is legitimate to say that the lack of universal frameworks presents an obstacle. However, I know firsthand from offering the Strategic Diversity Management Process as a universal approach that not much readiness exists for moving toward universal models. Even if such frameworks were widely available, I am not clear that they would be embraced.

Still another obstacle is a *preference for tactics*. When I am planning for a presentation, clients encourage me to be as tactical as possible—to make certain that participants take something away that can be used the next day. Rarely do they admonish me to take care to ensure that the audience leaves with an enhanced understanding of diversity.

Additionally, I am encouraged to keep abstractions at a "low level." Indeed, many diversity practitioners see little need for theory building or concept development. In part, this is because of the perceived urgency around finding solutions for the challenges of those they serve.

Nevertheless, this preference for tactics that can provide solutions can shortchange the concept building, theory building, and model building that also can generate understanding and effective problem solving. The field of diversity by and large appears to be challenged by the diversity mixture of theory *and* practice—that is, by the challenge of moving forward with both at once. Both have their place, and they complement and inform each other. Without this dynamic, the field will stifle the development of universal approaches.

Finally, *the significant baggage that the word* diversity *has picked up over the years* is an obstacle. Because of this baggage, practitioners in other arenas that could be viewed as part of the forest do not want that designation, or find it difficult to see the relevance of diversity. That is, they are not anxious to become "diversity practitioners." In some quarters, individuals not only are unreceptive to universal generalizations but are actively seeking to abolish the term and what it represents. Their likely response to the idea of universal frameworks would be "Why would we want to generalize diversity? Do we need to widen the use of that word? Can't we just ignore it and allow it to disappear?" To the extent that this attitude exists, it is a significant barrier.

Facilitating Factors

Awareness that "diversity" refers to differences and similarities of any kind, as well as their related tensions and complexities, is a major facilitator of this quadrant. Many of the issues that generate diversity gridlock do not carry the diversity label. For example, neither political divisiveness nor acquisition and merger disputes routinely qualify as diversity issues. As awareness and understanding grow about the forest of diversity, the demand for a universal approach-paradigm combination will increase.

As an aside, you can see where your organization stands with respect to its collective understanding with a simple exercise. Take an edition of a newspaper and ask a selected group of people to identify and count all the diversity issues that are mentioned. Most such exercises garner a count that ranges from the low teens to the thirties. The higher the count, the greater the tendency to think of diversity universally—that is, as referring to any type of differences and similarities.

Uncertain times also facilitate a more universal view of diversity. During these times, pressures mount for effective decision making in all settings, including those characterized by diversity of any kind. In sum, viability concerns increasingly will call for a universal capability for addressing diversity.

Globalism is a growing force that is placing diversity in many forms front and center on many organizations' agendas. Sometimes it is recognized as such, and at other times it is not. At a minimum, as organizations go global, they face the challenge of forging a cohesive, comprehensive diversity approach across nations. Increasingly, this challenge will lead to calls for a universal approach to diversity management.

Finally, as *our society becomes more receptive to differences of all kinds*, the need to understand better the forest of diversity will become evident. This, too, will foster movement toward a universal approach.

These forces and others suggest that organizations and individuals will need to make more use of this quadrant's approach and paradigm. As this occurs, the initial three quadrants will be able to use the knowledge gained, and overall progress with diversity management will be enhanced.

Desired Results

The central aspiration of Quadrant 4 and its undergirding paradigm is an ability to address *any* tree in the diversity forest. That is why this quadrant resonates with people—like CEOs—who have the big picture perspective. They operate at a sufficiently general level to see all kinds of mixtures of differences and similarities where diversity management might be useful. If these other mixtures happen to be challenging *and* critical to the bottom line, they have urgency for such a framework as Quadrant 4.

DISCUSSION

This quadrant addresses the reality of the *forest* of diversity; indeed, the forest demands this strategy—unless one concludes that most of the individual trees are irrelevant. Once the reality of a diversity forest with multiple dimensions that *can* be relevant is acknowledged, an urgency arises for a strategy by which they can be addressed.

The notion of the universal three-legged stool captures the required arenas for diversity management decision making about *any* diversity mixture: representation, relationships, and empowerment. Quadrant 4 presents a generalization of Quadrants 1, 2, and 3; so that *all* the trees in the forest can receive the attention they need, as appropriate.

Some don't see the need for generalization. However, once you attempt to apply workforce-specific approaches to non-workforce mixtures, you gain an appreciation for the potential utility of a universal approach.

I believe that Quadrant 4 is the key to the diversity management field's future development. It not only will facilitate focusing on

CHART 4-1. Core Diversity Management Strategies

Strategy / Variable	Managing Workforce Representation	Managing Workforce Demographic Relationships	Managing Diverse Talent	Managing All Strategic Mixtures
Undergirding Paradigm	Making Amends for Past Wrongs	Applying the Golden Rule	Maximizing Individual Engagement	Maximizing Stakeholder Engagement
Focus	Achieving Workforce Representation	Pursuing Harmony within the Workforce	Accessing Talent However Packaged	Accessing Potential of Elements in All Strategic Mixtures
Primary Motive	Civil Rights Social Justice Human Rights	Civil Rights Social Justice Human Rights	Business (Viability)	Business (Viability)
Universal Form	Managing Representation	Managing Relationships	Accessing Potential Contribution from Elements of All Strategic Mixtures	By Definition, Already Universal

non-workforce issues, but also will provide insights that advance the management of workforce diversity. Quadrant 4 and its universality are what make World-Class Diversity Management capability possible.

SOME TAKE-AWAYS

1. CEOs are likely to approach this quadrant in search of capability for generating solutions, rather than for the solution to a given diversity problem.

2. Competitive advantage for enterprises—or, for individuals, progress with personal diversity agendas—provides the driving motive behind this quadrant.

3. This quadrant is in an embryonic stage. While the recognition of diversity mixtures is broadening, development and adoption of a universal process are just beginning.

4. The three-legged stool approach for managing workforce diversity can be generalized for *any* mixture. It is *universal*.

5. The undergirding paradigm is Maximize Stakeholder Engagement.

6. As an overall take-away from this quadrant and the other three, Chart 4-1 compares highlights of each core strategy.

Part II

OPERATIONALIZATION

Now that we have discussed each of the four diversity management strategies—the paths to World-Class Diversity Management (WCDM)—what further can we say specifically about WCDM? What must be kept in mind when considering whether to work toward this status?

At this junction, CEOs should remember that they are *building* diversity management *capability*, and that they are not yet prepared to use the four strategies. They possess an intellectual understanding of diversity management but lack the wherewithal to actualize its strategies in practical applications.

Their situation at this stage is analogous to that of a would-be golfer who has taken in-depth, introductory tutorials from a golf professional. This novice golfer would have learned that golf consists of three basic strategies: a long game, a short game, and a putting game.

But she has not yet stepped onto a golf course. In other words, she has attained an intellectual understanding of golfing but has not addressed how to actualize her knowledge of the three strategies.

To actualize those golfing strategies, she will need three enablers:

1. **Proper equipment.** This includes a set of clubs and proper attire.

2. **The ability to read, assess, and manage the complexities** (which is what makes implementation difficult) **of a given course and of individual holes.**

3. **A mastery of strategy-paradigm dynamics.** Here I am suggesting that each of the basic golfing strategies is undergirded by paradigms and philosophies. For a variety of reasons—such as physical attributes and temperament—some golfers can have difficulty moving between the three strategies as dictated by the situations they encounter on a given course. Once, as an instructor was coaching me on my golf swing, he noted that many people were out working on their long game, but only a few were working on their short game or their putting. He was dismayed at how many were neglecting those critical aspects of golf. He, in essence, was bemoaning the reality that movement between the strategies and their related paradigms can be challenging for some golfers.

Effective actualization requires practice. Just *possessing* the proper equipment, *understanding* how to read golfing complexities, and *understanding* the strategy-paradigm dynamics are not sufficient for the development of the golfing craft. Mastery requires practice, which, in turn, permits pursuit of the three strategies for golfing excellence.

Aspirants to World-Class Diversity Management status must be concerned with actualization of basic strategies, as well. In particular, they will need the following:

1. **Mastery of the Strategic Diversity Management Process.** Analogous to golf clubs, this process equips CEOs to make quality decisions in each of the four core diversity management strategies. Chapter 5 details the attributes of SDMP.

2. **Mastery of managing complexity.** CEOs must be able to read and address the complexities (which make a situation difficult to understand, explain, or resolve) that come with diversity. Chapter 6 contends that the complexity associated with diversity can be conceptualized as diversity mixtures and addressed with SDMP.

3. **Mastery of the diversity management strategy-paradigm dynamics.** This is necessary if CEOs are to move between the four strategies as needed. Chapter 7 discusses these dynamics. CEOs must avoid the temptation to stop with understanding, or perhaps even worse, to jump into practice without understanding.

As is true for the would-be golfer, understanding alone is not sufficient for aspirants to World-Class Diversity Management status; it must be accompanied by practice. Actualization requires converting understanding to practical application.

5 STRATEGIC DIVERSITY MANAGEMENT PROCESS

A Universal Craft

After CEOs have recognized the Four Quadrants and determined that their core diversity management strategies might have utility, additional questions surface: "Are all strategies equally valued?" "Or is one more valued than another?" "How do we get our arms around the Four Quadrants?" "Where do we start?" "How do we actualize the core strategies?" "Are we, perhaps, overcomplicating matters?"

CEOs with these questions will find the Strategic Diversity Management Process (SDMP) to be invaluable. This process can both provide a lens through which these issues can be addressed, and help to implement the quadrants' core diversity management strategic prescriptions. To highlight the actualization role of the SDMP, I briefly review below what I have said about the four diversity management strategies.

I contended earlier that diversity management in the United States around race, ethnicity, and gender is evolving from three workforce-specific strategies: Managing Workforce Representation, Managing Workforce Relationships, and Managing Diverse Talent. Over the years, additional workforce dimensions have emerged. These include sexual orientation, age, geographic origin, physical ability, religion and national origin, class, education, and others.

Managing Workforce Representation and Managing Workforce Relationships have been operationalized by "traditional" practices based on concepts and thinking that emanated from advocacy efforts around civil rights, race, ethnicity, and gender. Not so for the emerging strategy of Managing Diverse Talent. Empowerment Management and organizational culture change are the most frequently used vehicles by which this emerging strategy is actualized.

However they are operationalized, I see the workforce-specific strategies as level 1 in the evolution of diversity management. This is where most organizations and individuals are; in particular, most function around Managing Workforce Representation and Managing Workforce Relationships.

I believe that level 2 for diversity management will begin when managers start to recognize that there are diversity mixtures other than the workforce, and that their workforce-specific strategies can be adapted for those mixtures. The more they adapt, the more they move toward generalizing these strategies. When this thinking-adapting process has evolved into the universal versions that can be applied to any diversity mixture, they will be operating at level 2:

Managing Workforce Representation ⟶ **Managing Representation**
Managing Workforce Demographic Relationships ⟶ **Managing Relationships**
Managing Diverse Talent ⟶ **Managing Empowerment**

Level 3 is reached when organizations and individuals are comfortable enough with these universal strategies to collapse them into one universal strategy—Quadrant 4's Managing All Strategic Mixtures. As with level 2, the implementation vehicle can and will be (in my opinion) SDMP or some other comparable process supporting universal applicability.

World-Class Diversity Management will be achieved when the individual or organization has mastered this universal strategy. Organizations and people operating at this level will be capable of addressing *any* type of diversity mixture *anywhere*. They will have achieved a world-class mastery of diversity management. The vehicle for achieving this capability will again (in my opinion) be SDMP. Figure 5-1

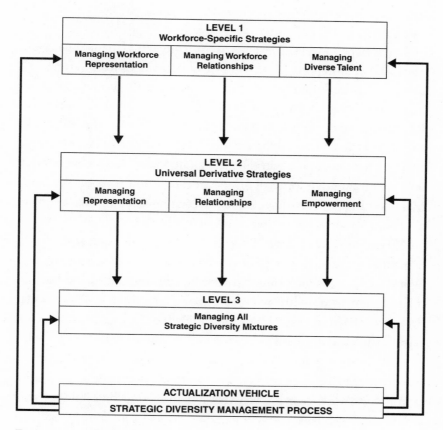

FIGURE 5-1. Evolution Toward World-Class Status

captures the recommended transition dynamics from level 1 to level 2 to level 3. The upwardly flowing arrows reflect my contention that SDMP can be used to actualize *all* levels.

The notion of "levels" has implications for determining which quadrants a leader might embrace. It's reasonable to ask, "Do we have to transition to levels 2 and 3?" Not necessarily. It depends on two things. The first is the extent to which you are concerned about *non-workforce* diversity mixtures. Managers who are primarily focused on *workforce* mixtures will have less need to transition. The greater the focus on non-workforce mixtures, the greater will be the need for levels 2 and 3.

It also depends on the level of risk you are willing to assume. Managers who *are* interested in expanding to non-workforce mixtures will benefit from working through level 2. Without the generalization of this second level, they will come to level 3 seeking to apply workforce-specific strategies to non-workforce mixtures. They might, for example, attempt to apply workforce-centric strategies to product diversity.

More fundamentally, without generalization, level 1 practitioners are often not aware that forms of diversity other than the workforce exist. Many level 1 managers have difficulty even envisioning that diversity can relate to something other than the workforce.

When one level 1 practitioner learned that this book argued that a parallel existed between World-Class Diversity Management and World-Class Manufacturing management, he responded, "What has diversity got to do with manufacturing?" This individual associated diversity with human resources so strongly that he could not even entertain the idea of a parallel.

This chapter describes the parameters of SDMP. I have devoted a full chapter to the process because its critical actualizing role in the transition to world class is so key that it merits as much visibility as possible. *To read this book and to understand the four core diversity management strategies without full awareness and comprehension of the actualizing vehicle (SDMP) would be like buying a new car without an engine.*

The description of SDMP in this chapter focuses on the *requirements* for making it a capability: Mastery of the process requires awareness, understanding, and operationalization of concepts, principles, and paradigms. It also requires development and mastery of skills and competencies. Finally, it requires maintenance of that mastery by continuous learning. For most, development of the SDMP capability (mastery of the SDMP craft) will require effort and commitment. Immersion in training alone will not suffice.

SDMP PARAMETERS

Universal Principles[1]

Conceptual clarity is a must. A definition of the most important universal concepts underlying the SDMP—diversity, diversity tension, complexity, diversity challenged, diversity capable, and diversity maturity—appear in the introduction to the book. It will be helpful to review these definitions as you continue with the chapter. However, it won't be enough. Mastering the SDMP requires the ability to incorporate these concepts personally and organizationally to the point of second nature.

Context is important. Knowledge of the organization's internal and external environments, mission, vision, strategy, and competitive challenges is essential. This knowledge allows the organization's leaders to identify where the organization is *strategically* diversity challenged, how it might be able to develop a compelling business case, and what its diversity management aspirations should be. As an illustration, if an organization has identified strategic partnerships or mergers as a priority, its leaders will need the ability to address the related diversity issues.

The specific core diversity management strategies selected must fit an organization's diversity aspirations. All diversity management strategies are legitimate. The critical issue is to determine the one most compatible with an organization's circumstances and aspirations.

An organization's dominant paradigm must match the primary strategy being used. When a mismatch exists, leaders must either position desired changes as supporting the dominant paradigm or move to bring about a paradigm shift. Otherwise, they risk compromising their chances for successful implementation of a new diversity management strategy. (More will be said about this in chapter 7.)

The organization's culture must support its diversity aspirations and diversity management strategies. If it doesn't, the odds are against sustainable diversity management progress.

Diversity efforts must be requirements driven. In the midst of differences and similarities and related tensions and complexities, quality decision making demands clarity about absolute requirements, as opposed to traditions, personal preferences, and convenience.[2] However, even that is not enough. Organizational leaders must not only identify requirements; they must be willing to be driven by them.

Empowerment Management meshes best with the engagement aspect of diversity management. The Empowerment Management model focuses on accessing the contributions of a mixture's elements in a way that the traditional Doer Model of command and control cannot.

Individual and organizational diversity aspirations must be in sync. Excellence with diversity management on the part of leaders and managers is not sufficient. Often I see situations where leaders "get it," and individual contributors remain unengaged. In one setting, the organization presented well-defined diversity principles and aspirations, yet associates' responses in interviews indicated a stark unawareness of the behavioral implications of their corporation's diversity statements. Leaders cannot take for granted that associates share their diversity management objectives; they must work toward congruence and commitment. Communication can be key here.

Leaders must create a readiness and capability for universal application. An inability to embrace the notion of a universal process with non-workforce mixtures can be a major obstacle. Organizations rooted deeply in workforce diversity will find it challenging to consider any other type.

SDMP Decision-Making Tool

Once organizations and their leaders are ready to address diversity issues, SDMP offers a decision-making tool to facilitate the process. Based on the principles and concepts articulated above, the framework prescribes five basic steps:

1. **Specify context.** This step is absolutely essential. Preparing to make decisions around a given diversity mixture requires "up front" answers to the following questions:
   - What is the organization's mission?
   - Vision?
   - Strategy?
   - Competitive challenges?
   - What are the "requirements" for achieving the organization's mission and vision and for addressing its competitive challenge? (This, of course, is in keeping with the requirements principle.)

2. **Recognize the nature and content of the diversity mixture in question.** Key questions are the following:
   - Who or what are the elements (individuals, groups, organizations, objects) in the mixture?
   - What are the elements' central differences and similarities? What are the demographic and behavioral differences and similarities?
   - What are the elements' interests, concerns, and priorities?
   - What "requirements" are related specifically to the mixture, as opposed to the organization?

3. **Assess the mixture's tensions.** All diversity mixtures contain some tensions.
   - What tensions do the elements experience?
   - What are the sources of the tensions?
   - What are the costs associated with the tensions? (This is key. If the costs are not significant, leaders can ignore this mixture.)
   - If individuals or groups are in the mixture, where are they diversity challenged?
   - What factors are causing them to be diversity challenged?

4. **Identify the desired state.** Ideally, how would you like to see circumstances resolved?
   - What would be the desired state and its characteristics?
   - What gains would accrue from achieving the desired state?
   - What problems would be minimized by realizing the desired state?
   - What existing cultural or situational factors might hinder progress toward the desired state?

5. **Apply the action response options.** This set of options provides generic alternatives from which to choose when addressing a mixture. They will be discussed under mastery requirements.

- How have the tensions been addressed before?
- What have been the benefits of past responses?
- What specific challenges remain to be addressed?
- Which action options offer the greatest possibility for achieving the desired state?
- What are the pros and cons of each?
- Which option(s) should be selected to address the remaining issues?

Depending on the issue, moving through the decision-making framework can take five minutes, five hours, five weeks, five months, or longer. The more complex the mixture, the greater the amount of time needed to determine a proper response. In some instances, gathering the necessary data can be time consuming. The framework ideally becomes second nature for individuals and institutionalized for organizations. Both outcomes will require mastery of SDMP concepts, principles, and decision-making tools.

PREREQUISITES FOR MASTERY

To master the SDMP decision-making tool, individuals and organizations must become competent with diversity management skills *and* achieve diversity maturity.

Diversity Management Skills

Three diversity management skills are critical to the mastery process:[3]

1. **The ability to recognize diversity mixtures.** Once developed, this skill must become a matter of routine. Several factors can block its development:

- Conceptual confusion about what constitutes a diversity mixture. Definitions not only define reality; they shape it. Those who define *diversity* only as race or gender will likely fail to see mixtures other than those involving race or gender.
- A belief that differences and similarities are irrelevant. During wartime, many United States soldiers have returned home with experiences that resulted in friendships across racial and ethnic groups, only to find that societal norms dictate that such differences and similarities still do matter.
- An overestimation of the progress that has been made with diversity. A typical example is when members of a community express surprise and even shock over a diversity incident. This kind of reaction is often seen when a corporation with a sterling diversity reputation is accused of or found guilty of a diversity misstep.
- Assimilation and color blindness that reduce the visibility of diversity mixtures. Assimilation seeks behavioral conformity, while color blindness—which can be generalized to any dimension—simply refuses to recognize differences. Where these two responses are in play, diversity mixtures often are not pronounced or recognized. (This potential downside of assimilation does not negate the fact that it is a legitimate response to diversity.)

Failure to recognize diversity mixtures can bring undesirable consequences. It can, for example, inhibit the ability to see and address a potentially detrimental or explosive situation (like an inability to retain executives of acquired companies). It can also obfuscate opportunities to use diversity management to leverage differences and similarities for strategic gain (for example, to bring about functional synergy). Diversity mixtures must be recognized before they can be addressed effectively.

2. The ability to determine whether action is required with respect to a particular diversity mixture. We can spend so much time trying to determine what is or is not a diversity mixture that we forget that many—if not most—do not merit action or attention. A frivolous example I have used is the amount of hair on the heads of men in an organization. This is a bonafide mixture, but not one that in most organizations merits attention. It is important to know when to act and when not to act.

3. The ability to select appropriate responses once you are sure that action is required. To facilitate development of this skill, I offer ten generic options from which to choose. All are legitimate; their appropriateness depends on the situation. The task is to use the option that offers the greatest gain in terms of organizational or personal objectives.

The basic definitions of the action options below are derived from discussions in three of my earlier books, *Building on the Promise of Diversity,*[4] *Building a House for Diversity,*[5] and *Redefining Diversity.*[6] The options are as follows:

Include. Increase the amount of diversity by adding a component or expanding the variability of the components in the mixture. This action option comes instinctively to mind when we speak of diversity. The leader developing a list of potential task force members, the hiring manager extending an offer, the executive deciding to acquire another company, two spouses deciding to adopt a child, national leaders setting immigration policies, politicians practicing wedge politics—all are examples of using the "include" option with respect to a diversity mixture. Simultaneously, however, they are making decisions to exclude.

Exclude. Decrease the amount of diversity by reducing the number of components or the variability of components in the mixture. We do not typically associate this option with diversity in the United States because of our historical interest in mainstreaming those who have been inappropriately excluded. Nevertheless, this remains a legitimate option. Indeed, as implied in the "Include" paragraph above, exclusion decisions are often—if not always—implicitly part of any inclusion discussion. "Who or what should be in the mix?" simultaneously and implicitly asks, "Who or what should *not* be in the mix?"

Deny. Minimize the diversity mixture by explaining it away. Prototypical here is the *decision* to be "blind" to differences of some kind. One example is the executive who introduces a leader of an acquired company by saying, "This is Bill. He's from the company we just bought, but he's okay. He's not like them."

A favorite example of mine is how more than forty years ago, potential employers told me, "We will not see you as a Negro." This blindness was convenient for them, since they would not have to deal with race, and also convenient for me, since I assumed their blindness meant I could go as far as my talent would take me. We both were in denial—I *was* a Negro.

To elect to be blind to a difference is to say implicitly or even explicitly that it is not relevant or is somehow distasteful. In recent years, to say that a person's race, gender, religion, or some other attribute is irrelevant has increasingly been viewed as insulting.

Isolate. Include and set "different" mixture components off to the side. Establishing functional silos or lines of business silos isolates them for reasons of effectiveness. Locating a distribution center away from headquarters in a region it serves is a form of isolation in pursuit of effectiveness and efficiency. Racial, gender, or ethnic segregation is still another form of isolation, albeit one that in most circumstances is deemed inappropriate.

Suppress. Minimize mixture diversity by assigning it to the unconscious—beyond immediate awareness. A prototypical example here is the military's approach to sexual orientation differences: "Don't ask, don't tell."

Acculturate. Minimize mixture diversity by insisting that "minority" components conform to the norms of the dominant one, no matter how they feel about those norms. Here credit is given for going through the motions. Using the golfing analogy again, gearing up once a year for required golf outings would be sufficient. Neither commitment nor excellence is required.

Assimilate. Minimize mixture diversity by insisting that "minority" components not only conform to the norms of the dominant one, but commit to them, as well. More than political correctness is required. If, for example, your company does considerable business on the golf course, assimilation requires not only that you play golf, but also that you become the best you can at it—regardless of how you feel about the game of golf. You cannot just go through the motions.[7]

Tolerate. Adopt a room-for-all attitude, but keep interactions among mixture components superficial and limited. Until recently, "tolerate" enjoyed considerable popularity; however, lately, most people understand that while being *tolerant* might be admirable, being *tolerated* is not a good feeling. Few people look forward to hearing at their retirement party, "For the last twenty years, it has been our privilege and honor to tolerate you." Such sentiments imply a less than wholehearted acceptance. Unstated but implied: "We really did not want you here." This can sometimes be seen among organizational units, where the last line of business acquired or launched is seen as less than. Here the message is "You're really not one of us, but you can stay as long as you make money."

Build relationships. Foster quality relationships, characterized by acceptance and understanding among the mixture components.

This option can be used to move beyond tolerance and into more intimate engagement. Leaders of two business units who "tolerate" each other may elect this option as a prerequisite for seeking synergistic opportunities they might exploit.

Foster mutual adaptation. Expect all components to adapt to "requirements." Here the goal is to identify where all components must conform (the requirements) and where they can be open to diversity (the non-requirements). The elements in the mixture adapt to requirements and are open to diversity in the area of non-requirements. Applying this option is easier said than done, especially for people who value conformity in the area of non-requirements, as well.

Diversity Maturity

Diversity maturity, the second requirement for mastery of the SDMP, refers to the degree to which an individual, manager, or organization understands and can act upon the universal concepts and principles. The premise is that the greater the diversity maturity, the more likely the entity will be effective with SDMP.[8]

While the concept can be used with respect to organizations, the discussion below refers to individual contributors and managers. Diversity mature people possess the following traits:

1. They acknowledge being diversity challenged. Individuals who refuse to consider themselves diversity challenged will lack motivation to master the SDMP.

2. They recognize the cost of being diversity challenged. The greater the costs, the greater the motivation will be to become diversity capable through SDMP.

3. They accept diversity management responsibility. This is critical. Individuals can be diversity challenged, or can see where their organization is challenged, but elect not to accept responsibility for moving themselves or their enterprises toward being diversity capable. These people are unlikely to be interested in mastering the SDMP.

4. They have a personal and organizational context. They know their priorities and those of their organization. Mature individuals have a strong sense of their aspirations and those of their organization.

5. They act on the basis of requirements.

6. They challenge conventional wisdom. Diversity mature people work to meet requirements even when that challenges the conventional wisdom of traditions, preferences, and conveniences that might not be essential.

7. They engage in continuous learning. This reflects recognition that the SDMP is a *capability* that requires maintenance through continuous learning.

8. They are comfortable with the dynamics of diversity, especially around related tensions and complexities. That is, they understand the SDMP and are comfortable with it.

As the list affirms, diversity mature individuals are better prepared for success with SDMP. Individuals and organizations typically have to strive to become diversity mature. For most, it is not natural.

LAUNCHING WORLD-CLASS DIVERSITY MANAGEMENT

The launching of World-Class Diversity Management involves three phases: (1) Talking the Talk, (2) Thinking the Talk, and (3) Walking the Talk.[9] (See figure 5-2.)

Talking the Talk

In this phase, the principal task is to gain clarity about World-Class Diversity Management and SDMP as the process that actual-

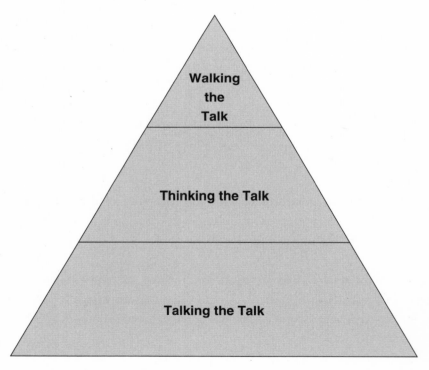

FIGURE 5-2. Three Launching Phases for World-Class Diversity Management

izes the pursuit of world-class status. Fundamentally, this is an educational step—developing or changing mindsets as opposed to training (developing skills). The *objectives* are to introduce World-Class Diversity Management and SDMP and to enroll key stakeholders in support of pursuing both.

Desired outcomes are that these stakeholders achieve the following:

- Become clear about the requirements for achieving World-Class Diversity Management.
- Appreciate the distinction between diversity and diversity management.
- Understand the notion of the "diversity forest."
- Recognize and understand the notion of "universal" as it applies to diversity.
- Appreciate the business rationales for diversity management and World-Class Diversity Management.
- Become motivated to pursue World-Class Diversity Management using SDMP as the actualizer.
- Understand the roles of managers and individual contributors in the pursuit of world-class status.
- Begin to internalize and commit to the process.

A *principal vehicle* for achieving these outcomes is the executive briefing (an interactive session between the presenter and the audience). Typically, this activity, which can last from one to four hours, is presented for an organization's senior leadership team or diversity council. It addresses at least the following:

- the notion of World-Class Diversity Management
- the Four Quadrants
- quadrant-paradigm dynamics
- SDMP and its universal components
- requirements for pursuing world-class status

Additional tools for educating include e-learning opportunities, traditional educational sessions, workbooks, books, and a variety of instruments. Although the initial education efforts target the organization's senior leaders or its diversity champions, once leaders decide to pursue World-Class Diversity Management, the launching process calls for extending some form of the educational process to rank-and-file associates.

"Talking the Talk" lays the foundation so vital to the pursuit of world-class status. Education here means not exposure, but rather understanding and internalization. This is so important to the endeavor's success that formal or informal assessments should be made to determine the effectiveness of the educational activities. If the education has not "taken," persistent remedial work is in order. As an example, one indicator of inadequate education would be persistent confusion about the definition of diversity. I am clear beyond question that if the educational foundation is weak, the pursuit of world-class status will be also.

The most successful launches I have seen have taken place when the CEOs and CDOs have taken the educational process seriously, to the point of attending several sessions of a given offering. They were signaling and modeling "I will stay at this until I get it."

Thinking the Talk

During this phase, leaders relate the educational results to organizational realities by asking, in effect, "So what now?" They have heard and understood what has been conveyed about World-Class Diversity Management, the Four Quadrants, and SDMP, and now must decide what it all means in the context of their particular mission, vision, culture, strategy, and competitive challenges.

Three steps constitute this phase: (1) strategic planning sessions, (2) research, and (3) planning. Through small-group experiences, two-day *strategic planning sessions* have as their *objectives* to allow participants to do the following:

- Relate World-Class Diversity Management to their mission, vision, culture, and competitive challenges.
- Relate World-Class Diversity Management to the organization's strategic thrusts (what it does to secure and maintain competitive advantage).
- Identify preliminarily the "trees" of their diversity forest that need the most attention.

Desired outcomes are that session participants achieve the following: ·

- Become aware of how World-Class Diversity Management capability can support the organization's mission, vision, strategy, and culture.
- Gain an initial sense of how their organizational culture will support World-Class Diversity Management.
- Identify how World-Class Diversity Management could be synergistic with the organization's other strategic thrusts.
- Gain clarity about the business motive for pursuing world-class status.

In contrast to the executive briefing session, where the expert presenter drives the discussion, participants drive the strategic planning session through their small-group work. Ordinarily, the organization's leadership team or diversity council is the first to experience a strategic planning session.

Step 2 of "Thinking the Talk" involves *research* and can be thought of as the diagnostic step. Among its *objectives* are to make preliminary determinations as to the following:

- where the organization is diversity challenged
- which of the Four Quadrants have been utilized by the organization
- what the organization's dominant collective paradigm has been
- whether the organization's culture will support its World-Class Diversity Management aspirations
- whether organizational leaders have sufficient information to answer the questions just above
- which research tools will be required to make the specified determinations for attaining information

The critical desired outcome is a significant, substantial, and sufficient amount of data to facilitate planning, the next step of this phase. A variety of research tools are available to generate these data if they are not otherwise available—for example:

- diversity research (reveals where organization is diversity challenged and diversity capable)
- quadrant audit (determines what the organization's experiences have been with the Four Quadrants)
- paradigm audit (reveals the organization's diversity paradigm structure)
- cultural audit (identifies the nature of the organization's culture)

Based on the data generated, *planning*—the third step in the phase—provides specifics for moving toward world-class status. Key data-driven *objectives* are to accomplish the following:

- Identify the trees of the organization's diversity forest that need the most attention.
- Decide where the organization needs to expand its involvement with the Four Quadrants.

- Determine where the organization needs to modify its diversity paradigm structure to support pursuit of World-Class Diversity Management.
- Develop a plan for making paradigm modifications that are needed.
- Identify where the organization's culture needs to be changed to support pursuit of World-Class Diversity Management.
- Develop a plan to bring about the necessary changes in culture.
- Ascertain when and where additional education will be necessary.
- Develop an education plan for all levels of the organization.
- Determine training needs around (1) skill building, (2) diversity maturity, and (3) application of the SDMP decision-making tool; and develop a training program around these areas.
- Agree on a plan for picking low-hanging fruit.

Clearly, several years will be needed for implementation—in both small and large enterprises. In this step, planning is the purpose. Frequently, internal and external resources collaborate around the planning activities. Most critical is that the planning be data driven.

The *desired outcome* is a comprehensive, detailed plan for launching the pursuit of World-Class Diversity Management, and a preliminary sketch of what will be needed beyond the launching process—especially with regard to education and training.

Walking the Talk

In this phase, the organization focuses on implementation. With respect to the launch, *implementation objectives* would be to accomplish the following:

- Begin paradigm modification as needed.
- Initiate the process of culture change.
- Continue to roll out World-Class Diversity Management education for all organizational members (training would be delayed until after initial educational efforts).
- Gain some introductory hands-on experience with applying the SDMP decision-making tool.
- Pick low-hanging fruit.

The *desired outcome* is a successful launch involving education, paradigm shifts, and cultural change as necessary; experimental application of the SDMP decision-making tool; and the harvesting of low-hanging fruit. Connected to these efforts would be measurement parameters that could assess the degree of success achieved and serve as a basis for future planning.

How long will the launch take? That depends on such factors as the size of the organization and the efficiency of its launch efforts. Education, for example, may require multiple iterations. Clearly, questions about duration are legitimate. But they may give a false sense that there is a definite "end point." *Keep in mind that we are talking about the launch, and also about a capability with requirements for continuous refinement and maintenance.* More than anything, World-Class Diversity Management is a *capability.* So more important than ongoing questions about the duration of the effort are perpetual inquiries about the strengths and weaknesses of this capability, such as "How strong is our capability?" "How might we strengthen or maintain our capability?"

GLOBAL PERSPECTIVE

Hopefully, the discussions of the launch process and the SDMP decision-making tool have indicated how World-Class Diversity Management can be applied globally. While the parameters might vary with respect to societal and organizational cultures, the World-Class Diversity Management and SDMP contexts would remain constant. As such, they are not peculiar to any geographical area or to any tree from the diversity forest.

DISCUSSION

I emphasize once again that optimal SDMP presumes a supporting organizational culture; an appropriate paradigm structure; and a clear understanding of SDMP and its universal concepts, principles, and dynamics. Further, prerequisite skills must be mastered, and diversity maturity must be attained. This context must be in place if the full potential of SDMP is to be realized.

Over the years, reaction to SDMP has varied. Some respond that it is too "complex," others that it is too time consuming, and still others that it does not capture how people experience diversity. I have found the last sentiment intriguing. My sense is that individuals do not experience diversity as something to which they can respond from a variety of legitimate options. Indeed, when managers are good with workforce diversity, peers and associates alike often describe them as "people persons" or individuals with "good hearts," as if their competency came about mysteriously and naturally. That very well may be true, but what about those of us for whom diversity capability is not "second nature"?

For these individuals, SDMP compartmentalizes the ways diversity mixtures can be addressed and provides a vehicle for developing diversity management capability. The thinking is not that users will spend the rest of their lives deliberately and methodically using this tool. It is, instead, that the tool's concepts, principles, and decision-making framework eventually will become second nature and be applied intuitively and instinctively.

I expect initially that users will apply the tool primarily to obviously complex diversity management challenges and that after several such applications, they will move to implement it routinely with less complicated challenges *and* opportunities. These applications will develop familiarity and confidence.

SDMP represents a marked departure from current practices because it is not just tactics or activities. It is a capability with concepts, principles, mastery requirements with respect to skills, and requirements for maintenance and advancement through continuous learning. This is what you would expect of any craft.

SOME TAKE-AWAYS

1. SDMP is the actualization vehicle for World-Class Diversity Management.
2. Evolution to World-Class Diversity Management can be seen as moving through three levels: level 1 (Managing Workforce Representation, Managing Workforce Relationships, and Managing Diverse Talent), level 2 (generalizing to Managing Representation, Managing Relationships, and Managing Empowerment), and level 3 (Managing All Strategic Mixtures).
3. SDMP is a universal process with a universal decision-making tool.

4. The launching of World-Class Diversity Management has three phases: (1) Talking the Talk, (2) Thinking the Talk, and (3) Walking the Talk.

5. For most enterprises, SDMP will mean a change in the method of operation.

6 MANAGING COMPLEXITY

An Inherent Capability

T his chapter places front and center a capability that is inherent in each of the diversity management strategies—
that of managing complexity. To effectively implement any of the
strategies, CEOs must acknowledge and accept that there will be sur-
rounding complexities, and be ready to address them.

The chapter has three objectives: (1) to examine the relationship
between complexity and diversity, (2) to explore the notion that many
complexities can be restated as diversity mixtures, and (3) to argue
that SDMP can be used to address these mixtures. These three objectives serve the broader one of preparing the reader for the realities of
diversity *and* complexity.

COMPLEXITY AND DIVERSITY

This preparation is important because a symbiotic relationship exists between the two: Where you have diversity, you have complexity;

and where you have complexity, you have diversity. Are the two concepts the same? They are not. But because diversity generates complexity, they are found in the same neighborhood.

I first affirmed this when a client requested an introductory, three-week seminar on diversity for managers from around the world. There was, he said, only one critical proviso—I could not use the word *diversity*. The client believed the word did not work outside of the United States. Although I knew from personal experience that *diversity*—as defined by me—worked perfectly well across nations, I did not argue the point; instead, I asked if we could replace it with *complexity*. The client agreed to that substitution.

My colleagues and I then went through our materials and dropped in "complexity" wherever "diversity" appeared. We provided no elaborations. This substitution allowed us to omit the word while effectively conveying the essence of diversity and diversity management as complexity and complexity management, and to have a very productive learning experience.

I came away from the session with a profound appreciation and respect for the relationship between complexity and diversity. Participants left with a deeper awareness and understanding of diversity and diversity management, having become acquainted with diversity through the lens of complexity.

What It Means to Be Complex

Webster's Dictionary defines *complex* as being synonymous with complicated, and it defines *complicated* as applying to that which "offers great difficulty in understanding, solving, or explaining."[1] Extrapolating, we can define *complex* as *that quality that makes it difficult to understand, solve, or explain a situation*. In the context of the four core diversity management strategies, we can designate obstacles as complexities.

What Contributes to Complexity?

Uncertainty, ambiguity, unpredictability, and emergent activity all contribute to complexity. To the extent that situations lack certainty and predictability, the degree of complexity increases. Similarly, the greater the ambiguity, the more complexity. Uncertainty, ambiguity, and unpredictability all set the stage for the emergence of the un-intended or the unexpected, which adds an additional degree of complexity

Diversity per se contributes to complexity, as well. I made this point in *Redefining Diversity*,[2] noting that diversity's propensity to gen-erate complexity can lead us to avoid diversity:

> Diversity generates complexity in terms of multiplicity and varia-tions. Imagine, for example, that you are juggling three balls and you are quite good at it. Your boss comes along and says that you are now required to juggle five. Clearly, this makes your task more com-plex. At a minimum, you will need greater hand speed.
>
> While you are learning to increase hand speed, your boss informs you that you will be juggling five *objects*, not five balls, and that these objects will differ in size, shape, and weight. This further complicates your juggling life. Not only will you need greater hand speed, you will also need to vary your grip for the different objects, and to take into account the varying weights so as to anticipate the speeds with which the objects will move through the air. You must make several calculations and adjustments simultaneously.
>
> How well you do this will depend on how well you can handle complexity. If these simultaneous adjustments are beyond your complexity capability, you will experience frustration and failure. If these circumstances persist, you may learn to dislike those objects that are so different from the balls you were once comfortable with and are contributing to your current difficulty.
>
> Diversity creates complexity, which, in turn, presents challenges for all individuals and creates resentments within those with limited capacity for complexity. In truth, that includes most of us. We prefer to avoid complexity, which means avoiding diversity.[3]

This excerpt implies that because of the intertwining of diversity and complexity, the ability to manage diversity can be positively or negatively affected by the ability to cope with complexity. If I am challenged by the complexity caused by diversity, I may decide to minimize the complexity by minimizing or avoiding the diversity that's involved.

For example, if I conclude that a mixture of races is too complex, I may try to reduce the number of racial groups present by excluding some until I reach a degree of complexity I can manage. Alternately, I could consider requiring assimilation as a way to reduce diversity and related complexity. Both options are legitimate, but neither fosters acceptance of racial diversity where it is desired or unavoidable.

On the positive side, the excerpt also implies that effective management of complexity can set the stage for more effective management of diversity. This chapter is based on the following premise: *Given that diversity leads to complexities, if we can isolate related ones and understand them as diversity mixtures, then we can apply SDMP to both the diversity mixtures in question and the complexities they generate.*

This is a key premise and reflects why I believe managing complexity is or should be implicit or inherent in the four core diversity management strategies. It suggests that before trying to minimize a type of diversity because it generates an uncomfortable level of complexity, organizations and individuals can isolate the complexity and understand it as a diversity mixture. Then—*before* dealing with the diversity issue in question—they can apply SDMP to the related complexity (more about this later in the chapter).

At that point, SDMP becomes a two-edged sword that can be used to foster quality decision making in the midst of diversity *and* complexity. Such decision making would not necessarily minimize either. It would, however, allow enterprise leaders to effectively pursue organizational objectives despite any discomfort they might experience with diversity or complexity.

This is not an academic discussion. Difficulty with complexity can lead managers to minimize the diversity of their associates. Consider, for example, the manager with a tight time frame for assembling a team and achieving an objective. Often, she will try to avoid unnecessary diversity that might generate progress-inhibiting complexity. As team selections are made, comments like the following may be heard: "I want him on the team; we're on the same page in our thinking." "If we can avoid her, it will be good. She can be way out there." "Do we really need someone from *that* department? They tend to be so critical and negative." "I don't want him. You never know which of his agendas he will bring."

A similar example can be seen around an acquisition. Say a large company bought an enterprise in an industry closely related to its own. However, despite sharing many technological similarities, the acquired company's culture differed substantially from that of the acquiring corporation. The acquired enterprise had a looser, less formal, more entrepreneurial culture that troubled leaders of the larger organization. They couldn't understand how it could be so poorly operated and yet be so successful. The puzzled executives considered two options for addressing the complexity of the operation they had bought. One was to "integrate" the smaller entity into the acquiring company; the other called for complete separation—"Out of sight, out of mind; just send the profits." Because the leaders believed that integration would destroy what made the company a viable business, they elected to leave it as a free-standing, largely independent, subsidiary. The acquisition thrived and sent plenty of profits to its new parent—whose managers remained perplexed by how it did that.

The unstated purpose in both examples is "Let's not make this too complex. Let's minimize the likelihood of uncertainty, unpredictability, ambiguity, and the emergence of the unexpected or the unintended." In neither case would that have been beneficial. If the effort to avoid complexity by minimizing diversity excludes people who could add value to the decision-making process, the result is detrimental to achieving organizational objectives. Or, if efforts to minimize complexity through "integration" had destroyed the special essence of the acquiree, the value added of the acquisition and its diversity would have been diminished.

The examples share another similarity. Both focused on minimizing disruptions in decision-making effectiveness and efficiency, not on social justice issues around being excluded or disadvantaged. In the team member selection example, for instance, the manager desired minimal tension and conflict so that decision making would flow more easily. Members of the acquiring company sought to minimize decision-making disruptions that would occur if they had to manage the acquiree.

These examples illustrate a basic really: Diversity comes with associated costs. It can complicate the decision-making and problem-solving process by presenting tasks that would not exist in the absence of diversity. For example, managers addressing diversity in a team setting must do the following:

1. **Access the desired diversity.** This means not only ensuring the presence of the desired diversity, but also extending extra effort to see that team dynamics promote and support the desired diversity—for example, that members do not shut down but rather remain engaged.

2. **Determine the degree of integration required.** For the diversity dimension in question, an analysis like the one done for race in chart 2-1, in chapter 2, would be helpful.

3. **Integrate the input from diverse elements in the mixture.** The task here is to accept and understand what each member is saying and how their inputs relate to each other. Critical here is suspension of judgment.

4. Process these understandings in search of solutions. In a requirements-driven fashion, participants must explore and test their understandings for an optimal solution.

Candidly speaking, this is what the manager with the tight time frame wanted to avoid. For her, timelines were more important than generating the best possible solutions through the vehicles of diversity *and* diversity management. My point here is not whether she was right or wrong, but rather that she did have to make a choice. If she had opted to pursue high-quality decisions through diversity, it may not have cost her timelines, but it most definitely would have required extra effort to ensure that her timelines priority was honored. She had to decide whether the *costs* of the extra effort would be less than the potential *benefits*. Again, diversity generates costs; its benefits are not free.

However, the "extra effort" should be seen as part and parcel of the managerial role, and the more effective a manager is with diversity and complexity management, the less extra effort is required. (The reader probably recognizes that this discussion of the costs-and-benefits analysis regarding diversity also applies to the example in the book's introduction of President Barack Obama's selection of his National Economic Council.)

Unfortunately, leaders who try to analyze these types of situations are often accused of bias, discrimination, pettiness, or personality clashes, which may or may not be accurate. Rarely is the desire to avoid complexity seen as the reason for excluding associates from the team or minimizing the integration of an acquisition. Becoming more comfortable with complexity would greatly help CEOs to get at diversity issues such as those in the examples.

CAPABILITY PARAMETERS

Definition

As noted above, we can best talk about the complexity of diversity as those things that make any diversity mixture difficult to understand, solve, or explain. Examples include the following:

Managing Workforce Representation

- Recruitment has become more complex. In the past, a plant foreman might simply invite staff to bring friends or relatives in to be considered for an opening. Under equal opportunity laws, appropriate outreach must be made to all demographic communities.

  A senior executive in a small business announced to her board that the firm had a key opening, and asked members to spread the word because she hoped to fill the position by word of mouth to minimize search expenses. In shock, an employment lawyer on her board responded, "You cannot do that! You will place yourself and the firm at great risk. Even if you were going to do it, you should not announce it." The executive thanked her board member and decided to incur significant search costs.

- Selection criteria have become more formal, extensive, and complex, as well. In the past, the earlier mentioned plant foreman two paragraphs back would have relied heavily on references from friends or relatives of applicants. As a child, I often heard people who were looking for jobs ask an employee at a site, "Are you hiring?" If the answer was yes, the next request would be, "Would you put a word in for me?" It was widely understood that references from current employees could be critical.

Today, selection criteria must be spelled out and applied consistently to all applicants. To neglect to do that is to risk being charged with making a hiring decision on the basis of a non-job-related criterion, which could lead to an equal employment opportunity challenge.

- Since recruitment and hiring activities are now pursued on all sides by descendants of slaveholders and those of slaves, bias must be avoided and fair play ensured—adding another level of complexity and tensions.

- Many organizations have struggled for more than forty years since the Civil Rights Era to achieve a "representative" workforce reflecting the general population. The length of this struggle shouts complexity, and many organizations remain unclear as to how to achieve their representation aspirations.

Managing Workforce Relationships

- In the past, managers could count on relatives and friends to integrate new hires into the workforce. As a result of integration, the on-boarding integration process now involves interactions between descendants of oppressors and those who were oppressed. As a result, the process can be more problematic and complex.

- Further, integration must now occur at two levels, that of the individual as a person, and that of the individual's talent (see chapter 3). This is more complex than initially anticipated.

- As organizational managers have sought to assure all new hires—especially minorities—that they are "equals" to anyone and are welcomed, they have unintentionally encouraged demographic and behavior diversity and discouraged the assimilation they preferred. A consequence has been much more complexity than expected or desired.

Managing Diverse Talent

- Many individuals still find it difficult to think of diversity in any but a civil rights, social justice, or human rights context. This has complicated efforts to make a compelling business case for diversity management. That, in turn, has compromised potential progress with cultural change and Empowerment Management.
- Cultural change is easier prescribed than done. While talk of true cultural change in pursuit of full employee engagement is common, examples are scarce.
- Similarly, despite several incarnations and rave reviews of its potential, Empowerment Management lags behind traditional managerial practices.
- Dealing with the three workforce-specific strategies simultaneously is daunting, given the unfinished business associated with the first two.

Managing All Strategic Mixtures

- Comprehending the notion of diversity mixtures beyond the workforce has proven challenging and presents a degree of complexity for which many are not prepared. Some simply cannot conceive of diversity referring to anything other than the workforce.
- Developing a universal diversity management strategy and applying it to *all* kinds of diverse mixtures represent a formidable task for those accustomed to dealing with one mixture, that of workforce diversity. "All" seems like an enormous amount of diversity, not to mention complexity.
- Individuals grounded in the civil rights context often see a "universal" strategy as far-fetched.

This partial list of complexities is substantial and parallels the obstacles and challenges discussed in each core strategy's respective chapter. Through the lens of complexity, these "challenges" become factors (complexities) that make it difficult to understand each strategy or to resolve implementation issues. Indeed, they often frighten people into accepting the status quo or settling into a frustrating pattern designed to illustrate good intentions, rather than to produce real change.

Just as I am absolutely clear that diversity can and does generate complexity, I also am beginning to understand that diversity-related complexities can be viewed through the lens of diversity. We therefore can speak of the diversity of a given complexity, or of complexity as diversity. So, for example, what is the diversity mixture inherent in the complexity of cultural change?

One way to get at the related mixture is to ask, "Complex compared to what?" The answer is compared to maintaining the status quo. Thus, the inherent related diverse mixture is that of the status quo *and* the new desired state. This mixture is characterized by differences, similarities, and related tensions and complexities.

Consider also the complexity of unanticipated demographic and behavior diversity with respect to the Managing Workforce Relationships strategy. If we ask the question "Complex compared to what?" the answer becomes, "Compared to the lack of diversity with respect to demographics and behavior." The inherent related mixture becomes that of a homogeneous workforce with respect to demographics and behavior *and* a workforce characterized by heterogeneity.

Here is the critical premise: *Because we can discuss complexities in terms of their inherent diversity mixtures, they can be addressed with the same diversity management tools used when dealing with the diversity mixtures that generated them.* This takes us back to the SDMP double-edged sword, which can be used to foster quality decision making in the midst of diversity and complexity.

In sum, diversity generates complexities, which in turn can be recast as inherent diversity mixtures. This allows diversity management tools to be used to tackle complexities that threaten to compromise the ability to address diversity mixtures.

The conclusion that diversity management tools can be used to break through complexities that compromise implementation of the four core diversity management strategies may seem straightforward. But it doesn't take into account that we typically try to avoid such complexity. The first step in applying this potential tool to complexity mixtures is to become more comfortable with complexity. Only then will we be ready to grapple with it.

Focus

Managing complexity focuses on effective utilization of universal diversity management tools to address complexities blocking the implementation of the four core diversity management strategies. This capability, therefore, becomes one that can empower the strategies within which it is implicit.

Motive

The overarching motive is to break through the complexities that can hamper implementation of the four core diversity management strategies. Organizations and individuals dislike complexity. Individuals often respond to my advocacy of Quadrant 4 with dismay. "Why would I want to take on *all* mixtures, when my hands are full with workforce issues?" they ask. "This is *too* theoretical for me. Give me the 'to-do's.'" "It cannot be *this* difficult." And, for me, the inexplicable "I don't have time for this; you're overcomplicating the issues. I need to get back to my real work."

Such comments reflect a fundamental misconception of many senior executives—namely, that "diversity management" constitutes something other than their "real work" and should be avoided or minimized as much as possible.

World-Class Diversity Management says that diversity of any kind and diversity management in the midst of any kinds of differences and similarities, and related tensions and complexities, are explicitly and implicitly part and parcel of the total sum of executives' and managers' work. This is true of complexity management, as well. This is the critical reality that justifies the pursuit of world-class status.

A second and supplementary motive is to be able to cope with increasing complexity. Over the past two decades, the complexities of diversity work have expanded substantially. We have moved from the Golden Rule context to one characterized by four basic strategies. Yet as our evolution and understanding have moved forward, our practice has not kept pace. If movement can be made with managing complexity, implementing the four core diversity management strategies should be facilitated.

Finally, the overarching motive is to secure competitive (viability) advantage. As "diversity gridlocks" become more visible in our society and its organizations, the importance of enhancing our collective diversity management capability—whether in pursuit of a competitive edge for organizations or vibrancy for our communities—becomes increasingly clear and urgent.

Principal Tool

As with managing diversity, the primary tool for managing complexity is the SDMP. The first step is to identify complexities inherent in the diversity mixture of interest by asking, "Complex compared to what?" Once you have determined the related mixtures, you can use the SDMP decision-making tool to address them.

If, for example, you are seeking to use Quadrant 3 (Managing Diverse Talent) with a group of employees, and the complexity of cultural change presents an inhibiting stumbling block, you can determine—as discussed above—that a related diversity mixture is one of the status quo *and* the new desired state. You can use the SDMP decision-making tool to diagnose the mixture and assess your action options. Once you have selected options and made progress with this complexity, you will have one less obstacle obstructing your ability to address the diversity mixture you were initially interested in.

The economies of effort and scale can be significant. The more you use SDMP, the more facility you achieve with it—which, in turn, leads to greater efficiency and effectiveness. Further, the more you use the tool, the shorter the time required to become adept with it.

Challenges

At least four challenges hinder the progress of managing complexity:

1. **Short attention span of organizations.** Managers prefer to deal with issues that can be resolved quickly and straightforwardly. In many instances, complexity will involve multiyear, multifaceted, complex action plans. A simple list of to-do's will not suffice.

2. **Lack of urgency to address complexity.** Because many see diversity as a workforce issue only and one driven by social justice–civil rights–human rights prescriptions, they do not view it as a business (viability) imperative and assign it and related complexities a relatively low priority.

3. **Lack of comfort with complexity.** Few people relish tackling complexity and its accompanying tension unless absolutely necessary.

4. **The denial or minimization of diversity-related complexity.** We prefer to pretend that diversity is not complex and still difficult for us. This is especially true with respect to race and gender diversity.

These factors individually and collectively work to interfere with addressing complexity and, in turn, the effective management of diversity. Although the benefits of greater diversity management are significant, inertia is a real threat. Without attention to complexity, progress will not come easily.

Facilitating Factors

No compelling facilitating factors currently exist, but there are some potential ones. One would be to *recognize that racial diversity remains a complex challenge for the United States.*[4] To acknowledge openly the complexity of this citizenry mixture would challenge the prevailing tendency to deny or minimize our country's continuing difficulties with racial diversity, and place complexity in play as a factor requiring attention if we are to progress further in this arena.

Another contributing factor would be *greater awareness and understanding of the nature and dynamics of diversity and diversity management.* The adoption of Quadrants 3 and 4 would foster movement toward a capability of managing complexity. In particular, this broader awareness would make visible the wide array of challenging diversity issues in which we are immersed.

Part of the challenge here is that very little *public* conceptual and theoretical structure exists with respect to diversity. There are theories and concepts; they simply are not that visible. As a consequence, *diversity* is simply a word that has picked up a lot of baggage and can be discarded with little regret. Obviously, this discourages learning more about diversity and diversity management. Nonetheless, enhanced awareness and clarification are needed if the third potential facilitator is to come into play.

The third potential facilitator is *the reality of diversity gridlocks*— situations that occur when two or more diverse forces converge at a junction, create intense heat, and then recede, leaving the unsatisfactory status quo essentially intact. The net result is poor decision making and problem solving in the midst of differences, similarities, and related tensions and complexities.

Examples of such gridlocks abound. In organizations, we have the case of acquisitions and mergers that readily and easily consummate, only to frequently dissolve a few years later after major disruptions and costs to people individually and collectively. In the public arena, talk shows as public service or entertainment routinely foster diversity gridlocks around any number of personal, economic, social, or political issues. In the political arena, vicious and uncivil debate over issues such as health care, immigration, and the conduct of war result in diversity gridlock.

Once identified as diversity issues, these gridlocks and others would highlight the cost we are paying for poor diversity management capability. At present, they are acknowledged and regretted, but not as diversity matters. Assembling such incidents under the umbrella of diversity gridlocks would promote and encourage readiness to deal with the complexities of diversity. This won't happen, however, until we understand diversity better.

I am cautiously optimistic that an understanding of the Four Quadrants will help by generating a broader perspective around diversity. If it does, it will have succeeded against the odds. Much is at stake.

GLOBAL PERSPECTIVE

The managing complexity enabler is global. It can be used to facilitate diversity management with *any* type of diversity mixture, in *any* setting, and in *any* geographic location.

DISCUSSION

Organizational leaders wishing to progress with managing complexity must first shed their propensity to avoid or ignore it. They must demystify the notion of complexities so that they and others are more willing to address them. At present, to describe something as complex or complicated is to imply that it should be left alone. Nothing could be further than the truth.

In reality, organizational leaders must become comfortable with recognizing, naming, and addressing the complexity that accompanies a given diversity mixture as a prerequisite for managing that mixture. Managing complexity is not a panacea for complexity. However, it can highlight options, stimulate problem-solving creativity, and minimize the likelihood of feeling overwhelmed. Just as important, it can eliminate the phenomenon of the elephant in the room—the unspoken but ever present perception of a problem too threatening to name or address but too dangerous to ignore.

In one presentation, I noted acquisitions and mergers as examples of diversity mixtures. An executive came up afterward and said, "You tried to get us to talk about acquisitions, didn't you?" It turned out that the client company had just made an acquisition—something I had not known—and had retained only one of the acquiree's senior executives, the individual who approached me after my presentation. Reportedly, the client company had wanted the departing executives to remain, and its leaders were disappointed when they left. This had happened with other acquisitions, as well. At the time of my speech, they had relegated the issue to the "complex" pile as something too difficult to discuss. As a result, the inability to keep senior executives of acquired entities became the elephant in the board room that no one wanted to discuss.

In another setting, integration proved elusive among functional silos at a time when collaboration could generate some significant economic and strategic benefits. A variety of mechanisms had been used to achieve integration, but none had succeeded. When senior managers were asked about it, they would shake their heads and mumble something about personality clashes that were too complex to be resolved. The organization accepted the undesired status quo and avoided talking about it. The issue became the increasingly expensive elephant that no one would acknowledge.

In several enterprises, I have seen issues with implicit racial undertones that no one wanted to address. Perhaps they involved recruiting, hiring, or promoting minorities. While multiple causes may have been in play, a reasonable hypothesis would have included the possibility of relationship challenges being driven by racial ill will. Because these were too "complex," however, or were unable to identify with absolute certainty, all other possibilities were examined. Even when the alternative possibilities failed to account for the challenges, the issues of race and racism remained unaddressed. These elephants were too complex to discuss.

My hope is that this chapter will encourage readers to acknowledge complexities, help readers to become more familiar with their characteristics, and motivate readers to work toward greater capability in addressing complexities as diversity mixtures. To the extent that this happens, they will enhance their knowledge of how to manage diversity.

Some Take-Aways

1. To address diversity with optimal effectiveness, CEOs must acknowledge and address related complexities.
2. A complexity is that which makes something difficult to understand, solve, or explain.
3. Diversity and complexity go hand in hand. Where you have one, you have the other.

4. Diversity incurs costs. (Diversity of any kind can complicate—bring complexities to—decision making and require "extra effort.")

5. Managing complexity effectively sets the stage for managing diversity successfully.

6. The "extra effort" required for managing diversity and complexity should not be seen as extra, but rather as part and parcel of the managerial role. In reality, diversity management and managing complexity are inherently part of managerial work. The more proficient executives become with this "extra effort," the more it becomes recognized and accepted as a legitimate managerial task, not something to be ignored.

7

THE DYNAMICS OF STRATEGIES AND PARADIGMS

CEOs seeking effectiveness with all four of the core diversity management strategies (quadrants) must master the dynamics of strategies and paradigms. Otherwise, their ability to move between the strategies as required by World-Class Diversity Management will be hampered. World class will require that an organization's prevailing paradigms and intended strategies are in sync.

This chapter examines some of the dynamics of using the four diversity management strategies and their undergirding paradigms in pursuit of World-Class Diversity Management. It particularly explores how the core strategies and paradigms provide a path to World-Class Diversity Management capability.

As noted earlier, I see this capability as the ability to employ best practices from *anywhere* to address any diversity mixture, in any setting (workforce, workplace, marketplace, community, family, for example), and in any geographic location. This status is dynamic, not static. As practices inherent in the strategies that contribute to the universal approach continue to evolve, so will those associated with World-Class Diversity Management.

STRATEGY DYNAMICS

Point of Departure

An excellent way to become familiar with the Four Quadrants construct is to use it to take stock and to organize. For example, an organization's senior managers might request a list of the company's diversity
interventions and categorize them by the diversity management strategy they serve. They would find it instructive to note where they have
and have not been active and to ponder the implications of their strategy utilization patterns.

Some executives have found that just listing their diversity management practices is beneficial. One vice president of human resources
said, "We have so many diversity activities that I sometimes forget
what we are doing, and why we are doing it."

Paths to World-Class Status

As noted earlier, the diversity field's evolution—and that of most
organizations and individuals—will likely transition through the three
workforce-specific strategies, then transition through the three derivative universal ones, and finally collapse into the universal strategy,
Managing All Strategic Mixtures (Quadrant 4). This is not the only
path to world-class status, but since most enterprises have launched
their diversity efforts with the workforce-specific strategies, it is likely
to be the most practical.

Organizations just launching diversity thrusts and aspiring to
world-class status can begin with either the three derivative universal
strategies or the Quadrant 4 alternative, Managing All Strategic Mixtures. *Enterprises that choose either of these paths will need to take deliber-*

ate care that appropriate supporting paradigms are in place. You cannot assume that they are.

Movement Among Strategies

Since all of the core diversity management strategies are legitimate, organizations can move among them as needed and desired and can operate in more than one simultaneously. *But they can do this only if they have the paradigm flexibility to make that movement possible.* Let's look at the path most United States organizations would likely take in pursuit of world-class status.

Beginning with Managing Workforce Representation and then moving subsequently to Managing Workforce Relationships would require a paradigm structure encompassing both Make Amends for Past Wrongs *and* Apply the Golden Rule. Without such a structure, making and sustaining the move would be difficult.

Similarly, transitioning to Managing Diverse Talent would necessitate a paradigm structure that included Make Amends for Past Wrongs, Apply the Golden Rule, *and* Maximize Individual Engagement. To get to the three strategies derived from these workforce-specific approaches, organizations would have to generalize their workforce-specific paradigms into mindsets appropriate for *any* setting—not just the workforce.

Once this tweaking was completed, they would be ready to expand the paradigm structure to include Make Amends for Past Wrongs, Apply the Golden Rule, Maximize Individual Engagement, *and* Maximize Stakeholder Engagement. This would set the stage for developing the three transitional strategies and for adopting the universal strategy, Managing All Strategic Mixtures.

Critical Strategic Questions

Because of the dynamics between strategies and paradigms, leaders must *continuously* ask two sets of questions and be *continuously* aware of their responses. These questions must be asked in the context of their organization's overall mission, vision, strategy, and competitive challenges, and also its corresponding diversity aspirations

Set 1: Strategy Questions

- What diversity management strategies has my organization used in the past?
- With what strategies is it currently involved?
- With what strategies does it need to be active?
- What is it losing by being inactive with these identified strategies?
- What would it gain by becoming active with these strategies?

Set 2: Paradigm Questions

- What is the organization's paradigm structure?
- Is this structure aligned with the diversity management strategies being used by the organization?
- If not, how big is the alignment gap?
- How might the organization close the alignment gap?

These questions highlight the reality that achieving world-class status is a dynamic process of strategic and paradigmatic adjustments—all intended to ensure that an organization's diversity management efforts are "world best" in pursuit of viability objectives. As such, organizations pursuing world-class status likely will have to make multiple strategic and paradigmatic modifications. Their success in achieving this status will be determined in large part by their ongoing ability to modify their paradigm structure as needed.

The Nature of Predispositions

Paradigms are so important because they constrain our thinking and predispose us to related behavior patterns. Recently, I experienced this aspect of paradigms.

My earlier reported experience in the men's room of the new Jacksonville, Florida, airport is instructive of this phenomenon (see the introduction). On reflection, the paradigm shock—and resulting frustration and anger—that I experienced were out of proportion to the magnitude of the change.

Similarly, as was noted earlier, undergirding paradigms powerfully predispose individuals individually and collectively toward a given diversity management strategy—namely, the following:

- Make Amends for Past Wrongs predisposes us toward Managing Workforce Representation.
- Apply the Golden Rule predisposes us toward Managing Workforce Demographic Relationships.
- Maximize Individual Engagement predisposes us toward Managing Diverse Talent.
- Maximize Stakeholder Engagement predisposes us toward Managing All Strategic Mixtures.

Predispositions vary in the degree that they are embedded within individuals or organizations. Some are deeply entrenched and intertwined with an individual's belief and value systems. Others are simply intellectual constructs that have been adopted without significant connections to belief and values. Where predispositions are deeply entrenched, individuals and organizations experience great difficulty going against them. This does not mean they will not, however, or that they cannot be persuaded to do so.

I clearly would have preferred a traditional arrangement of the sinks in the airport men's room. But I had no choice, so I reluctantly acted against the predisposition of my existing paradigm. Of further note, however, is that because the Jacksonville airport is the only place where I have seen the new arrangement, and because I rarely go through that airport, my original paradigm remains intact. Sustained paradigm adjustment requires frequent reinforcement.

Although my experience with culture shock at the Jacksonville airport suggests that movement among the core diversity management strategies can be challenging, that is not always so. Moving from a strategy that one feels deeply about and is accustomed to can provoke confusion, frustration, and anger. Where predispositions are not deeply entrenched, however, fostering such shifts can be significantly easier. Nonetheless, understanding paradigm structures and designing change strategies with them in mind is critical to navigating among the diversity management strategies.

IDENTIFYING PARADIGMS

Paradigm Structures

One way to identify paradigms is to use an inventory developed by Dr. Elizabeth Holmes.[1] This inventory, titled *Personal Diversity Paradigm: A Tool for Exploring Your Orientation to Diversity*, is designed to identify both individual and organizational paradigm structures. Through a series of questions, the tool develops a frequency profile that indicates the number of organizational participants for whom each of the four paradigms is dominant. Knowing this allows individuals or organizations to determine their *paradigm structure*. For organizations, the tool can serve as the heart of a paradigm audit.

Why not simply say "paradigm profile" instead of "paradigm structure"? Profile implies more fluidity than typically exists with respect to allegiances to a given paradigm. "Structure" more closely portrays the rigidity I have seen with respect to diversity management paradigms.

Because most organizations are still preoccupied with Managing Workforce Representation and Managing Workforce Relationships, I had expected the inventory to reveal that most organizational paradigm structures would reflect dominant allegiance to Make Amends for Past Wrongs and Apply the Golden Rule. Yet researchers have found a surprising skew toward Maximize Individual Engagement and Maximize Stakeholder Engagement. Further, while Apply the Golden Rule has tended to attract the greatest allegiance, results indicate relatively little allegiance to Make Amends for Past Wrongs.

In one setting, for example, we found a distribution of dominant paradigms as follows:

- Paradigm 1 (Make Amends for Past Wrongs)—5%
- Paradigm 2 (Apply the Golden Rule)—32%
- Paradigm 3 (Maximize Individual Engagement)—39%
- Paradigm 4 (Maximize Stakeholder Engagement)—24%

These results are presented in figure 7-1.

What respondents reported in completing the instrument does not mesh with what I see as I move through corporations. It is as if respondents' practices have not caught up with their paradigm shifts.

This is a distinct possibility. Thinking and frameworks are much more developed around Quadrants 1 and 2 than around Quadrants 3 and 4. As a result, there may be an operational gap between the emerging paradigms and the diversity management strategies actually being used.

I do not want to overstate what I am seeing. Most surprising has been the low scoring for Make Amends for Past Wrongs. Although Maximize Individual Engagement and Maximize Stakeholder Engagement have attracted more allegiance than anticipated, Apply the

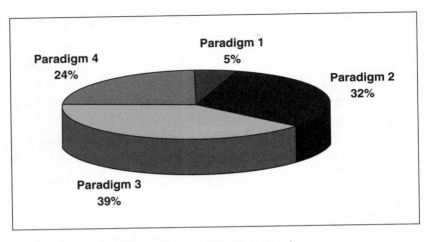

Paradigm 1
5%

Paradigm 2
32%

Paradigm 4
24%

Paradigm 3
39%

FIGURE 7-1. Illustrative Distribution of Paradigm Results

Golden Rule has still ranked as the dominant paradigm across the audits that I have seen to date.[2]

Paradigm Continuums and Grid

The four paradigms can be collapsed into two continuums (see figures 7-2 and 7-3). The first carries the label "Social Justice/Civil Rights" and reflects the paradigms Make Amends for Past Wrongs and Apply the Golden Rule, while the second carries the label "Productivity" and reflects the paradigms Maximize Individual Engagement and Maximize Stakeholder Engagement. Figure 7-2 presents the social justice–civil rights approaches that can support it. Figure 7-3 does the same for productivity.

On either continuum, intensity of focus can range from low to high. To facilitate simultaneous consideration of both, you can combine the content of the two figures to form a grid that conveys the intensity of focus for both continuums (figure 7-4).

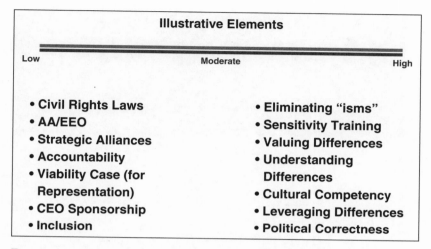

FIGURE 7-2. Focus on Social Justice–Civil Rights Diversity Paradigms

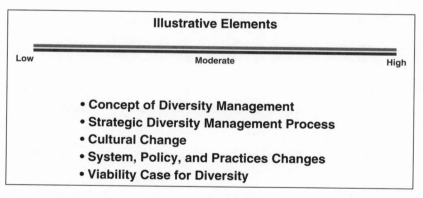

FIGURE 7-3. Focus on Productivity Diversity Paradigms

In the future, researchers might seek to empirically determine the dynamics of organizations in the four grid areas. I anticipate that they will find the following:

Area 1 (High Social Justice and Low Productivity). This is where many—if not most—enterprises are. They have strong commitments to social justice and civil rights and give little or no

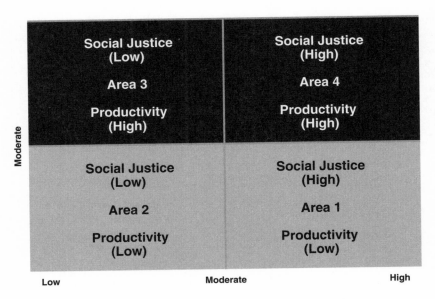

	Social Justice (Low) Area 3 Productivity (High)	Social Justice (High) Area 4 Productivity (High)
Moderate	Social Justice (Low) Area 2 Productivity (Low)	Social Justice (High) Area 1 Productivity (Low)
	Low	**Moderate** **High**

FIGURE 7-4. Diversity Paradigm Grid

thought to diversity management and productivity. Many organizations that continue to win awards for diversity work are in this area.

Area 2 (Low Social Justice and Low Productivity). Organizations here range from those with little or no focus on either continuum to those with a lukewarm focus. These might include enterprises just launching diversity management initiatives or those experiencing a shift of focus after a period of high intensity. They may also be enterprises in the compliance mode with respect to legal requirements and political correctness.

Area 3 (Low Social Justice and High Productivity). Included in this area would be organizations that formerly focused on social justice–civil rights efforts but currently are focusing on ensuring maximum engagement of their diverse workforce. These are organizations that are discovering the Managing Diverse Talent leg of the three-legged stool with respect to workforce diversity.

Area 4 (High Social Justice and High Productivity). These would be organizations that historically have maintained high focus on social justice and civil rights and are currently complementing that interest with an equally high intensity on productivity. Those operating in this area would reflect a comfort level with all four paradigms. This is where World-Class Diversity Management aspirants must be if they are to utilize all four core diversity management strategies effectively.

Managers should not worry about being in the "right" area, but rather should be concerned about whether their current area supports what they wish to achieve with diversity and diversity management. If not, the question becomes how to move the organization to a more supportive area. This does not reflect absolutes like "high" is better than "low." Rather, it reflects the compatibility of the chosen area with the strategic direction in which the organization wishes to go with diversity and diversity management—and ultimately with World-Class Diversity Management. An organization's overall diversity management aspiration is a key contextual factor.

IMPLICATIONS FOR MANAGING PARADIGM STRUCTURES

Because CEOs desiring to achieve world-class status must have the capability to use *all* of the core diversity management strategies, they must foster the development of a supportive paradigm structure. One ultimate possibility—not immediately doable for most organizations— would be to shift everyone's dominant allegiance to the Maximizing

Stakeholder Engagement option. That would ensure paradigm support for the universal strategy required for utilization of SDMP and pursuit of World-Class Diversity Management.

Organizational leaders wishing to change their enterprise's paradigm structure would need to begin with the following steps:

Step 1. Conduct a paradigm audit.

Step 2. Determine where their paradigm structure is incongruent with their diversity management aspirations.

Step 3. Determine what type of paradigm structure would best support their diversity management aspirations.

Step 4. Develop a plan for closing the gap between the organization's current paradigm structure and its preferred one. A critical part of this plan would be education regarding what the paradigm alternatives are and why a given choice is preferred. Sometimes individuals are unaware of alternative paradigms and their potential benefits. I've been told, "I didn't even know there *was* more than one diversity paradigm."

Education can help bring about a paradigm shift, but to do so, it must be persistent and continuous over a period of time. At a minimum, such education must work toward acceptance of a paradigm structure that reflects *organizational* flexibility and comfort with all of the paradigms. Success here would be minimizing the dominance of paradigms 1, 2, and 3 and enhancing the dominance of paradigm 4, since it inherently fosters flexibility.

An alternative option to modifying the paradigm structure would be to position any diversity management strategy change in terms of its benefits to subscribers of the paradigms related to the other strategies. For example, a CEO championing a major Managing Workforce Relationships push might explain to advocates of the Make Amends for Past Wrongs paradigm that quality relationships would facilitate the Make Amends process. Similarly, the CEO might point out to subscribers of Managing Diverse Talent that social integration ultimately supports talent integration.

These two strategies—education and effective marketing—are not mutually exclusive. They can be used simultaneously. However, since World-Class Diversity Management ultimately requires a comfort level with all four paradigms and core strategies, at some point the "What's in it for everyone" approach might reach its limits.

GLOBAL PERSPECTIVE

The dynamics noted here are found directionally outside the United States, as well. However, the nomenclature is different. For that reason, I recommend that instead of Make Amends for Past Wrongs, the social justice–civil rights paradigms might be labeled "Social Justice–Human Rights." This terminology would be general enough to include both the U.S.-specific Make Amends *and* other countries' paradigms that reflect a commitment to social justice and human rights.

Once terminology issues have been settled, the directional dynamics—though not the details—described in this chapter should be valid globally.

DISCUSSION

I believe that the diversity paradigms and their dynamics with the four core strategies will be key to the future development of the field. They cannot be ignored.

Collapsing the four paradigms into two categories highlights how much they differ. My experience of paradigm shock over an insignificant change in the Jackson airport men's room has helped me to see clearly and empathetically how subscribers to the social justice–civil rights paradigms would experience significant trauma when introduced to the productivity paradigms.

The analogy of my airport experience with the paradigm shock associated around the civil rights–social justice paradigms (to which many are deeply committed) and productivity paradigms is not intended to dismiss the magnitude of the change from one to the other. It is meant only to point out that paradigms constrain us around what is mundane as well as what is obviously critical. In both cases, paradigm shock can be a reality.

I believe that I underestimated the role of paradigm shock in my earliest diversity work. When I began talking about diversity and managing diversity in the late 1980s and early 1990s, I had in mind a capability that could be borrowed or developed from practices in other areas—especially that of Complex Organizations theory—where scholars and managers had been grappling with achieving organizational objectives in the midst of differences and similarities.

I particularly was influenced by the work of Paul R. Lawrence and Jay W. Lorsch, as they explored the concepts of differentiation and integration with respect to functions.[3] Their key question was "How do you ensure sufficient differentiation in the organization of functions to reflect their different tasks, while simultaneously achieving the integration necessary for synergy?" Along this same line, Lorsch and Stephen A. Allen wrote a book entitled *Managing Diversity and Interdependence*, exploring the same question with respect to lines of business.[4]

I thought that individuals and organizations concerned about racial, ethnic, and gender mainstreaming in the workplace could borrow from these explorations and, indeed, similar prescriptions from others in the field for achieving purposeful cohesiveness in the midst of differences and similarities. Doing that might allow them to fashion a perspective that could be useful in the same way with respect to the workforce. I believed that such a perspective might *complement and support* traditional civil rights–social justice efforts.

Things did not quite turn out that way. In the 1980s and 1990s, advocates for desegregation and integration with respect to race, gender, and ethnicity strategically adopted the packaging of managing diversity for their traditional efforts but ignored its substance. So *diversity* became synonymous with having representation of minorities and women and something to be embraced and valued. This represented a marked departure from *diversity management* relating to differences and similarities of *any* kind—so much so that to mention the possibilities of other types of diversity brought cries against "broadening" the definitions, as if diversity originated with civil rights efforts in the 1960s.

In the context of my paradigm change, I see the adoption of diversity terminology (packages) as a reaction to being in paradigm shock. The appropriation acted to minimize the perceived gap between the civil rights–social justice paradigm and the one I was perceived to be offering.[5]

Finally, a clear thread throughout my discussion of diversity paradigms has been the possibility of having to change paradigms. Clearly, this can happen only if organizations and individuals are willing to check their paradigms, especially when encountering diversity gridlock, paradigm shock, or frustration in achieving their diversity aspirations. Without this willingness, individuals and organizations can become prisoners of their paradigms. Paradigm management is a key factor in effective strategic diversity management.

SOME TAKE-AWAYS

1. CEOs wishing to be effective with diversity management in pursuit of world-class status must learn to manage the dynamics of core strategies and their related paradigms.

2. CEOs continuously must ensure that their personal and organizational diversity paradigm structures support their diversity management aspirations.

3. Because paradigms predispose individuals to certain behaviors, plans for going against those predispositions will require positioning the desired change as beneficial to subscribers to all paradigm(s), or modifying the paradigm structure so that the paradigm congruent with the desired behavior becomes dominant or, at a minimum, a level of comfort with that paradigm evolves.

4. Paradigm audits can be critical for understanding an organization's paradigm structure and providing a context for changing or positioning a paradigm structure.

5. Paradigm management will be one of the critical keys for advancing the practice of diversity management.

Part III

APPLICATION

T he two-part case included in this section reflects a composite of actual individuals, organizations, and situations that
I have interacted with over the past twenty-five years. Overlaid on that
composite portrayal are the World-Class Diversity Management framework, the Four Quadrants Model, and the Strategic Diversity Management Process. The result is a disguised accounting and extrapolation of
the efforts of one CEO (Jeff Kilt) to achieve world-class status. While
the characters and situations are composites, any resemblance to actual
persons or organizations is purely coincidental and unintentional.

As readers prepare to read the case, they will likely ask, "Has any
organization ever achieved world-class status? If not, how much of the
process has any organization completed?"

To my knowledge, no organization has achieved world-class status.
Further, I believe that this book is the first published representation of

world-class diversity work and the requirements for achieving that status.

Another question about composites in general might be "How realistic is the material?" I feel that the depiction of Jeff Kilt is very representative of real-time diversity dynamics. I base this claim on four considerations:

1. My colleagues and I have more than twelve years' experience with two critical components of the World-Class Diversity Management approach: the Four Quadrants and the Strategic Diversity Management Process.
2. Participants in the American Institute for Managing Diversity's Diversity Leadership Academy have applied SDMP to more than a hundred situations, ranging from traditional race, gender, and ethnicity issues to nontraditional issues.
3. I have facilitated at least ten workshop discussions of part I of the Jeff Kilt case, in which participants debated about what Jeff has done, should do, and will do.
4. While my colleagues and I have just started working within the context of World-Class Diversity Management and have used it with only a handful of clients, those limited interactions have provided fodder for our compositing efforts. Early reactions to this framework have been well received.

In sum, the composite is based on a rich collection of experiences and data. Because of this abundance of source material, I am confident that Jeff Kilt represents a realistic portrait.

I have seen at least 90 percent of the characters, organizations, and circumstances in the case in real life; however, that does not mean that any organization has completed 90 percent of the journey to world class. Specifically, I have not seen any organization move forward under the banner of "world class." This should not be surprising, given that World-Class Diversity Management is just emerging.

The first part of the case, "Jeff Kilt: In Pursuit of World Class," presents a picture of a CEO coping with the traditional issue of race in the workforce. The second component of the two-part case, "Reflections of Jeff Kilt," looks at what the composite Jeff Kilt might do if he decided to pursue world class. Of the two, this part contains the most extrapolation beyond actual experiences, specifically with respect to World-Class Diversity Management. But even here, because World-Class Diversity Management so heavily leans on the Four Quadrants and SDMP, we have ample data from which to draw.

Why present this composite accounting and extrapolation? I wanted to convey that while much is required to reach world-class status, it is doable. I also wished to present these requirements in the most realistic fashion. As part of the realism, I wanted to capture dialogue between key players, as well.

While this case does not reflect any actual circumstance, it does portray a collective reality and an extrapolation of how that actuality might play out in pursuit of World-Class Diversity Management capability.

8 JEFF KILT

Coping with a Nagging Challenge

Inevitably, CEOs experience a crisis that tests them. To respond effectively, they have to draw upon their personal strengths, their sense of what is right, and also the wisdom and practices of others. This chapter presents a picture of Jeff Kilt, CEO of Bjax Corporation, as he struggles to control a crisis that could harm his company's image and, indeed, threaten its viability. It begins with descriptions of the company and Kilt and their efforts to look at the nagging challenge and examine how it has been handled.

BJAX: THE COMPANY

Bjax Corporation offers a wide variety of consumer products that are manufactured and sold around the world. While the bulk of its customers are in the United States, in recent years it has grown rapidly through acquisitions and now manufactures, sells, and distributes products worldwide. Since its 1915 founding in Philadelphia, the company has enjoyed a reputation for high quality and competitively priced goods. In several niches, Bjax's products offer the greatest value per dollar spent.

Looking toward the future, Bjax expects to continue its world expansion and, in particular, to accelerate the strategic, global placement of manufacturing operations in pursuit of the lowest costs possible. Key to this strategy will be the ability to manage human and other resources in a cohesive, comprehensive, and effective manner. Competitors have long admired Bjax's ability over the past two decades to manage and grow its operations worldwide cost-effectively. For Bjax the benefits have been an increase in overall sales and profits.

A contributing factor to Bjax's global success has been a pioneering and ongoing interest in world-class management practices. This interest dates back to when Total Quality's popularity propelled a focus on manufacturing practices worldwide. Bjax executives adopted many innovations growing out of those efforts; indeed, several of the company's leaders now attribute the corporation's success with globalism to its commitment to be world class in manufacturing. The visibility of those efforts motivated other Bjax functions to pursue world-class status—all of which worked to improve managerial practices at Bjax.

JEFF KILT: THE LEADER

The current CEO, Jeff Kilt, grew up in manufacturing during the time Bjax first became interested in world-class status. During his twenty-five years with the company, he has served in a number of capacities—the last six years as CEO. His track record illustrates the up-through-the-ranks, promote-from-within approach Bjax has adopted for the development of managers and executives. During his time as CEO, the corporation has experienced enormous sales and profit growth.

Jeff enjoys a sterling reputation within and outside of the company. Internally, Bjax associates see him as professional and technically competent, as well as skilled at motivating and relating to people. Known as an idea person who is well read, he frequently is referred to as a "practical thinker" who gets things done. He also has earned recognition as a fair person, someone committed to equal opportunity for everyone, and a manager with a "good heart."

Reflecting this "good heart," during Kilt's tenure as CEO, Bjax has enhanced its Affirmative Action (AA) efforts to the point that the company is the envy of its peers. Wherever AA issues have arisen, Jeff has insisted on thorough investigations and timely resolutions. The prevailing sentiment among Bjax executives is that their house is in order with respect to AA, and that Jeff "gets it."

Externally, community leaders see him as strongly committed to community service on the part of individuals and corporations. He participates on a number of community organizations' boards and has facilitated the involvement of Bjax executives in some creative community initiatives. Further, with respect to the minority communities, he enjoys an image as someone who genuinely cares and puts his money where his mouth is, both personally and for his company.

THE NAGGING CHALLENGE

About five years ago, a group of minority employees calling themselves the Alternative Management Development Committee (AMDC) confronted Jeff about the lack of people of color in the company's managerial ranks. Very few could be found in the upper and middle levels of the hierarchy. Even in the entry-level managerial ranks, where the presence of people of color was significant, it was not proportionate to their representation among the corporate rank-and-file employees. The AMDC argued that this was unacceptable for a company located in the Philadelphia area.

Jeff agreed that the complaints had some validity and indicated that he had been concerned about Bjax's success in attracting and retaining minority employees. True to his reputation as one who acts, he moved quickly to develop a comprehensive action plan. After benchmarking other corporations with reputations for outstanding equal opportunity efforts, he took several actions.

Plan of Action

First, he established an Office of Diversity. The benchmarking study suggested that this was a "best practice." While firmly committed to AA, Jeff sensed that "diversity" was different—perhaps more proactive and less compliance driven than AA. In any event, he felt that setting up the office would be a strong sign of his serious intent.

Second, to enhance this signal, and to give the new office as much clout as possible, Jeff made the position of vice president of diversity a direct report to him. He also decided to keep "diversity" and AA separate by leaving the latter in Human Resources (HR). In his mind, this differentiation would facilitate the development of diversity at Bjax—although even he was not clear about the direction this evolution would take.

Third, Jeff recruited an African American man named Mark Bronson, the second-ranking manager in the Benefits Department of the Human Resources Division, to fill the position of vice president of diversity. Mark, who had joined the company the same year as Jeff, had performed well and moved up the HR ladder at a steady, though not rapid, pace. Jeff and Mark had worked on several community projects together, and, indeed, Mark had represented Jeff at various external events.

Jeff liked Mark for the post of vice president of diversity for several reasons. He saw Mark as having a strong passion for racial justice but also an ability to express and pursue that passion without unnecessarily offending white males. His managerial colleagues saw him as a straight shooter who "called it like he saw it." Mark enjoyed wide respect throughout the Bjax internal community.

Externally, the various communities held him in similar high regard—in part, no doubt, because he was often the one to show up with the Bjax check. He had warm professional and personal relations with many critical community leaders. Even more so than Jeff, Mark attracted the label "Mr. Bjax." In any event, Jeff considered Mark to be the person for the position.

Mark, however, did not readily agree. He saw the position as a promotion that offered an opportunity to serve and to make a significant contribution to Bjax and its external constituencies, but he worried about the risk of offending senior individuals and damaging his career options. He had two relatively young children from his second marriage and wanted to work at Bjax through their undergraduate years. The last thing he desired was to leave Bjax and start anew at another organization. He also did not want to stagnate and remain in the new position solely because he had nowhere to go because of burned professional bridges. He particularly wanted to keep his HR options open.

Jeff appreciated Mark's concerns, and they in no way diminished his enthusiasm for his choice. As an enticement, he informally committed to make certain that Mark remained whole. With that commitment and his confidence in Jeff's integrity, Mark accepted the position as Bjax's first vice president of diversity.

Fourth, once Mark was on board, he and Jeff established a Diversity Council. Diverse with respect to race, gender, ethnicity, hierarchical level, function, and geographic location, the council has earned high marks for its performance. Its role has primarily been one of coordinating activities and programs, not one of problem solving. It has also served as a communications vehicle for issues that rank-and-file associates want addressed. A lingering frustration for Mark and Jeff has been an inability to get the council to accept leadership responsibility for problem solving, instead of passing the buck. They had envisioned that the council would be more proactive and accountable for the evolution of diversity at Bjax. Employees currently see diversity as Mark and Jeff's responsibility, with the council serving in an advisory capacity.

Fifth, in cooperation with HR, Mark used his connections to establish corporate-wide programs for minorities. He did this through targeted recruitment efforts, mentoring programs, and high-potential identification mechanisms. While HR managed these programs, Mark's office provided counsel and support—so much so that many thought the programs were operated by the vice president of diversity.

Sixth, Mark and Jeff upgraded relationships with and support for minority groups in the community. They sought to invest Bjax resources strategically where the greatest amount of goodwill would be generated. Within three years, Bjax had reinforced its already significant role in the Philadelphia area. Word quickly circulated that Bjax was serious about diversity.

Seventh, internally and in conjunction with related external groups, Mark and Jeff initiated "cultural celebration days." These were elaborate events drawing from internal and external resources. In addition to these internal activities, Bjax sponsored and supported similar efforts in the broader community.

The results of these initiatives have been impressive. Generally, people of color within the company have credited Bjax for good-faith efforts to bring about change and, in a recent survey, indicated "good feelings" about working at Bjax. Community organizations now hold Bjax in even higher esteem than before these initiatives. On a recent diversity best practices list, Bjax ranked in the top ten.

Outcomes

To Jeff's surprise, the AMDC did not share in the good feelings about Bjax's diversity thrusts. In a recent meeting with Jeff, AMDC members noted that, while the presence of people of color in the entry-level managerial ranks had been enhanced, little or no change had occurred in the higher ranks. Stated differently, even during a period of special initiatives and tremendous growth, people of color were not getting their share of promotions. They cited this as proof of racism and the systematic oppression of people of color. Even more disturbing, the AMDC threatened to move forward in pursuit of class-action remedies.

Jeff vehemently denied that he or any senior Bjax official was racist. He repeatedly offered these denials publicly and privately. The AMCD contended that the denials themselves were proof of racism.

Jeff convened an ad hoc committee of himself, the vice president for diversity, the corporation's general counsel, and the head of the Diversity Council, all white males except Mark. Their task was to craft a response to the AMDC challenge. As a first step, they asked the Diversity Council chair—a senior, well-respected executive—to look at recent deliberations of the Management Development Committee (MDC). This was a group of eleven senior executives (nine Caucasian males, one Caucasian female, and one Hispanic male) who met once a year to identify entry-level managers who were ready for development or promotions to the middle and upper ranks.

Bjax executives made recommendations to the MDC, which reviewed applicants and made decisions as to who qualified for high-potential designation. What was especially galling to the AMDC was that the MDC was supposedly making a special effort to foster upward mobility for minorities. Though Jeff knew the eleven individuals to be free of racism, he wanted the Diversity Council chair to review the MDC's deliberations, just as a precaution, in case there were any shortcomings.

After the review, the council chair reported that, although few people of color had earned approval, the MDC had based its reasons for denial on solid grounds. He saw no evidence of prejudice or illegal discrimination.

Jeff's Basic Options

With the review from the Diversity Council chair in hand, Jeff asked Mark for a report that detailed their most viable options. Mark responded by contacting several of his peers and attending three best practices workshops. He then counseled Jeff that Bjax had three basic options:

1. Prepare to defend against class-action efforts. In essence, Bjax would stand on its commendable, nationally recognized record over the past five years. The general counsel noted that while Bjax's efforts were impressive, its numbers would make a defense against a class-action suit problematic.

2. Initiate a cohesive set of interventions to minimize or eliminate Bjax's "oppression of people of color." While the vice president for diversity did not believe the corporation was guilty of oppression, an anti-oppression campaign might prevent a class-action suit.

Indeed, some had suggested racism and sexism awareness training before, but Jeff had repeatedly rejected it because he did not see himself, or his executives and managerial colleagues, as racists or sexists. Bjax's general counsel has informed Jeff on numerous occasions that, legally speaking, "impact" not "intent" determines whether "institutional racism" exists. Jeff's response has been that he refuses to be governed by legal definitions that do not fit reality. In his view, "It makes no sense to call people racists or sexists when they don't have a racist or sexist bone in their body. I refuse to do it!"

3. Initiate diversity management. While Mark admitted to being unclear about this option, he was intrigued by some recent articles on "World-Class Diversity Management" and a "Four Quadrants" universal approach. He felt that perhaps those notions would mesh well with Bjax's other world-class aspirations.

Jeff requested that Mark pass the identified three options by the AMDC. When approached, members of the AMDC unanimously declared, "They're all the same. We're not interested in any semantic games or meaningless 'special efforts' for people of color. We want the issue of racism to be hit hard!"

Jeff turned to his special committee and asked that they consider the following questions:

1. Given Bjax's recent, award-winning, nationally recognized equal opportunity efforts, do we still have problems with people of color? If so, does this mean that we should discontinue these special interventions?
2. Are the three options being considered really different, or, are they truly all the same?
3. If they are significantly different, what would be the initial steps for each?

4. If they are significantly different, what would be the likely ultimate outcome for each?

5. What should we (Bjax) do?

As the special committee deliberated, twelve disgruntled African Americans who had been passed over by the MDC volunteered to spearhead the movement toward a class-action suit. Also, Mark's contacts warned him that unrest was building in the community, and that Jeff should expect a visit from a delegation of African Americans concerned about Bjax's best practices.

JEFF'S RETURN TO THE CLASSROOM

While these events were evolving, one of Jeff's former MBA professors, Andrew Jones, approached him about writing a case on Bjax's success with diversity issues. Jeff had always sought to be supportive of his alma mater, so he readily agreed. However, as matters deteriorated further, he wished he had not. The professor wrote a case that encompassed much of what is in this chapter and invited Jeff to be present for the discussion. His visit proved to be memorable.

After the professor announced their visitor, his class engaged in a lively discussion. To Jeff's surprise, a large contingent of the class felt that Bjax had engaged in window dressing and had changed very little. Jeff could not understand how anyone could say that nothing had changed.

Another segment believed that Bjax had demonstrated good faith and had made great progress. This group counseled that Jeff and Bjax should stand firm on their accomplishments. Jeff observed that this group contained the largest number of African Americans. A third component of the class argued that Bjax had not addressed the real issue of racism. They adamantly contended that Bjax's semantic gymnastics had not addressed the need to eliminate racism and pursue social justice.

At the end of the class, Jeff engaged in a dialogue with the students. When he expressed consternation over the assertion that Bjax really had done little, proponents of that view started talking about the need to look at organizational culture. They said that real change called for examining an organization's culture and diversity paradigms, and for making modifications as needed. These class members specifically condemned as window dressing the establishment of an office of diversity, the appointment of a "safe" African American to run it, the creation of a less than effective Diversity Council, support of community groups, and elaborate cultural celebrations. In their view, these window dressings changed little.

These accusations stunned Jeff. He could accept the different interpretations of Bjax's progress, but the contention of window dressing really bothered him.

MORE TURMOIL

When he arrived back at his office, a message awaited him saying that some African American community leaders were seeking a meeting with him. Jeff then called Mark, described the class visit, and notified him of the upcoming meeting with the community leaders. He asked Mark to be present for the meeting.

DISCUSSION

Jeff is where many executives have found themselves at one time or another over the past forty years. He is seeking to move from Quadrants 1 and 2 to Quadrant 3, and like many similarly situated leaders, he has no inkling of the quadrants or of a universal approach.

Further, Jeff's primary paradigms are Making Amends for Past Wrongs and Apply the Golden Rule. He appears to be on the verge of becoming aware of Maximize Individual Engagement, but his motivation for enhancing the engagement of African Americans seems more related to issues of fairness and doing the "right thing" than to productivity. He has a way to go before fully recognizing and adopting the Maximize Individual Engagement paradigm.

Jeff finds himself in a diversity gridlock. He, his fellow white executives, white employees, African American employees, and African American community leaders have converged repeatedly on the issue of representation for African Americans at senior levels, generated significant heat, and then disengaged with the undesirable status quo intact. Neither party is clear about how to move beyond this diversity gridlock.

Paradigm shocks are emerging. Jeff is struggling to go beyond "fairness" associated with Apply the Golden Rule, while African American employees are grappling with how to move beyond "racism" associated with Make Amends for Past Wrongs. Trauma from these shocks can be seen in Jeff's frustration and confusion, and also in the growing anger of African Americans as they demand that perceived racism be addressed. Of course, these shocks and traumas only intensify the gridlock.

Also reflected here is a trap around racism that many CEOs, CDOs, and other senior executives experience. Jeff and his senior Bjax colleagues appear to be moving toward a preoccupation with proving they are not racists, as opposed to managing diversity in pursuit of organizational objectives. Unfortunately, they will never be able to *prove* they are not racists. This is a rabbit they cannot catch.

Similarly, proving that Jeff and his executive team *are* racist is a rabbit that Bjax African American associates cannot catch. In all likelihood, the situation will degenerate into dysfunctional shouting matches of countering claims: "You're racist!" "No, I'm not!" These dynamics will intensify the gridlock.

Finally, Jeff feels some frustration over the fact that one external school of thought—and probably some internal critics—argue that he and his colleagues have accomplished little. This is not an uncommon reaction of executives facing what appears to be a spiraling and insatiable set of expectations. Yet, in truth, it is not so much that the expectations cannot be satisfied, but rather that Jeff and his senior colleagues lack the strategies or paradigms that would allow them to meet the associates' requests. This too will intensify the gridlock.

In sum, Jeff and Bjax are galloping toward possibly even more challenging times. Their situations are not atypical in the diversity arena. Having a "good heart," enjoying external praise, and implementing a variety of diversity activities are often not enough to avoid immobilizing gridlocks.

Some Take-Aways

1. A CEO's "good heart" may not be enough.
2. Impact, not intent, can be critical in legal deliberations.
3. CEOs must not assume that their values are shared by managerial colleagues.
4. CEOs should keep in mind that benchmarked best practices may not generate the desired results.
5. External praise may not be sufficient.
6. Without clarity about what constitutes "success," CEOs can find it difficult to get credit for their accomplishments in the diversity arena.
7. CEOs must avoid becoming preoccupied with proving their corporation is not racist, as opposed to focusing on the building of a diversity management capability.

9 REFLECTIONS OF JEFF KILT

In Search of World Class

Six years after his business school classroom visit, Jeff and his professor friend Andrew Jones reflected on the changes Jeff and Bjax went through as he worked to revive both the enterprise's and his own reputation following the diversity fiasco. These reflections were part of a presentation to a CEO roundtable on diversity convened by Andrew. What follows is a summary of Jeff's reflections, which Andrew presented in the alumni magazine. Andrew also intended to use the article in his class.

Roughly six years before, Jeff had received a group of African American community leaders, who sided with African American Bjax associates in their concerns about inadequate upward mobility for people of color at Bjax, and also the failure of Bjax to address "raw" racism. About a month later, these individuals and a small group of African American employees set up and walked a picket line in front of Bjax headquarters.

Reactions came swiftly. Internally, the Bjax community by and large felt betrayed and considered the picketing action unwarranted. Most whites felt that Jeff had been very responsive to concerns of African

Americans, and that he would have worked through the current issues if he had been given a chance. The African Americans who did not join the protest line also thought such an action was premature. Those who did march cited as their motivation Jeff's "semantics mumble jumble about diversity and whatever" as opposed to practical hard-hitting attacks on "runaway racism" at Bjax.

Jeff took these developments personally and agonized over them. He felt that neither he nor the company deserved this kind of treatment. While some within Bjax did support him, his Board of Directors pressed hard for him to get the marchers off the streets. With the growing economic uncertainty, members believed that this kind of stain was the last thing Bjax needed. Some even expressed personal embarrassment—which Jeff saw as an implicit indication that they believed the protesters had a valid argument. The protests set off a chain of events that led Bjax to once again become a corporate diversity leader.

Jeff and Andrew talked first of Jeff's response to the picketing. Jeff had met daily with the protesters for about a week. They had refused to back off their "non-negotiable" demand that Bjax address alleged racism. Jeff had been clear that he did not feel racism was an issue, but he was under a lot of pressure from the board to bring the matter to a close, and the protesters refused to come in without an agreement. So he offered to initiate racism training for all levels of management, but not the total population. He reasoned that this could be completed quickly on a limited basis and then put behind them.

After some wrangling, the protestors agreed to the "management only" training. Jeff then solicited a proposal for a "bias-reduction" training program and presented it to the protesters. They overwhelmingly rejected it, stating that they wanted something that directly and unequivocally targeted racism. Jeff next proposed a consulting firm that specialized in a confrontational approach to racism. The marchers wholeheartedly endorsed the firm's proposal, and Jeff reluctantly went along.

Once they reached this settlement, everyone reverted to their previous positions as members of a mutual admiration society. All apparently was forgiven.

But Jeff was still struggling. He kept thinking, "We are not racists! Yet we are being forced to go through a program based on the declaration that we are." He had gone along, but he was not happy about it.

The trainers turned out to be excellent and professional—though hard hitting. Even Jeff credited the training with having significant consequences. One, participants had learned something about what is racially inappropriate and come away with greater sensitivity. Two, the African American community leaders were happy with Bijax again. Three, several managers went out of their way to ensure that African Americans were considered for the upper-middle levels of management as openings surfaced. Four, white males became bolder in expressing backlash sentiments. Essentially, their message was "Surely we've done enough for blacks now!"

In spite of these mostly positive consequences, Jeff was dissatisfied. He remained convinced that he and the other Bjax managers were not racists, and that if they were, it was only a portion of the picture. It just didn't explain some of the challenges the organization had had. He kept thinking, "It's not the whole story."

In addition to implementing training activities, Jeff placed the Management Development Committee's operations on hold in an effort to appease the AMDC. To his surprise, AMDC members wrote him frequently asking that the MDC start up again, and things went more or less well for a while. Jeff began to relax.

While attending an alumni meeting, Jeff bumped into Andrew, who invited Jeff to his current class for their discussion of the Bjax case. Andrew knew nothing of the training classes but had been so pleased with Jeff's first visit that he had hoped for a repeat performance. Jeff accepted Andrew's invitation with some trepidation, as the first visit had been both provocative and stressful for him.

His return visit went much as the first. The dynamics were essentially the same, with camps similar to those of the previous group of students. When Jeff updated the case by reporting on the recently conducted bias-reduction training, one group gave him high marks, as before. However, the window dressing sentiments also surfaced and, once again, stumped him. He had been certain that the racism training would count for more than window dressing. To have two different groups of students—in significant numbers—accuse the organization of window dressing was quite disturbing.

In his closing dialogue with the class, Jeff challenged those contending that only window dressings had been put in place. They responded with the same arguments Jeff had heard from the previous class—that he and his managers had not examined the organization's culture. Jeff became frustrated and angry, and it showed. One white male student—who was as angry as Jeff—told him, "You just don't get it!"

After class, as Jeff turned to leave, the student rushed up to him and apologized for his rudeness. Jeff acknowledged that his own behavior had not been exemplary and told him no apology was needed. As a peace token, the student offered Jeff a copy of a book being used as a reference for the class, suggesting that it might give him a different perspective. Jeff resisted accepting it, but the student insisted. With mixed feelings, Jeff reluctantly agreed to take the book.

Andrew, who had overheard the exchange, explained that the book was one of several being studied by the class and that the zealous student was a new, enthusiastic convert. He also offered to admonish the student to become more skilled in dealing with thought diversity, as he considered his interactions with Jeff to be rude. Again, Jeff protested that that was not necessary, as he too needed to improve his ability to deal with thought diversity. The next day, he took the book to his office and put it on one of his bookshelves, where it stayed for about six weeks.

The next thing that happened was that Jeff learned that four high-potential African American engineers from different divisions had left Bjax unexpectedly. Exit interviews revealed that their departures were unrelated and that they had left to accept exceptional offers. They reportedly did not leave out of dissatisfaction with Bjax. Nevertheless, their departures left the organization in shock. Each of their division heads had penciled them in for promotions and much greater responsibilities and opportunities. Their departure told Jeff that perhaps they had not licked this issue yet.

The Pursuit of World-Class Status

Jeff again approached Andrew for help—this time for consulting expertise. Andrew asked Jeff if he had read the book the student had given him. When Jeff said no, he suggested that he start there as a way to expand his thinking on diversity. Jeff read the book, along with an article secured for him by a staff member. The results were twofold: The claims of both about the importance of organizational culture rang true for him, *and* he developed a sense of the differences between Affirmative Action and managing diversity. He was ready to consider the need for a full-blown cultural audit.

When Andrew and Jeff met again, Andrew saw that Jeff was connecting with this new perspective and invited him to a panel presentation by three or four academicians, all of whom had expertise in diversity management. At the presentation, one talked about World-Class Diversity Management and compared it to World-Class Manufacturing. This professor also mentioned the Four Quadrants as a vehicle that could be used in pursuit of world-class status.

Jeff was intrigued by the notion of being world class in diversity, given Bjax's experience with the pursuit of World-Class Manufacturing practices. He knew that the company's manufacturing capability really had improved as it introduced World-Class Manufacturing practices. But he had no idea how that would work with diversity.

Given Jeff's interest, Andrew recommended that Jeff ask his diversity people, the Diversity Council, and senior executives to use the

Four Quadrants Model to categorize Bjax's diversity work. He also suggested that Jeff engage the panelist who had talked about the Four
Quadrants to assist in the analysis. His thinking was "This will be a
good way to initially test the practicality and relevancy of the World-
Class Diversity Management concept."

Although Jeff was intrigued, he was not won over. "Interesting," he
thought. "Good theory, questionable practicality." Nonetheless, the old
remedies weren't working all that well, and he trusted Andrew's judgment. He did as Andrew had suggested and brought in the panelist.

Overwhelmingly, Bjax's activities were in the first two quadrants,
around representation and relationships. He thought about Bjax's
situation—especially the "window dressing" comments from both of
Andrew's classes—and wondered what the company might be missing
by not utilizing Quadrants 3 and 4. Still, he did nothing for a couple
of months.

About that time the MDC rebooted its efforts, and so did the
AMDC. Once again, AMDC members came to Jeff with complaints
about the lack of color at the higher levels of the hierarchy. Jeff thought,
"What else can I do?"

When he told Andrew about the AMDC's renewed complaints,
Andrew suggested that Bjax retain the panelist who had helped with
the Four Quadrants analysis and also a professor with expertise and
reputation in World-Class Diversity Management. Andrew felt that this
tandem would be ideal as Jeff moved toward world class in diversity.

Jeff still questioned the practicality of World-Class Diversity Management but felt that engaging the professors might give him some
cover with the AMDC. He was right. When he told the head of the
AMDC about his plans to invite the two professors in, she seemed
impressed and asked to be kept in the loop.

Jeff and Andrew spent a day with the professors, and Jeff came away
with mixed reactions. On the one hand, he felt that the world-class
concept was more practical than he had realized at first glance. He was

impressed that the manufacturing professor felt that a parallel world-class movement in diversity was not unrealistic and that a wide variety of tools was emerging that potentially could help in such an effort.

Also, going world class with diversity potentially would help the company not just with the workforce, but also with diversity in areas such as acquisitions and mergers, functional integration, and global expansion. Jeff knew Bjax had diversity challenges beyond the workforce.

Yet he was also very concerned. Implementation would be a huge and complex multiyear challenge. Just getting internal and external buy-in and support would be difficult and time consuming. And they already had committed so many resources to diversity. Could they afford to embark on this challenging journey? It wasn't just about money, but also about time, energy, and focus.

Andrew agreed with Jeff about the magnitude and complexity of the effort that would be required and reminded him that Bjax would be pioneering—that this "world class" thing was a new concept. He also told him that the potential benefits could be huge, as well. He had consulted with Bjax the previous year on the implementation of an acquisition, and, without a doubt, the diversity perspective would have been helpful.

After going back and forth for about two months, Jeff decided that the benefits would be worth the effort. Interestingly, he was more confident about benefits associated with non-workforce diversity than with workforce issues. He continued to be puzzled about the AMDC.

Jeff was clear that he wanted Andrew to be his lead consultant, for two reasons: Andrew and he had had a relationship for several years, and others in the company trusted him. In addition, Andrew was Philadelphia based, and Jeff wanted to avoid negativity about a non-Philadelphia consultant. Andrew was delighted. Not only was the opportunity exciting, but Jeff had agreed to help develop another teaching case based on their joint work.

Initial Preparation: Securing Internal Support

Together, the two men began the internal buy-in process. First on the agenda was to talk with Mark Bronson, Bjax's vice president of diversity. They decided to include him at their next meeting. Mark, who had been kept informed about Jeff and Andrew's thinking, was not surprised. But he wasn't supportive, either. On the contrary, he doubted whether "this world class notion" truly was different from traditional civil rights–social justice efforts. And if it were different, he didn't want any part of it—least of all as a leader. He felt he could not endorse focusing on non-workforce areas when there were still significant workforce challenges. He offered his resignation as VP of diversity.

Jeff refused to accept it. He knew that Mark had not bought in to the world class perspective, but he had played a critical role with the company's diversity work. As its first vice president, he had gotten things off to a good start. He was particularly competent in the areas of community affairs and relationships with and across the demographic groups within Bjax. Everyone trusted him. To lose Mark would create a major obstacle.

Mark countered by observing that he would lack credibility in areas such as acquisitions and mergers and global expansion. His background was benefits management. Andrew agreed that going world class would require credibility beyond workforce issues. As the three men talked, Jeff was mentally doing a rapid scan of HR leaders to see who might have this broader credibility. He could not identify a viable candidate. When he said as much, Andrew asked why the person needed an HR background.

Mark was incredulous. He could not see how you could have a VP of diversity who did not have an HR background, even if he was dealing significantly with non-workforce issues.

Jeff complicated the conversation further by stating that he could not think of an African American male or female who would have the needed credibility. Andrew wanted to know whether the VP could be a white male. Mark countered by questioning what the selection of a white male would signal to the AMDC. Jeff agreed with Mark's point. And Andrew acknowledged that he wasn't excited about having a white male as VP, either.

Mark remained adamant about resigning his position, though he did not necessarily wish to return to HR. Jeff asked if he could help get internal buy-in before leaving the VP role. Mark wanted to know how he could he could sell something he did not believe in.

Andrew observed that it appeared they were going through one of the "paradigm shifts" that one of the professors had mentioned—moving from diversity as race, gender, and ethnicity to diversity as differences and similarities and related tensions and complexities. As their thinking had shifted, so had their views about the position of VP of diversity.

The other two men were not impressed. Jeff thought Andrew was making sense but worried that this paradigm shifting was taking them into uncharted waters. Mark did not buy in to either the emerging paradigm shift or the change in thinking about the VP of diversity position.

After considerable discussion and some heat, Jeff asked Mark to serve as senior vice president of community affairs, reporting to his office. The position built on Mark's strength in relating to community groups but also entailed managing the corporation's foundation. The foundation responsibility represented a growth opportunity for Mark, while the community affairs responsibility kept him close to the company's diversity work.

Mark remained neutral, at best, about the new world class direction. But he trusted Jeff's good intentions and was determined not to hamper his efforts. In addition, the new responsibility offered a promotion and new challenges. He also felt that Jeff had treated him with respect by, in essence, rewarding him for his work as the first VP of diversity and understanding his reservations. He accepted the position.

Resolving this issue was only part of the initial internal buy-in process. They still had to achieve accommodation with the MDC and AMDC. Jeff and Andrew designed a strategy calling for Mark to meet with both groups in Jeff's absence. They hoped that this would facilitate candor. Mark had several meetings with the combined groups. They established an agenda for developing feedback to Jeff on his evolving world class aspirations. Once the group understood that their purpose was not to find fault, but to assist Jeff in his thinking about what Bjax should do, things went fairly well.

Members of the MDC found the world class notion to be exciting. They remembered how beneficial world class efforts had been in other areas, and how positive ripple effects had traveled throughout the company. They agreed to champion the effort in any way they could.

The AMDC did not readily become excited about the world class concept, and members continued to express frustration with the relative lack of progress in increasing the presence of people of color at the higher levels. However, they did somewhat ease off the allegations of racism. They assumed a posture of "Why not? We've tried everything else."

What progress was made was in large part due to Mark's efforts. He was very straightforward with the AMDC members about his reservations, and equally so about his convictions regarding Jeff's good intent. Jeff saw Mark's efforts as representing an endorsement.

Collectively, the MDC agreed to be supportive. Individually, they were all over the place. Several were very interested in the possibility of becoming world class in diversity. Others went along out of frustration and a lack of better ideas. All had heard of the two professors and had read some of their writings.

Once Jeff had touched some of the most critical internal bases, he turned to his board. At Bjax, the board's Social Responsibility Committee had oversight for diversity. This committee presented a challenge for Jeff. Its members did not take readily to the "broader definition of diversity." Only when he assured them that he was not abandoning traditional issues did they grant him their tentative endorsement. He was helped by the fact that one member was CEO of a company struggling to get traction with diversity. This individual expressed appreciation for Jeff's leadership and the potential benefits for Bjax internally and externally. He asked to be kept closely informed, so that he might share the experience of Bjax with his company.

Securing External Support: Mr. Ollie Floyd

Having attained major internal, preliminary buy-in, the three men turned to securing external support. They all agreed that minimizing external concern that would work against diversity management and the pursuit of world-class status was essential.

There were three civil rights organizations in Philadelphia—one local and two national. Most influential was the local one, headed by a man named Ollie Floyd. Mark counseled that Floyd's support would be critical to achieving their buy-in goal. He described the powerful man whom they must convince:

"Mr. Ollie Floyd, an attorney, is approximately eighty years old and an esteemed civil rights veteran," he said. "In all the significant Philadelphia civil rights struggles, he has played a major behind-the-scenes role. He is a critical power broker here in the city.

"Mr. Ollie Floyd exudes integrity. His word is his bond. He's respected by all—black, white, whatever, and he's careful about what he supports. Very formal, he refers to everyone as Mr., Mrs., or Ms., and he expects to be called Mr. Ollie Floyd—*not* Mr. Floyd, Mr. Ollie, Ollie, or Floyd, but *Mr. Ollie Floyd*.

"Very, very bright, a voracious reader, his mind often runs ahead of your thoughts. He does not tolerate small talk or foolishness easily, and he's sensitive to perceived slights, but not overly so. Also extremely careful to avoid offending anyone unnecessarily. When necessary, however, he can be very aggressive and—indeed—vicious. He does not smile easily but has a sense of humor and laughs more easily than he smiles. In sum, Mr. Ollie Floyd is an interesting legend."

The three talked long about how to approach Mr. Ollie Floyd. Though Jeff and Andrew knew *of* him, only Mark had been with him personally. As they sought a meeting, they debated who should attend. Jeff felt Mark should be present, since he had dealt with him before. Mark thought that, given the magnitude of their proposed project, Mr. Ollie Floyd might feel slighted if Jeff were not involved. Both felt that Andrew should be in attendance, since he was the Philadelphia-based lead consultant.

Mark's connections came in handy, and he secured an appointment for two weeks away. All—including Mark himself—were impressed as he worked his connections.

At the appointed time, the three arrived at Mr. Ollie Floyd's office, where his assistant of thirty years greeted them. Then Mr. Ollie Floyd appeared and welcomed them cordially.

Mark made the introductions, but he had a feeling that Mr. Ollie Floyd had done his homework on everyone. Then they proceeded without any small talk. Jeff briefly described Bjax's experiences with diversity and the world class approach they now were considering. Mr. Ollie Floyd said nothing.

Jeff continued talking and then asked Andrew to say more about his work and the notion of world class. Andrew spoke for about thirty-five minutes on different aspects of the process. When he paused, Mr. Ollie Floyd said quietly and deliberately, "Mr. Jones, why should I be interested in diversity? For me, the focus has always been about justice." And then he and Andrew looked at each other for about thirty seconds without speaking. Finally, Andrew talked about how diversity management complemented social justice efforts and made them more sustainable.

The room became completely silent. Then Mr. Ollie Floyd stood and said, "Let's meet again." He cordially ushered them out of his office. They had no idea how things had gone.

The three men returned once a week for four more weeks in a row, and each time they went through a version of the first meeting. At the end of the fifth meeting, to everyone's surprise, Mr. Ollie Floyd turned to Jeff and asked, "How can I be of help?" Jeff was so surprised that he was speechless. Fortunately, Mark spoke up.

He noted that some civil rights and community leaders saw a conflict between civil rights and diversity management and did not recognize the complementary benefits. He asked Mr. Ollie Floyd if he could help them make the case for that complementary relationship. He agreed to do so. "Just ask them to give me a call," he said, "and keep me posted on your progress."

The three subsequently made several one-on-one presentations to individual civil rights and community leaders, ending each with a reference to Mr. Ollie Floyd and his invitation for them to call. The leaders were impressed that Mr. Ollie Floyd had agreed to personally endorse World-Class Diversity Management. His endorsement meant a lot.

Planning

Having secured internal and external support, it was possible to move forward in pursuit of World-Class Diversity Management. The challenge was determining how to do it.

Jeff particularly wanted to make sure that what the professors had talked about was doable. He asked Andrew to work with Daniel Miller, the new VP of diversity, and the professors to sketch out a multiyear plan. He did not want anything in stone, but he did want to see signs of feasibility.

In spite of early reservations, Jeff had hired a white male as the new VP of diversity. Daniel Miller had been chair of the Diversity Council in Bjax's largest division and one of the company's most effective line managers. When he heard of the company's world class aspirations, he jumped on board. He approached Jeff, who had noticed earlier what a quick study he was on the specifics of the professors' perspectives. The two hit it off really well. Jeff asked Mark to check him out with African Americans in the AMDC and on the diversity council. Surprisingly, these individuals unhesitantly endorsed him. There was no flack about his being white.

Jeff, Andrew, and Daniel invited the professors back. They asked the two experts to walk them through the implementation of World-Class Diversity Management. The professors detailed the change stages as "Talking the Talk," "Thinking the Talk," and "Walking the Talk."

Daniel focused on what the three stages meant in time requirements. The professors replied that they varied for each organization. When Daniel pressed for more specific information, the manufacturing professor said, "We recommend that you take a year at a time, and after each year evaluate progress and assess what appears appropriate for the next year."

The group began to map out what each phase would target and identified the following initial efforts:

1. For Jeff and his direct reports and for each divisional head and their direct reports
   - executive briefing (1/2 day)
   - strategic planning session (2 days)
   - introduction to SDMP

2. For managers
   - town hall executive briefing (2 hours)
   - introduction to SDMP (2 days)

3. For individual contributors
   - town hall meetings (2 hours)
   - introduction to SDMP (1 day)

4. For the organization
   - cultural audit
   - paradigm audit

- research on diversity (defined broadly) at Bjax
- establishment of diversity management infrastructure

The Bjax executives continued to be unnerved by the uncertainty about how long all of this would take. Pressed, the professors told them, "Given your size and geographic dispersion, and your desire for managers to experience the material before individual contributors, we see three years as a reasonable projection for your first phase."

Pressed further about the possibility that individuals who attended educational programs early would "sit out" the next few years, the professors responded, "That's not what is intended. The hope is that as a result of their education experience, managers will have concepts that could be used as tools for diagnosing and understanding, even in the absence of skills." This, in fact, did become a key challenge—encouraging the use of such concepts.

OUTCOMES

The three-year plan work worked well—although it turned out to take five years. After a year, the three men realized that completing the training did not necessarily mean that participants had an understanding of World-Class Diversity Management, the Four Quadrants Model, or the Strategic Diversity Management Process. They learned this after employing a self-coaching tool that provided feedback on the user's understanding of World-Class Diversity Management and the SDMP. It quickly revealed considerable room for improvement. They had to decide whether to go forward with skill building and application training, even though conceptual understanding was weak. Jeff and Daniel argued that without a good conceptual foundation, sustainability would be difficult.

As a remedy, they started the Bjax Diversity Institute (BDI), which offered minicourses on various aspects of World-Class Diversity Management. Further, they required all managers to demonstrate through several assessment instruments that they had a solid conceptual grasp of the material. They also encouraged managers to take a similar tactic with their individual contributors.

The BDI was also used to encourage utilization of the concepts by providing facilitated application sessions. Some sessions focused on major business issues such as acquisition implementation, functional integration, or strategic partnerships. Others looked at special interest areas such as parenting and the SDMP, religion and the SDMP, and politics and the SDMP.

Because setting up the institute and requiring remediation and application took considerable time, Jeff and his cohorts fostered credibility and maintained momentum by circulating written reports of successful utilization.

At the end of the five years, they had gained much ground—and had considerably more to go. Most important, they now had a world class infrastructure. At the top was the *Champions Council*, consisting of Jeff, division heads, and heads of staff departments. They set the tone and affirmed Bjax's World-Class Diversity Management aspirations. Also, based on their learnings from the results of the cultural and paradigm audits, this group endorsed the development and implementation of strategies for modifying Bjax's culture and diversity paradigms.

Results from the cultural audit indicated that a major operational assumption was that everyone should be treated as if they were members of the Bjax family. The challenge uncovered was that minorities and women did not feel part of the "family." The Champions Council commissioned a task force to identify and propose an alternative assumption. The task force is charged with answering two questions: "If we are not family, what are we?" and "Is the recommended alternative to family more inclusive with respect to minorities and women?"

Reporting to the Champions Council was an *Accountability Board* that heard, reviewed, and evaluated each division's annual plans and progress. The board's rotating membership was composed of four division heads and Andrew. This group had teeth. If a division's plan was not approved, or if its progress report was deemed inadequate, compensation and assignment consequences could be serious.

At the *implementation level* were the division heads and their directors of diversity. They were responsible for implementation. Each head was responsible for presenting plans to the Accountability Board and also for reporting on progress. Competition was keen here. No one wanted to be seen as lacking.

Finally, there were the facilitators: Andrew and his staff. Included here also were the director of the institute and the director of diversity management planning. Their task was to keep the process moving.

This structure meant that Bjax now had the solid beginnings of a commitment that was not dependent on Jeff—a major accomplishment. The company also had good, positive footings—indeed, partnerships—with community groups. Community leaders did not fully understand what the company was doing, but they liked the excitement and intent. They no longer were looking over Bjax's shoulders.

Bjax fostered its partnership with community groups by sponsoring World-Class Diversity Management and SDMP training for community and political leaders. As Bjax associates were learning how to create a world-class organization in diversity, its community leaders also were exploring how to become world class in diversity. These two developmental processes proved to be mutually reinforcing.

Considerable conceptual clarity was emerging, along with modified diversity paradigm structures. People talked across paradigms and respected all diversity mindsets. Also, in meetings you could hear talk about "diversity gridlocks," "diversity challenges," "paradigm shocks," "diversity tensions," "paradigm shifts," "requirements vs. preferences vs. traditions," and "diversity maturity."

The company had seen some significant business benefits, as well. Integration managers for a recent acquisition had not only applied diversity management concepts, but also had requested skill training ahead of schedule so that they might be better prepared to assist on a continual basis. This generated such significant strides that teams were established to address lingering integration problems of earlier acquisitions.

Finally, a troubled relationship with a critical supplier was resolved by a team consisting of players from both sides, who had mastered and applied diversity management concepts. The savings here exceeded $50 million.

Next Steps

No one is ready to call this a success story. The prevailing sentiment is that Bjax has a long way to go. However, Jeff and his executive colleagues believe that they have built a great foundation, and they are convinced that their organic approach, calling for planning and evaluating as they went along, was the right approach. They credit the professors for steering them well in that regard. They continue to provide Mr. Ollie Floyd with quarterly updates, and he continues to sing their praises. The trust level is high. Finally, there has been minimal—if any—white backlash. White males are engaged in a wide variety of SDMP applications that benefit them and Bjax. They are clear that diversity includes them.

Bjax still has inadequate representation of people of color at senior levels, but its managers are seeking out systemic and cultural factors that might be in play. AMDC members are involved in the process and have not charged the company with racism in over two years.

As a part of this systemic approach, the MDC and AMDC are collaborating on research to determine whether "requirements" or "traditions, personal preferences, and conveniences"—all of which may not be requirements—have been the basis for management development. All parties believe that clarity regarding this question will be a firm basis for performance management system changes in pursuit of talent integration at all levels.

Plans are to continue with the organization's culture and paradigm changes. Skill building and application are also on the agenda, as is giving attention to institutionalizing the progress already realized. But Jeff is determined to proceed one year at a time—always with the goal of universal capability in mind.

Jeff and his senior colleagues have experienced how difficult the challenges of gaining conceptual clarity, changing paradigms, and modifying culture can be, and they are convinced that an infrastructure must be put in place early. In addition, they recommend that CEOs seeking to pursue World-Class Diversity Management spend the necessary time to win internal and external buy-in as a foundation for their efforts.

DISCUSSION

Jeff Kilt's experiences offer a view of how World-Class Diversity Management implementation decisions might be approached. Below, I explore some of the critical considerations.

The Commitment Decision

Jeff Kilt spent a lot of "soaking time" with the world class possibilities. He proceeded very deliberately, refusing to rush to judgment. When the AMDC pressed with allegations of racism, he clung to his belief that those claims were false. Also, he did not rush to embrace the "new" notion of diversity that Mark was hearing about, or even the emerging thinking about World-Class Diversity Management capabilities the professor was speaking about. In addition, the criticisms of the MBA classes did not precipitate a rush to judgment.

As he approached a commitment decision, he took care to learn as much about implementation as possible. He also did not rush the buy-in process. He did his homework and paid his dues in pursuit of internal and external support. Even after commitment, he moved carefully and patiently

This deliberateness and care were appropriate. After all, he was pioneering. He was advancing down a path that was not well trodden. His behavior provides a useful decision-making model for those considering a similar commitment for their enterprise.

The Role of Concepts

In the diversity arena, because of our passion for our work, we sometimes overlook the importance and utility of concepts. We want *tools* that generate "action." Hence, the perpetual quest for "the silver bullet" or "the five to-do's." Concepts, however, can be powerful tools for securing understanding and diagnosing—both of which can shed light on what might constitute appropriate and effective actions. Jeff shared this sentiment. Indeed, I suspect that his decision to slow the process in pursuit of greater conceptual clarity was a key one. Understanding and sound diagnosing can generate a lot of commitment that in the long run can pay great dividends.

Low-Hanging Fruit

The racism training represented low-hanging fruit for Jeff because it could be implemented relatively easily and had the potential for a quick return on his effort. He implemented the training, recognized its strengths, enjoyed the results, and, yet, avoided seeing it as a silver bullet. He kept the training in perspective and maintained a realistic view about the issues still in play. He did not permit the low-hanging fruit to become a distraction.

The Role of Outsiders

Outsiders like the students, the professors, Mr. Ollie Floyd, and other community leaders can each in their own way play a facilitating role in the pursuit of world-class status. The trick for CEOs is to be receptive to interacting with outsiders and processing the input of outsiders without compromising their own integrity.

Jeff handled this task well. While being open to input, he did not rush to judgment about what was wrong or right. CEOs sometimes appear too eager to please everyone, or to hold everyone at bay. Jeff welcomed and considered input, but more as fodder to be weighed in determining the right thing to do, not as something that was dictated. He accepted the responsibility for determining what was appropriate to do.

Selection of a CDO

Many CEOs stress over this selection, even as Jeff did. They feel constrained to at least look first for a minority or woman associated with Human Resources. Jeff did, too, but he appeared to be requirements driven; specifically, he sought someone who bought in to the paradigm shifting around the definition of diversity, and who would have credibility in the nontraditional diversity areas. This eventually led him to Daniel Miller, a white male without an HR affiliation.

Those criteria differed from the criteria for the selection of Bjax's first CDO. Then, Jeff sought someone who had credibility with community groups and African American associates and could advocate for African Americans without offending white males. Mark Bronson provided a good fit in that case.

In both instances, requirements drove Jeff's action and produced two good, effective choices. CEOs pursuing world-class status will have to be prepared to be requirements driven when selecting a CDO and to go against past selection practices when appropriate.

Securing External Support

Increasingly, CEOs and CDOs are beginning to think of the community and its leaders as partners in their diversity efforts. They invite the public to company diversity events or find vehicles for partnerships around specific diversity activities. Jeff knew well that he had an external constituency and sought a relationship with that constituency. This was true beyond Mr. Ollie Floyd, but it definitely was reflected in his relationship with that icon. His efforts resulted in a relationship of mutual respect and mutual benefit.

Planning

Within a structured framework of Talking the Talk, Thinking the Talk, and Walking the Talk, Jeff planned carefully in an attempt to determine what he was signing up for. He wanted to know what was involved and how long it would take. Yet, once into implementation, he was cautious about getting into a "check it off" mode. When he discovered that conceptual understanding remained low, he delayed moving to skill building and application training in favor of activities that likely would foster greater conceptual clarity. He was appropriately sensitive to whether his organization was truly ready to move forward.

Another sign of his flexibility was that he did not become imprisoned by the planning process. While the organization was not prepared for Walking the Talk, he encouraged application as a means of becoming more familiar with SDMP. He used rudimentary Walking the Talk to foster Talking the Talk.

This is analogous to a golfing newcomer, playing a round of golf with little preparation. With careful monitoring and coaching, playing golf prematurely can create an enhanced sense and appreciation of the game and awareness by the newcomer of what he does not know. In addition, if the newcomer sees benefit in the game, he becomes motivated to learn.

This dynamic appeared to be in play at Bjax. Before they were technically ready to Walk the Talk, managers and associates were engaged in experimental and wide-ranging application and realizing significant benefits. In turn, the employees gained an appreciation for SDMP and a greater willingness to continue the training and education.

This combination of serious planning and flexible implementation serves pioneering CEOs well in pursuit of World-Class Diversity Management capability.

Pioneering

Make no mistake, CEOs electing to pursue World-Class Diversity Management at this point are pioneers. Several signs affirm this:

- Ambiguity exists as to what World-Class Diversity Management would look like in action. Jeff's experience with World-Class Manufacturing no doubt helped him to deal with this ambiguity.
- Ambiguity exists as to what the optimal route to world-class status in diversity is. Jeff dealt with this by using aids that were available, but also by staying in touch with reality.

- Ambiguity surrounds the issue of time. Jeff answered this challenge with patience.
- Ambiguity exists with respect to the definition of success. Jeff appears cautiously optimistic about the progress that has been made but reluctant to embrace it as a success. He continues to stay in touch with reality.

Jeff has a temperament that meshes well with pioneering. He works to stay on an even keel—not too high, not too low. Many agree that this is ideal when you do not know what lies ahead on your pioneering journey.

Integrity

Through it all, Jeff has maintained his sense of who he is and what his priorities are. He remains convinced that neither he nor his managerial colleagues are racists. He persists in his desire to be fair and to do the right thing. He kept his promise to take care of Mark Bronson. He accepted some responsibility for the confrontation with the challenging student and asked Andrew not to chastise the newly converted learner. Throughout his interactions, he has remained in touch with who he is.

Am I saying that Jeff Kilt is *the* model CEOs pursuing World-Class Diversity Management should emulate? No, I am not.

Jeff provides many opportunities for criticism. Some would argue that he moved too slowly to cope with the possibility of racism. Others would contend that he never really got in touch with even the possibility that racism might be in play. Still others would suggest that he does not know what he is doing—that he's muddling through indecisively toward a murky destination called World-Class Diversity Management.

What Jeff offers is not perfection, but rather *one* illustration of the type of implementation decisions that can be related to the pursuit of world class and *one* example of how they might be addressed.

SOME TAKE-AWAYS

1. CEOs pursuing World-Class Diversity Management must be prepared to pioneer.
2. They also must be prepared to deal with ambiguity.
3. Despite ambiguity, these CEOs should seek as much clarity as possible about World-Class Diversity Management and the routes for attaining it.
4. Pioneering CEOs pursuing World-Class Diversity Management must maintain their integrity.
5. Pioneering CEOs must be open to a variety of inputs while retaining the ultimate decision-making authority.
6. Pioneering CEOs must keep in mind the notion of organizational readiness, as opposed to moving with the dictates of a change model. Moving ahead in the absence of readiness can lead to a stall.

CLOSING THOUGHTS

I wrote this book for organizational leaders who desire to sustain their progress with diversity and build on past accomplishments. Particularly, I wrote it for leaders aspiring to exploit fully the potential of diversity management as a managerial *and* leadership tool. These are the individuals who have inspired me to continue efforts to clarify the nature of diversity and diversity management.

World-class status will appeal to CEOs and others who wish to expand their capability and that of their organization to cope with differences and similarities of *any* kind and in *any* setting or geographical location. Leaders focused primarily on diversity with respect to race, ethnicity, and gender in the workplace likely will not have an urgency to pursue World-Class Diversity Management.

For leaders determining whether to pursue world-class status, the critical question becomes this: Given my organization's mission, vision, strategy, and competitive realities, would an enhanced ability to address differences and similarities make a difference—that is, would it add sufficient value to make it worthwhile to develop a world class capability? This is the crux of the decision as to whether to commit to pursuing world-class status.

If you can readily identify mixtures other than the workforce that need better management, then you likely would benefit from World-Class Diversity Management. *If* you find yourself and your senior colleagues speaking frequently about the breadth of diversity and yet inevitably returning to workforce "numbers," world-class status likely would enhance your effectiveness with nontraditional mixtures.

If you see diversity mixtures related to globalism; acquisitions, mergers, or strategic partnerships; functional synergy; or expansion of your product portfolio in your strategic future, then pursuit of World-Class Diversity Management likely would be advantageous for you and your organization.

On the other hand, *if* you are firmly committed to the advancement of civil rights, human rights, and social justice through equal opportunity employment, and *if* that is unquestionably the most important—if not the only—diversity matter for you and your organization, then pursuit of world-class status likely would not generate sufficient added value. World-Class Diversity Management capability, even applied narrowly, would add significant benefits but not as many or as significant as those achieved through application of the capability to *any* of your organization's diversity mixtures, in *any* setting and in *any* geographical location. Without broad application, I question whether the gains would be worth the effort.

Organizational leaders who are intrigued by the notion of World-Class Diversity Management may now be wondering, "What's next?" My suggestion is that both they and their leadership teams think deeply about the situation. This introspection should be in terms of not just benefits and costs, but also their own and their team's willingness and ability to lead—indeed to pioneer—in uncharted waters.

If you do decide to proceed, reread chapter 5 on the SDMP and the Jeff Kilt chapters, with a keen eye for learnings that might be useful in your organization's environment. Because this is pioneering territory, sequencing and other particulars might not be the same for all world class aspirants.

Some, for example, might find it useful to first master SDMP, while others might start by focusing on the four core diversity management strategies. Still others might begin with the dynamics of the diversity management paradigms and their strategic implications.

Organizational leaders who elect not to pursue World-Class Diversity Management still can make great progress with diversity, albeit probably on a narrower field of play. Everyone does not need to be world class as defined in this book.

For those proceeding, I wish you well with your pioneering. I hope the chapters on the enablers, and also on the experiences of Bjax and Jeff Kilt, provide a framework for effectively planning how to best move forward in your particular situation. I am confident that your gains will add great value for you.

ACKNOWLEDGMENTS

As with my previous writing endeavors, a number of individuals have contributed to making this book possible in a variety of ways. I am indebted and appreciative to each of them.

Once again, I thank my wife, Ruby, and our family for their love, support, and also indulgence of my passion for the work of diversity management. Without their backing, my writing of this book would have been much more challenging.

I acknowledge an ongoing intellectual indebtedness to the work of Harvard Business School professors Paul R. Lawrence and Jay W. Lorsch. Their work on functional differentiation and integration in organizations continues to inspire my thinking on diversity management.

I appreciate the CEOs and other senior leaders who have been encouraging. From the beginning of my involvement with the diversity arena, these individuals have provided some of the most rewarding consulting experiences I have had.

In this vein, I also thank the many workshop participants who have helped me refine my understanding of the Four Quadrants Model and the Strategic Diversity Management Process. These opportunities have played a pivotal role in the evolving of my thinking.

Several individuals read parts or all of the book proposal or manuscript and offered comments. My Berrett-Koehler reviewers Patrick Hehir, Danielle Scott, and Leigh Wilkinson provided very valuable feedback, as did Melanie Harrington, David Kravitz, and James Daniels.

Similarly, members of the Roosevelt Thomas Consulting and Training Community offered extremely useful input. They are Willard Eng, Albert George, Elizabeth Holmes, John Hutcheson, Terri Kruzan, Kathy Lee, Mikell Parsch, David Rupp, Jill Schichter, and Richard Smith. Additionally, Albert George first started me thinking about World-Class Diversity Management, while Jill Schichter helped in the collection and synthesizing of feedback from the various parties.

I thank Berrett-Koehler's publisher, Steve Piersanti, who served as my editor, for his suggestions that helped shape the book's development. Also, I am grateful to Jeevan Sivasubramaniam, executive managing editor of Berrett-Koehler, for his assistance with the logistics of bringing the book to publication.

With respect to word processing the manuscript, I thank Yolanda Washington, Sharon Dwyer, Lonna Jennings-Carter, and Sheila Savage.

This is the fifth book I have written with the editorial assistance of Marjorie Woodruff. As usual, it has been a pleasure to work with her. She consistently has demonstrated a high level of professionalism and commitment.

I also acknowledge the late Ann Billingsley, who in the kind, encouraging spirit of my grandmother Lela Potts, would ask occasionally, "Well, Doc, when are you going to write your next book?" I think of her encouraging words from time to time.

While engaged with this project, I felt the influence of my grandfathers, Ollie Robert Potts and Floyd Thomas, both of whom I never really knew. As I researched the challenges that threatened black men in the twenties, thirties, and forties, I thought of them. They shared the similarity of having suffered through work-related injuries. I named one of the fictitious characters in the composite case study—Mr. Ollie Floyd—after them.

While I express appreciation for the many forms of direct and indirect assistance I have received, I fully accept responsibility for the book.

NOTES

INTRODUCTION

1. William B. Johnston and Arnold H. Packer, *Workforce 2000: Work and Workers for the 21st Century* (Indianapolis, IN: Hudson Institute, 1987).

2. The New York Times, "Times Topic: Larry Summers," http://topics.nytimes.com/top/reference/timestopics/people/s/lawrence_h_summers/index.html?scp=1-spot &sq=Lawrence%20H.%20Summers&st=Search.

CHAPTER 1

Managing Workforce Representation

1. R. Roosevelt Thomas, Jr., *Beyond Race and Gender: Unleashing the Power of Your Total Workforce by Managing Diversity* (New York: AMACOM, 1991).

2. Wikipedia, "Affirmative Action in the United States," http://en.wikipedia.org/wiki/Affirmative_action_in_the_United_States.

3. *Stanford Encyclopedia of Philosophy*, "Affirmative Action," http://plato.stanford.edu/entries/affirmative.action/.

4. Ibid.

5. University of Michigan, "Amicus Briefs Filed with Sixth Court of Appeals in Grutter vs. Bollinger-Fortune 500 Corporations," www.vpcomm.umich.edu/admissions/legal/grutter/.

6. Free Legal Information: Nolo, "Federal AntiAdministration Laws," www.nolo.com/legal-encyclopedia/checklist-29451.html.

7. *CBS News*, "High Court Clashes over Voting Rights Case," www.cbsnews.com/stories/2009/04/29/supremecourt/main4977755.shtml.

8. Comments made at a meeting of civil rights activists in summer of 2009.

9. *Stanford Encyclopedia of Philosophy*, "Affirmative Action." This paper presents a comprehensive review of the evolution of Affirmative Action, its political difficulties, and other challenges.

10. Raymond A. Winbush, ed., *Should America Pay? Slavery and the Raging Debate on Reparations* (New York: Amistad / Harper-Collins, 2003). This book contains a comprehensive set of articles on the topic of reparations.

11. *Stanford Encyclopedia of Philosophy*, "Affirmative Action." The crux of the legal challenges to Affirmative Action is that it means preferential treatment for protected groups and reverse discrimination against white males. This article provides a good account of the evolution of the debate on this issue.

12. Douglas A. Blackmon, *Slavery by Another Name: The Re-Enslavement of Black Americans from the Civil War to World War II* (New York: Doubleday, 2008).

13. George Davis and Gregg Watson, *Black Life in Corporate America: Swimming in the Mainstream* (Garden City, NY: Anchor Press / Doubleday, 1982), pp. 17–32. A chapter entitled "Tokens: The First Decade" explores the experiences of African American corporate pioneers as they sought to fit in.

14. Alternet, "Affirmative Action in Other Countries," Puong Vongs, www.alternet.org/rights/16391/. Vongs offers a comparative analysis of "diversity initiatives" in Malaysia, India, Brazil, and South Africa. Harish C. Jain, Peter J. Sloane, and Frank M. Horwitz, with Simon Taggar and Nan Weiner, *Employment Equity and Affirmative Action: An International Comparison* (Armonk, NY: M.E. Sharpe, 2003). This book examines policy approaches in Canada, South Africa, Malaysia, India, the USA, and Britain and Northern Ireland.

15. Krissah Thompson, "Senate Backs Apology for Slavery," *Washington Post*, June 19, 2009.

CHAPTER 2

Managing Workforce Relationships

1. William H. Whyte, Jr., *The Organization Man* (New York: Simon & Schuster, 1956).

2. Law.JRank, "Black Power Movement," http://law.jrank.org/pages/4776/Black-Power-Movement.html.

3. Wikipedia, "Black Is Beautiful," http://en.wikipedia.org/wiki/Black__is_ beautiful.

4. Metrolyrics, "I Don't Want Nobody to Give Me Nothing (Open Up the Door, I'll Get It Myself)," James Brown, www.metrolyrics.com/I-don't-want-nobody-to -give-me-nothing-open-up-the-door-ill-get-it-myself-lyrics-jamesbrown.html. Lyr-icsdownload, "Say It Loud, I'm Black and I'm Proud," James Brown, www.lyrics download.com/james-brown-say-it-loud-im-black-and-im-proud-extract-lyrics .html.

5. Wikipedia, "Say It Loud—I'm Black and I'm Proud," http://en.wikipedia.org/ wiki/Say_It_Loud_%E2%80%93_I'm_Black_and_I'm_Proud.

6. Echelonmagazine, "Understanding Diversity Fatigue," Jene Keys, www.echelon magazine.

7. Thomas Kochman and Jean Mavrelis, *Corporate Tribalism: White Men / White Women and Cultural Diversity at Work* (Chicago: University of Chicago Press, 2009), p. 6.

8. Ibid.

9. Think Humanism, "The Golden Rule," www.thinkhumanism.com/index.php? option=com_content&view=article&id=59&Itemid=69.

10. Ibid.

11. R. Roosevelt Thomas, Jr., *Building on the Promise of Diversity: How We Can Move to the Next Level in Our Communities and Our Society* (New York: AMACOM, 2006), p. 157.

12. Martin Luther King, Jr., "The Ethical Demands for Integration," in *A Testament of Hope: The Essential Writings of Martin Luther King, Jr.*, ed. James M. Washington (San Francisco: Harper & Row, 1986), pp. 117–125.

13. Ibid., p. 118.

14. Ibid., pp. 118–119.

15. Ibid., p. 119.

16. Wikipedia, "The Golden Rule," http://en.wikipedia.org/wiki/Ethic_of_reciprocity.

17. Tamar Jacoby, *Someone Else's House: America's Unfinished Struggle for Integration* (New York: Free Press, 1998), p. 8.

18. Square Wheels, "The Platinum Rule," Tony Alessandra, www.squarewheels .com/articles2/platinum.html.

19. Paul R. Lawrence and Jay W. Lorsch, *Organization and Environment* (Boston: Harvard Business School Press, 1967).

20. Jay W. Lorsch and Stephen A. Allen, III, *Managing Diversity and Interdependence: An Organizational Study of Multidivisional Firms* (Boston: Harvard Business School Press, 1973).

21. Ibid., pp. 16–17.

22. Ibid., p. 16.

23. Ibid., p. 17.

24. Off K Street, "Racial Profiling: Henry Louis Gates vs. James Crowley—Who's Right, Who's Wrong, or Can They Blame the Nosy Neighbors?" http://offkstreet .blogspot.com/2009/07/racial-profiling-henry-louis-gates-vs.html. *New York Daily News*, "Sgt. James Crowley, Cop Who Arrested Harvard Professor Henry Louis Gates, Jr., Denies He's Racist," Beverly Ford and Rich Schapiro, www.nydaily news.com/news/national/2009/07/23/2009-07-23_sgt_james_crowley_cop_who_ arrested_henry_louis_gates_denies_hes_a_racist.html. Krissah Thompson, "Professor Says He's Victim of Racial Bias," *Atlanta Journal-Constitution*, July 2, 2009, p. A2.

25. Jacoby, *Someone Else's House*, p. 45.

CHAPTER 3

Managing Diverse Talent

1. Stephen L. Carter, *Reflections of an Affirmative Action Baby* (New York: Basic Books, 1991), pp. 47–50.

2. From my days as a student at Morehouse College in the 1960s, I remember then president Benjamin Elijah Mays exhorting students to do what was necessary to compete, including possibly working longer and harder than your competition. Students perceived "burning the midnight oil" to be not only a useful practice for collegiate success, but also a practice that might necessarily be extended to the world of work.

3. An additional word about nomenclature is in order. What I call Managing Workforce Representation (Quadrant 1) and Managing Workforce Relationships (Quadrant 2), many call Managing Diversity or Managing Workforce Diversity. I, however, reserve Managing Diversity, Managing Workforce Diversity, and Managing Diverse Talent for Quadrant 3.

4. Thomas, *Beyond Race and Gender*, p. 9. Here I posed this question as being analogous to having to burn a nontraditional fuel mixture in an automobile. The question becomes "As the available fuel changes in terms of composition, will you be able to burn this new mixture in your engine designed for the traditional mix, or will you have to modify your engine in order to utilize the new blend?"

5. Ibid.

6. Ibid., p. 12.

7. Edward E. Lawler, III, *Talent: Making People Your Competitive Advantage* (San Francisco: Jossey-Bass, 2008), pp. 22–26.

8. Thomas, *Beyond Race and Gender*, pp. 46–47.

9. Ibid., p. 50.

10. Ibid., pp. 46–47

11. Ibid., p. 46.

12. Ibid., p. 47.

13. SDMP is a process for making quality managerial decisions in the midst of diversity. While it can be used with any strategy, this quadrant is the first to require it. I devote chapter 5 to SDMP.

14. R. Roosevelt Thomas, Jr., *Building a House for Diversity: How a Fable about a Giraffe and an Elephant Offers New Strategies for Today's Workforce* (New York: AMACOM, 1999), pp. 3–4.

15. Thomas, *Beyond Race and Gender*, pp. 50–59.

16. Ibid.

17. These steps capture the essence of the cultural audit process.

18. Business Management, Suite 101, "Organizational Culture and Climate: The Personality and Mood of Organizations," Mitch McCrimmon, http://business management.suite101.com/article.cfm/organizational_culture_and_climate.

19. Lawler, *Talent: Making People Your Competitive Advantage*, pp. 22–26.

20. Adams Six Sigma, "Employee Empowerment," Adams Associates, www.adams sixsigma.com/Newsletters/employee_empowerment.htm.

21. Thomas, *Beyond Race and Gender*, p. 164.

22. Thomas, *Building on the Promise of Diversity*, pp. 44–46.

23. Lawler, *Talent: Making People Your Competitive Advantage*, p. 22.

24. Terrence E. Deal and Alan A. Kennedy, *Corporate Culture: The Rights and Rituals of Corporate Life* (Reading, MA: Addison-Wesley, 1982).

25. Thomas J. Peters and Robert H. Waterman, Jr., *In Search of Excellence: Lessons from America's Best-Run Companies* (New York: Harper Business Essentials, 1982).

26. Edgar H. Schein, *Organizational Culture and Leadership* (San Francisco: Jossey-Bass, 1985).

27. Ibid., p. 6.

28. Thomas, *Beyond Race and Gender*, pp. 12–14.

29. Ibid., pp. 50–71.

30. Ibid.

31. Ibid., pp. 10–11.

32. Ibid., pp. 3–9.

33. Elizabeth Holmes, *"Personal Diversity Paradigm": A Tool for Exploring Your Orientation to Diversity* (Atlanta: Roosevelt Thomas Consulting & Training, 2008), p. 17.

34. Lawler, *Talent: Making People Your Competitive Advantage*, p. 23.

35. Lawrence and Lorsch, *Organization and Environment.*

36. Thomas, *Beyond Race and Gender*, p. 4.

37. Gene Levine, "Is Empowerment Right for You," Gene Levine, www.genelevine.com/Merchant/merchant.mv?Screen=PROD&Store_Code=4273A&Product_Code=Reprint14. About.com: Human Resources, "Top Ten Ways to Make Employee Empowerment Fail," Susan M. Heathfield, http://humanresources.about.com/od/involvementteams/a/empowerment.htm.

CHAPTER 4

Managing All Strategic Diversity Mixtures

1. R. Roosevelt Thomas, Jr., *Redefining Diversity* (New York: AMACOM, 1996).

2. Ibid., pp. 45–46.

3. Thomas, *Building on the Promise of Diversity*, pp. 103–105.

4. Ibid., pp. 130–131. In this earlier book I referred to these questions as relating to representational diversity.

5. Ibid., pp. 131–132. Similarly, in this same work, I wrote of these questions as relating to behavioral variations.

6. Mark Douls, "On Medical Coverage, Many Agree to Disagree," *Atlanta Journal-Constitution*, August 23, 2009, pp. A1, A17.

7. Ibid., p. A1.

8. Arun A. Elias and Robert Y. Cavana, "Stakeholder Analysis for Systems Thinking and Modeling," http://portals.wi.wur.nl/files/docs/ppme/BobCavana.pdf. In a

review of the stakeholder literature, Elias and Cavana cite "those groups without whose support the organization would cease to exist" as the first definition of stakeholders to appear in the literature.

9. York University / Principia College, "Stakeholder Theory: From Theories Used in IS Research," http://fsc.yorku.ca/york/istheory/wiki/index.php/Stakeholder_theory.

CHAPTER 5

Strategic Diversity Management Process

1. Thomas, *Building on the Promise of Diversity*, pp. 119–135. In these pages, I present an earlier discussion of some universal principles as "fundamentals."

2. Ibid., pp. 126–129.

3. Ibid., pp. 155–159.

4. Ibid.

5. Thomas, *Building a House for Diversity*, pp. 229–231.

6. Thomas, *Redefining Diversity*, pp. 19–36.

7. I acknowledge that some may assign to the words *acculturate* and *assimilate* different meanings than I have, while others may agree with my definitions. Regardless of terminology, the net is that one action option calls for surface conformity, while the other related one requires conformity on and below the surface.

8. Thomas, *Building a House for Diversity*, pp. 11–20; Thomas, *Building on the Promise of Diversity*, pp. 159–161.

9. Thomas, *Redefining Diversity*, pp. 216–234. These pages contain an earlier discussion of Talking the Talk, Thinking the Talk, and Walking the Talk.

CHAPTER 6

Managing Complexity

1. *Merriam-Webster's Collegiate Dictionary*, 11th ed. (Springfield, MA: Merriam-Webster, Inc., 2003), p. 254.

2. Thomas, *Redefining Diversity*, p. 83.

3. Ibid., pp. 83–84.

4. Thomas, *Building on the Promise of Diversity*, pp. 21–46. Here I discuss some of the challenges associated with the United States' diverse body of citizens.

CHAPTER 7

The Dynamics of Strategies and Paradigms

1. Holmes, *"Personal Diversity Paradigm."*

2. In the example presented, paradigm 3 (Maximize Individual Engagement) ranked as the dominant paradigm closely followed by paradigm 2 (Apply the Golden Rule). Nevertheless, across audits that I have seen to date, paradigm 2 has prevailed as the dominant option.

3. Lawrence and Lorsch, *Organization and Environment*.

4. Lorsch and Allen, *Managing Diversity and Interdependence*.

5. Thomas, *Building on the Promise of Diversity*, pp. 35–46. I distinguish in these pages between diversity and diversity management and the civil rights movement.

INDEX

Accountability, 31, 255
Acculturation, 112, 116, 171, 279n7
    workforce relationships and, 65–66,
        68–70, 72
Adaptation, 115–116, 172
Affirmation motive, 49–50
Affirmative Action, 28–30, 36–37, 42,
    58, 274n11
African Americans
    diverse talent and, 87–90
    workforce relationships and, 45–46,
        49, 55, 60, 76–77
    workforce representation and, 25–27,
        33–36, 41, 44
    See also Discrimination; Integration;
        Mainstreaming; Racism
Allen, Stephen A., 218
Ambiguity, 161–262
American Institute for Managing
    Diversity, 128, 222
Application, 221–223
    composite case study of, 225–263
Apply the Golden Rule, 60–84,
    211–212, 236, 280n2

Assimilation, 38, 188
    diverse talent and, 108–109, 112,
        116, 118
    SDMP and, 168, 171, 279n7
    workforce relationships and, 54–56,
        58, 65–66, 68–70, 72
Audits, 100, 178, 243, 254, 277n17

Behavioral variations (diversity)
    diverse talent and, 92, 108, 112,
        122
    workplace relationships and, 47, 56
    workplace representation and,
        29–30, 42–43
Benefits of diversity, 8–12, 29–30, 33,
    47, 53, 245, 256
Beyond Race and Gender (Thomas),
    90–91, 95, 110–111, 118
Black Is Beautiful movement, 55
Blackmon, Douglas A., 37–39
Black Power movement, 55
Brown, James, 55
Building a House of Diversity (Thomas),
    97–98

Building on the Promise of Diversity
(Thomas), 131
Business rationale (case)
diverse talent and, 94, 103–104,
118–119, 121
strategic mixtures and, 126–127, 145
workforce representation and, 27–28,
30
See also Competitive advantage

Capability, 2–3
data gathering, 5
See also Management capability
Case study composite, 225–263
Cavana, Robert Y., 278–279n8
CDO (chief diversity officer), 259–260
Civility, 52, 62, 74
Civil Rights Law of 1964, 28, 35
Color blindness, 168, 170
Commitment decision, 257–258,
265–267
Competitive advantage, 9, 94, 114, 130,
143–144, 197
See also Business rationale (case)
Complexity, 2, 138, 186, 245
contributions to, 187–191
diverse talent and, 88–89, 97–98
workforce relationships and, 45–46
See also Managing complexity
Complex Organizations theory, 114, 218
Compliance, 27, 31
Concepts
clarity of, 163, 174–175, 255
role of, 258, 260
Context, 7, 101, 128, 136
SDMP and, 163, 165, 173, 181
Core strategies. *See* Four Quadrants
Model
Corporate social responsibility, 27,
36–37
Craft of strategic diversity, 131–132
Cultural archetypes, 57–58
Cultural competency approach, 52
Culture. *See* Organizational culture

Demographic tension, 33, 48, 54,
69–71
Denial, SDMP and, 169
Differences. *See* Diversity
Differentiation, 75–77, 84
Differentiation-integration tension, 76
Dimensions of diversity, 2
diverse talent and, 93–94, 111, 116
strategic mixtures and, 127–128,
145–147
workforce and non-workforce,
125–131, 159–160, 162
Discrimination
laws against, 31, 36
legacy of, 38–39, 68–69, 89, 120–121
"Diverse hire," 111
Diversity, 2
acculturated, 84
broad focus and, 114–115
changing attitudes toward differences and, 69, 71, 84, 118, 150
common patterns and dynamics of,
146–147
costs of managing, 190–191, 245
demographic, 48, 54, 69–71
thought, 242–243
See also Behavioral variations
(diversity); Benefits of diversity;
Dimensions of diversity
Diversity aspirations, 164–165
Diversity awareness, 5–7, 12, 52,
129–130, 149–150, 199
Diversity challenged people, 172–173
Diversity fatigue, 43, 56–57
Diversity field, 58–59
baggage and, 149, 199
preference for tactics in, 148–149
Diversity forest, 11–12, 146–147, 151
Diversity gridlock, 139–140, 149–150,
197–200, 236–237
Diversity management, 2–5
complexity and, 196–197
levels of, 160–162, 161
skills, 167–172

strategic mixtures and, 129, 131–132, 138, 147, 151–152
See also Strategic Diversity Management Process (SDMP)
Diversity maturity, 147, 173
Diversity mixtures
    complexity and, 188, 195, 197–198
    SDMP and, 160, 162, 168–169, 182
    strategic mixtures and, 125–126, 138–139, 142, 145–146
Diversity practitioners, 82–83
Diversity tension, 2, 33, 166
Divisiveness in society, 53–55, 58, 84
Doer Model of management, 91, 95–96, 106, 109, 119

Education
    in composite case study, 253–255
    paradigms and, 216–217
    SDMP and, 175–176, 180
"Eggshell" situations, 80–82
Elias, Arun A., 278–279n8
Empowerment, 92
Empowerment Management
    diverse talent and, 91, 95–97, 109, 115–116, 119–120, 123
    SDMP and, 164
    strategic mixtures and, 138, 142–143
Engagement, 90–92, 106–107
    Maximize Individual, 108–122, 211, 236, 280n2
    Maximize Stakeholder, 142–151, 211
Equality, 63, 67–68, 70, 76–77, 109, 118
Exclusion, 169, 188–190
Executive briefings, 175
External support, 249–251, 259–260

Face validity, 8
Four Quadrants Model, 13, 23–24, 24, 93, 152
    Diverse Talent and, 87–124
    Strategic Mixtures and, 125–153
    Workforce Relationships and, 45–85
    Workforce Representation and, 25–44

Generalization (of strategies), 144, 147, 151, 160, 162, 207
Glass ceiling, 33, 53, 58, 94, 112
Globalism, 150
Global perspectives, 41, 141, 181, 200, 217
    diverse talent and, 108, 122
    workforce relationships and, 59–60, 83
"Groupthink," 54–55

Harmony
    aspirations for racial, 46, 61
    demographic tension and, 54, 56
    as integration, 62–63, 67, 71, 74–79
High-Involvement Management, 109, 113, 119
Holmes, Elizabeth, 112

Inclusion, 31, 52, 104–105, 169
Institutionalization of cultural change, 102
Institutional racism, 233
Integration
    complexity and, 190, 201–202
    need for, 74–79
    workforce relationships and, 65–68, 70–73, 78f, 79–80, 83–84
Integrity, 262–263
Internal support, 246–249
Isolation, SDMP and, 169

Jacoby, Tamar, 70–71, 82–83
Justice
    diverse talent and, 94
    paradigms and, 212–215, 213, 214, 217
    strategic mixtures and, 138, 141
    workforce relationships and, 63, 67
    workforce representation and, 25, 27, 31, 33–36, 38

Kennedy, Anthony M., 32
King, Martin Luther, Jr., 66–67
Kochman, Thomas, 57

Lawler, Edward E., 109, 113
Lawrence, Paul R., 74–75, 114, 218
Leadership, 201, 208, 216
    SDMP and, 165, 172–173, 175–176
Level playing field, 88–89
Lorsch, Jay W., 74–75, 114, 218
Lowery, Joseph, 34

Mainstreaming
    aspiration, 25–27, 33, 36, 38, 40–41
    diverse talent and, 113, 116–117
    workforce relationships and, 60, 62,
        67, 70–73, 79–80, 82–83
Make Amends for Past Wrongs, 25,
    34–43, 211, 236
Management
    absence/illegitimacy of, 88, 96, 106, 119
    Doer Model of, 91, 95–96, 106, 109,
        119
    equated with controlling, 121
    High-Involvement, 109, 113, 119
    Total Quality (TQM), 4
    See also Diversity management;
        Empowerment Management;
        Strategic Diversity Management
        Process (SDMP)
Management capability
    diverse talent and, 95, 107
    SDMP and, 173, 180, 182
    strategic mixtures and, 131–132, 141,
        144–145
    See also Managing complexity
Managing All Strategic Mixtures,
    125–153, 152, 194
    challenges to, 137–139
    obstacles to, 148–149
    parameters of, 129–141
    undergirding paradigm of, 142–151
Managing complexity, 2, 14, 15, 17,
    185–203
    avoidance of, 189–191, 195–197, 201
    challenges to, 198–199
    diversity and, 185–192
    parameters of, 192–200

Managing Diverse Talent, 87–124, 134,
    152, 194
    challenges to, 106–107
    obstacles to, 119–122
    parameters of, 92–108
    undergirding paradigm of, 108–122
Managing diversity, defined, 129
Managing Workforce Relationships,
    45–85, 133–134, 152, 192–193
    accomplishments of, 52–54
    challenges to, 54–58
    obstacles to, 68–71
    parameters of, 47–60
    undergirding paradigm of, 60–84
Managing Workforce Representation,
    25–44, 132–133, 152, 193
    challenges to, 32–34
    obstacles to, 38–39
    parameters of, 26–34
    undergirding paradigm of, 34–43
Marketing, paradigms and, 216–217
Mavrelis, Jean, 57
Maximize Individual Engagement,
    108–122
Maximize Stakeholder Engagement,
    142–151, 211
Mays, Benjamin Elijah, 276n2
McCrimmon, Mitch, 101
Moral imperatives
    workforce relationships and, 58–59,
        61, 67, 71
    workforce representation and, 35,
        38, 40

National Economic Council, 12, 53

Obama, Barack, 12, 53
Operationalization, 155–157
    dynamics of, 205–220
    managing complexity and, 185–203
    SDMP and, 159–183
Organizational culture, 52, 102, 164
    archetypes and, 57–58
    change in, 99–102, 106, 109–110, 120

in composite case study, 235, 242–243
diverse talent and, 88, 91, 98–99,
110, 115
Outcomes, 177–180, 231, 253–257
Outsiders, role of, 259

Palmer, Judith, 24
Paradigm imprisonment (confinement),
9–11, 148
Paradigms, 205, 210–219, 247
continuums and grid of, 212–215, 214
core strategies and, 23–24
distribution of dominant, 211–212,
212, 280n2
diverse talent and, 108–122
managing and, 215–217
strategic mixtures and, 142–151
strategy dynamics and, 207–210
workforce relationships and, 60–84
workforce representation and, 34–43
Paradigm shock, 218–219, 236
Paradigm structures, 210–212, 215–217,
255
Personal development seminars, 51
Personal Diversity Paradigm (Holmes),
210
Pioneering, 161–262
Planning, 102, 177–179
in composite case study, 228–231,
251–253, 260–261
Platinum Rule, 73–74
Pluralism
workforce relationships and, 47, 54,
56, 67
workforce representation and, 28–
29, 39–40, 42–43
See also Diversity, demographic
Political correctness, 52, 56, 79–81
Powell, Lewis, 29
Predispositions, 209–210
Premature plateauing, 33, 53, 58, 94, 112
Productivity, 46, 48–49, 67
Productivity paradigm, 212–215, 213,
214

Questions, critical strategic, 208

Racial harmony. *See* Harmony
Racism, 202, 233
in composite case study, 231–236,
239–241, 248
workplace relationships and, 48–51,
64–65
workplace representation and, 34,
39
Racism seminars, 50–51, 64–65
in composite case study, 240–241,
258–259
Reciprocity, 61, 67–68
Redefining Diversity (Thomas), 128–129,
187
*Regents of the University of California vs.
Bakke*, 29
Relationships, workforce
representation and, 73
SDMP and, 171–172
See also Managing Workforce
Relationships
Reparations, 37, 41–42
Representation, workforce
benefits of, 33
diversity and, 27
relationships and, 73
See also Managing Workforce
Representation
Requirements, 164, 166, 172–173
in composite case study, 256–257,
259
Research, SDMP and, 177–178
Revolving door, 32–33, 53, 58, 94, 112

Schein, Edgar H., 110
SDMP. *See* Strategic Diversity
Management Process (SDMP)
Sensitivity, 77, 80–82
training, 51, 240–241, 258–259
Slavery by Another Name (Blackmon),
37–39
Social justice. *See* Justice

Social Justice/Civil Rights paradigm, 212–215, *213*, *214*
Social Justice/Human Rights paradigm, 217
Stakeholders, defined, 279n8
Stakeholder theory, 142–143
Stereotyping, 57
Stigmas, 88–89
Strategic Diversity Management Process (SDMP), 13, 97, 159–183, *161*, 277n13
   complexity and, 197–198
   Decision-Making Tool of, 165–167
   launching process of, *174*, 174–180
   mastery and, 167–173
   universal principles of, 163–165
Strategic mixtures. *See* Managing All Strategic Mixtures
Strategy, universal. *See* Universalization (of strategies)
Strategy dynamics, 205–210
   paradigms and, 207–219
Suppression, SDMP and, 171

Talent management, 11
   See also Managing Diverse Talent
Talk
   talking the, 174–176
   thinking the, 176–179
   walking the, 179–180
Thomas, R. Roosevelt, Jr.
   Beyond Race and Gender, 90–91, 95, 110–111, 118
   Building a House of Diversity, 97–98

Building on the Promise of Diversity, 131
Redefining Diversity, 128–129, 187
Toleration, SDMP and, 171

Underutilization. *See* Utilization of human resources
Universalization (of strategies), 5, 138, 144, 147, 151–152
   lack of frameworks for, 148
   strategy dynamics and, 206
Utilization of human resources, 24, 43
   diverse talent and, 87–91, *93*, 93, 105, 107, 117–118, 122–123

Valuing differences approach, 51–52

Walking the talk, 179–180
Whyte, William, 54–55
Window dressing, 234–235, 242, 244
Women
   glass ceiling and, 33, 53
   underutilization of, 123
Workforce relationships. *See* Managing Workforce Relationships
Workforce representation. *See* Managing Workforce Representation
World-Class Diversity Management, 3–5, *14*
   obstacles to, 6–8
   potential benefits of, 8–12
   requirements for, 5–6
World-Class Manufacturing, 4

ABOUT THE AUTHOR

DR. R. ROOSEVELT THOMAS, JR. is chairman and CEO of Roosevelt Thomas Consulting and Training (RTCT) and founder of the American Institute for Managing Diversity (AIMD). Considered to be the foremost thought leader in the diversity arena for over twenty-five years, Dr. Thomas has been at the forefront of developing and implementing innovative concepts and strategies for maximizing organizational and individual potential through diversity management.

In 1984, concerned about the inability of America's organizations to maximize the contribution of *all* employees, Dr. Thomas founded AIMD as a non-profit research and education enterprise. He and his staff became known as the seminal source for managing diversity concepts and strategies. The AIMD team focused initially on workforce diversity and later expanded their focus to creating a diversity management framework for addressing general management issues, such as change management, functional coordination, the integration of multiple lines of business, and acquisitions and mergers.

In 1996 Dr. Thomas founded Roosevelt Thomas Consulting and Training. Translating his thought leadership into practice under the rubric of the Strategic Diversity Management Process™, the RTCT team has developed an array of skills, based on training and consulting services, and created a supportive body of e-learning modules and a variety of measurement and assessment instruments. These offerings have helped organizational leaders make quality decisions in the midst of diversity, develop diversity-capable managers, foster collaboration and innovation, and achieve desired business outcomes.

Dr. Thomas is the author of six published books including the highly acclaimed *Beyond Race and Gender: Unleashing the Power of Your Total Workforce by Managing Diversity*, and *Building a House for Diversity: How a Fable about a Giraffe and Elephant Offers New Strategies for Today's Workforce*. He contributes regularly to periodicals and trade magazines and has authored numerous articles. His seminal 1990 *Harvard Business Review* article titled "From Affirmative Action to Affirming Diversity" alerted corporate America to the need for supplementing EEO in addressing the challenge of empowering *all* employees. He is also a contributing columnist to *Diversity Executive* magazine.

In 1998, the National Academy of Human Resources elected and installed Dr. Thomas as a Fellow. He has also been recognized in *Wall Street Journal* as a top business consultant, cited by *Human Resource Executive* as one of "HR's Most Influential People," and has received the Distinguished Contribution to Human Resource Development Award from the American Society for Training and Development, and the Trailblazer in Diversity Award from Bennett College.

He holds a D.B.A. in Organizational Behavior from the Harvard University Graduate School of Business Administration and an M.B.A. in Finance from the University of Chicago Graduate School of Business Administration. He also served as Secretary of the College at Morehouse College, dean at the Graduate School of Business Administration at Atlanta University, and as an assistant professor at the Harvard Business School.

Dr. Thomas provides consulting services to numerous Fortune 500 companies, professional firms, government entities, non-profit associations, and academic institutions. A sought-after speaker, Dr. Thomas offers practical, action-oriented presentations grounded in his research and writings.

asae & the center™
for association leadership

ASAE & The Center for Association Leadership provide organizational leaders and staff an array of educational programming, services, and published resources focused on contemporary thinking in association and nonprofit management. Our members—who work at some 10,000 membership organizations that represent more than 287 million people and organizations—find in our offerings the strategic and tactical insight needed to improve performance now and in years to come.

ASAE & The Center's decision to co-publish and support *World Class Diversity Management* derives from our commitment to helping associations and other nonprofit organizations more effectively draw upon the diverse talents of their workforce. We commend *World Class Diversity Management* as a roadmap for any organization seeking a disciplined approach to defining why diversity matters, to harnessing its untapped potential for better business outcomes, and to achieving the significant benefits of diversity well beyond traditional demographic dimensions. While many of the examples in the book reference race and gender, the author's four-quadrant model applies to any dimension of diversity (e.g. religion, ability/disability, LGBT, etc.) and thus this book presents a universal model that can be adapted for the benefit of any organization and any reader regardless of prior expertise in diversity management.

www.asaecenter.org

Berrett–Koehler
Publishers

Berrett-Koehler is an independent publisher dedicated to an ambitious mission: *Creating a World That Works for All*.

We believe that to truly create a better world, action is needed at all levels—individual, organizational, and societal. At the individual level, our publications help people align their lives with their values and with their aspirations for a better world. At the organizational level, our publications promote progressive leadership and management practices, socially responsible approaches to business, and humane and effective organizations. At the societal level, our publications advance social and economic justice, shared prosperity, sustainability, and new solutions to national and global issues.

A major theme of our publications is "Opening Up New Space." Berrett-Koehler titles challenge conventional thinking, introduce new ideas, and foster positive change. Their common quest is changing the underlying beliefs, mindsets, institutions, and structures that keep generating the same cycles of problems, no matter who our leaders are or what improvement programs we adopt.

We strive to practice what we preach—to operate our publishing company in line with the ideas in our books. At the core of our approach is stewardship, which we define as a deep sense of responsibility to administer the company for the benefit of all of our "stakeholder" groups: authors, customers, employees, investors, service providers, and the communities and environment around us.

We are grateful to the thousands of readers, authors, and other friends of the company who consider themselves to be part of the "BK Community." We hope that you, too, will join us in our mission.

A BK Business Book

This book is part of our BK Business series. BK Business titles pioneer new and progressive leadership and management practices in all types of public, private, and nonprofit organizations. They promote socially responsible approaches to business, innovative organizational change methods, and more humane and effective organizations.

Berrett–Koehler
Publishers

A community dedicated to creating
a world that works for all

Visit Our Website: www.bkconnection.com

Read book excerpts, see author videos and Internet movies, read our authors' blogs, join discussion groups, download book apps, find out about the BK Affiliate Network, browse subject-area libraries of books, get special discounts, and more!

Subscribe to Our Free E-Newsletter, the *BK Communiqué*

Be the first to hear about new publications, special discount offers, exclusive articles, news about bestsellers, and more! Get on the list for our free e-newsletter by going to **www.bkconnection.com**.

Get Quantity Discounts

Berrett-Koehler books are available at quantity discounts for orders of ten or more copies. Please call us toll-free at (800) 929-2929 or email us at **bkp .orders@aidcvt.com**.

Join the BK Community

BKcommunity.com is a virtual meeting place where people from around the world can engage with kindred spirits to create a world that works for all. BKcommunity.com members may create their own profiles, blog, start and participate in forums and discussion groups, post photos and videos, answer surveys, announce and register for upcoming events, and chat with others online in real time. Please join the conversation!

DATE DUE

DEC 0 8 2010			
3.18.16			

Demco